Praise for *AI-Powered Business Intelligence*

After 15 years in the data world, this book has turned my view of classic BI upside down. *AI-Powered Business Intelligence* is excellently designed and structured. I wish I had a book like this much earlier.

—*Kai Aschenbach, Head of Financial BI-Tools, HDI Global SE*

AI-Powered Business Intelligence is the definitive book for anyone who wants to understand what it takes to improve business intelligence with AI. From conceptualization to operationalization, Tobias has done a terrific job in creating a practical playbook that outlines a step-by-step approach to managing data-driven intelligent solutions for your business.

—*Ram Kumar, Chief Data and Analytics Officer, Cigna*

Tobias writes at a level of technical sophistication that works very well for me, a non-technically trained person. There is a healthy amount of coding, but not too much, and it is all integrated effectively with related business principles.

—*George B. Moseley, Professor,*
Harvard T.H. Chan School of Public Health

AI-Powered Business Intelligence is one of the best books for anyone wanting to apply data science and machine learning concepts to the world of BI.

—*Himanshu Yadav, Head of Data,*
Commonwealth of Massachusetts

AI is a daunting discipline with many intricate pieces needing to come together. With *AI-Powered Business Intelligence* at your disposal, you'll have the foundations to confidently build AI capabilities into your data analytics products.

—*Mathias Halkjær, Principal Architect, Data & AI, Fellowmind*

AI-Powered Business Intelligence

Improving Forecasts and Decision Making
with Machine Learning

Tobias Zwingmann

Beijing · Boston · Farnham · Sebastopol · Tokyo

AI-Powered Business Intelligence

by Tobias Zwingmann

Published by O'Reilly Media, Inc., 1005 Gravenstein Highway North, Sebastopol, CA 95472.

O'Reilly books may be purchased for educational, business, or sales promotional use. Online editions are also available for most titles (*http://oreilly.com*). For more information, contact our corporate/institutional sales department: 800-998-9938 or *corporate@oreilly.com*.

Acquisitions Editor: Michelle Smith	**Indexer:** Judith McConville
Development Editor: Rita Fernando	**Interior Designer:** David Futato
Production Editor: Christopher Faucher	**Cover Designer:** Karen Montgomery
Copyeditor: Sharon Wilkey	**Illustrator:** Kate Dullea
Proofreader: Piper Editorial Consulting, LLC	

June 2022:   First Edition

Revision History for the First Edition
2022-06-10:   First Release

See *https://www.oreilly.com/catalog/errata.csp?isbn=0636920584834* for release details.

978-1-098-11147-2

Table of Contents

Preface

Pop culture has had a huge impact on the way we view AI. If there's anything that sci-fi movies such as *The Matrix* and *The Terminator* have taught us, it's that AI is out to get us and that AI has a human touch. Arnold Schwarzenegger's Terminator showed us what an AI-turned-human could look like. From *The Matrix*, we learned that we might not even recognize that our lives are all controlled by a superior artificial intelligence.

While I think that both of these takeaways are problematic, I do believe they convey some truth in the context of *business intelligence* (*BI*). AI *is* coming to get us and it *might* have a human touch. But before we get into the details, let's first clarify some key terms. What is BI, exactly? BI is difficult to define because it depends on who you ask, when, and in what context.

The definition of BI for the context of this book, however, is fairly straightforward. I define BI from a systemic point of view: *business intelligence is a system or software that enables business users and analysts to look at data from multiple sources within an organization with the goal of making better-informed decisions.* So when I refer to BI, this term is closely related to BI systems such as Microsoft Power BI, Tableau, and Looker, and the underlying infrastructures that run these systems.

Let's take a quick look at *AI*, a term that we will explore in much broader detail in the course of this book. First, AI fuels all kinds of business processes today. More than 50% of all companies worldwide are on an AI journey, with at least some small use cases or early proof-of-concept (PoC) projects. The most popular AI use cases include the following:

- Search engines
- Churn prediction
- Demand forecasting
- Document processing

- Predictive maintenance
- Customer segmentation and personalization
- Quality control and process monitoring in manufacturing

If you look at the breadth of AI use cases, it would be naive to think that the impact of AI initiatives would skip the domain of BI. It's inevitable and only a matter of time that a proportion of traditional BI tasks such as planning and forecasting will be outperformed by AI. If you try to beat AI at finding patterns in data, good luck! You'll probably lose.

Second, when we think about AI, we often think about technology replacing our jobs. However, how realistic is this concern, really? Ask yourself, when do you expect an automated end-to-end AI system or robot to be good enough to take over 100% of your daily job? Five more years? Ten more years? Never? On the other hand, when do you think a colleague sitting next to you could use AI to outperform you on important tasks? Next year? Next month? Is that person already in the company? It's important to realize that AI itself is not replacing our jobs. Rather, people who know how to harness AI are entering organizations and changing the status quo. This is where data scientists come into the picture.

Shortly after the term *data science* was coined in 2008, a wave of aspiring data scientists popped up, with a wide variety of training, ranging from online courses and bootcamps to specialized college degrees. They were hired by world-leading companies in the hope of generating a meaningful business impact with data. Data scientists were even named the "sexiest job of the century" by the *Harvard Business Review*.[1]

All of a sudden, "traditional" data professionals such as business analysts and BI professionals found themselves standing on the sidelines, while new data scientists were brought in to work on exciting AI use cases. This led to a disconnect between the two sides.

When I became the first data scientist in an enterprise organization, I faced high expectations from top management as well as suspicious looks from the more "estab-lished" data departments. I must admit, the beginning was a rough ride. When I first looked into the company's data warehouse, I thought, how difficult can it be to generate static reports from what I called "small data"? On the other side, my BI colleagues were just as skeptical about my work: how could I even come up with a single metric reliably from raw data sources without an armada of specialists? And how could I even work without a fixed project scope and clearly defined deliverables?

---

1 Thomas H. Davenport and DJ Patil, "Data Scientist: The Sexiest Job of the 21st Century," *Harvard Business Review*, October 2012, *https://hbr.org/2012/10/data-scientist-the-sexiest-job-of-the-21st-century*.

It took a considerable amount of effort on both sides to appreciate each other's goals, challenges, and skills. But eventually it clicked. The BI team, for example, helped me get a better understanding of how metrics can be calculated consistently over time, considering permanent changes in IT systems and business processes. On the other hand, I suggested techniques that could help us provide better forecasts, get quicker insights, and generally provide a better BI experience, thanks to automation.

It's time to tear down the wall between "data tribes" in organizations and bring them together for the most profound impact. I wrote this book to help those on the BI side understand how they can benefit from the outputs of data scientists (e.g., models and algorithms) and how they can use machine learning (ML) to improve their BI experience. Also, I am going to explain the relevant methodologies for identifying good AI use cases and how to implement them in an Agile way so you can directly get started and lift your BI to the next level.

To do this, I'm not going to focus too much on details such as training or deploying ML models—that's something you can leave to the data scientists. Instead, you'll discover how to use the models effectively for your purposes and build first prototypes or quick PoCs. Thanks to technologies such as AI as a service (AIaas) and automated machine learning (AutoML), we will be able to cover *a lot* of AI services without worrying too much about the underlying details.

This book won't turn you into a data scientist, but it will bring you closer to understanding their role and how they can help you with yours. You will capitalize on your existing knowledge and learn how to implement AI services effectively into your own workflows and dashboards. By the end of this book, you should be able to collaborate even more effectively with your data science colleagues, or even fulfill some of the genuine data science tasks on your own.

Who Should Read This Book

This book will provide the most value if you are already an experienced data professional or a data-savvy businessperson in an organization. I assume that you know your business data (or at least the parts you work with) pretty well and that you are aware of the pitfalls and caveats it can have. In your role as a BI professional, business analyst, data analyst, or data-heavy software developer, you have a good understanding of the value of your organization's data in a particular use case.

What you still want to figure out is how AI can add value to your business, improve processes, or provide better insights. You want to gain hands-on experience by building an end-to-end AI use case yourself, or at least understanding it from start to finish. You are not yet an AI expert, but you want to learn more in this area.

To get the most out of this book, do not be afraid to do a little programming yourself. While we will stick to no-code tools in most cases, in certain areas it is simply easier to run a small Python or R script to ensure smooth operations. For example, we will be pulling data from HTTP REST APIs to build AI predictions into our dashboards. Or we will do some basic data processing in Python's pandas or R's Tidyverse. If you are open and willing to learn some of these practices, this book will give you everything you need to create a first version of an AI use case prototype on your own, without any hand-holding, thanks to ready-to-use code templates.

Although I do not assume much from a technical standpoint, I do expect you to be familiar with basic data analysis workflows. For example, you should know how to analyze data across multiple dimensions, create line and bar charts, and conceptually understand how a CSV file works. Terms like *descriptive statistics* or *linear regression* should not scare you too much.

All BI examples in this book are shown using Microsoft Power BI. If you already know Power BI, this is a great advantage. If not, this book will introduce you to the main concepts, but it might be worth reading one of the additional resources listed in the next section.

Microsoft Power BI and Azure

While all concepts and methodologies in this book are written to be universal, the exercises are explained within a single tech stack. For the purpose of this book, I am using Microsoft software, particularly Power BI Desktop as the BI frontend and Microsoft Azure for cloud and AI services. If you prefer other tools, you should easily be able to switch context, since most interfaces and workflows are quite similar in other BI tools such as Tableau and Qlik, or for cloud AI services from Amazon Web Services or Google Cloud Platform.

To follow the examples in this book, you will need to have access to the following software:

Microsoft Power BI Desktop
> The free version will be enough to follow the examples. You can download Microsoft Power BI from its website (*http://www.powerbi.com*). If you've never worked with Power BI before, it might be worth checking out the "Introduction to Power BI" (*https://oreil.ly/KseuL*) guide.

Microsoft Azure Cloud Services
> For this book, we will use AI services from the Microsoft Azure cloud platform. You should be able to work completely within your free subscription tier. You can sign up for a free Azure account (*https://azure.microsoft.com/free*) if you don't have one yet. Depending on how often you run the exercises and the size of your datasets, however, you might hit the boundaries of the free tier. Check out the Microsoft Azure pricing calculator (*https://oreil.ly/4tez1*) when you are in doubt of any associated costs.

Learning Objectives

By the end of this book, you should understand the following:

- How AI can generate business impact in BI environments
- What the most important use cases for AI in business intelligence are
- How to get started with AI through rapid prototyping
- What prototyping tools are available in the context of AI
- How to build AI-powered solutions in the context of BI
- How to build an end-to-end prototype to verify AI return on investment
- How to go from prototype to production

You will be able to do the following:

- Use AutoML for automated classification and improved forecasting
- Implement recommendation services to support decision making
- Draw insights from text data at scale with natural language processing services
- Extract information from documents and images with computer vision services
- Build interactive user frontends for AI-powered dashboard prototypes
- Implement an end-to-end case study for building an AI-powered customer analytics dashboard

Navigating This Book

Now that you understand the background of this book and what I hope for you to achieve, let's take a look at its structure.

The book is divided into two parts. Part 1 (Chapter 1 through Chapter 4) gives you the theoretical basics. Part 2 (Chapter 5 through Chapter 11) provides practical examples that demonstrate how to build better dashboards and forecasts, and to unlock unstructured data with the help of AI.

Chapter 1, "Creating Business Value with AI", looks at the impact AI has on the BI landscape and how you can typically use AI within a BI context. You'll also get to know a framework that helps you prioritize AI/ML use cases according to their business impact.

Chapter 2, "From BI to Decision Intelligence: Assessing Feasibility for AI Projects", focuses on technical feasibility of AI projects. You will get to know typical AI solution patterns and get an intuition of how AI services are built. By the end, you will be able to assess the feasibility of an AI project that enables you to create a prioritized use case roadmap for your BI use cases.

Chapter 3, "Machine Learning Fundamentals", covers some fundamental ML concepts that allow you to not only apply AI techniques, but also understand what they are doing and how this all fits into a bigger picture. We will also cover some basic pitfalls of ML.

Chapter 4, "Prototyping", introduces you to one of the most powerful tools of Agile project management and data science: prototyping. You will learn what prototypes are, why they are important, and how to build impactful prototypes for AI systems.

Chapter 5, "AI-Powered Descriptive Analytics", kicks off Part 2, the hands-on part of the book. You'll learn how to implement AI capabilities to help you run descriptive analytics faster and provide a more intuitive and seamless way to interact with large datasets.

Chapter 6, "AI-Powered Diagnostic Analytics", goes one step further in not only describing data, but also making sense of it by supporting diagnostic analytics to reveal interesting patterns automatically so you have more time to focus on the interpretation of data.

In Chapter 7, "AI-Powered Predictive Analytics", you will learn how to look beyond historical insights and how to implement AI-powered predictive analytics by using various examples from classification, forecasting, and anomaly detection.

Chapter 8, "AI-Powered Prescriptive Analytics", goes one step more to not only predict outcomes, but also prescribe the next best actions to take by using recommendation systems.

In Chapter 9, "Leveraging Unstructured Data with AI", you will finally learn how to leave the realms of tabular data and explore how AI can help you to automate processing of unstructured data such as text, document, and image files.

Chapter 10, "Bringing It All Together: Building an AI-Powered Customer Analytics Dashboard", pulls all this together. You'll build an AI-powered customer analytics dashboard that builds on the individual building blocks you've learned in previous chapters.

Having celebrated the success of your first AI-powered BI PoC, Chapter 11, "Taking the Next Steps: From Prototype to Production", discusses the next steps required to scale from prototype to production and wrap up what you've learned.

This book has an accompanying website (*http://www.aipoweredbi.com*), which contains all the demo files and code snippets used for the practical exercises. Be sure to bookmark this website to follow along smoothly. Each chapter has direct references to resources on this website.

Are you ready? Take the keys and jump into the front seat. I'll be at your side with directions, navigating you through the landscape of AI-powered business intelligence.

Conventions Used in This Book

The following typographical conventions are used in this book:

Italic
> Indicates new terms, URLs, email addresses, filenames, and file extensions.

`Constant width`
> Used for program listings, as well as within paragraphs to refer to program elements such as variable or function names, databases, data types, environment variables, statements, and keywords.

`Constant width bold`
> Shows commands or other text that should be typed literally by the user.

`Constant width italic`
> Shows text that should be replaced with user-supplied values or by values determined by context.

 This element signifies a tip or suggestion.

 This element signifies a general note.

 This element indicates a warning or caution.

Using Code Examples

Supplemental material (code examples, exercises, etc.) is available for download at *https://www.aipoweredbi.com*.

If you have a technical question or a problem using the code examples, please send email to *bookquestions@oreilly.com*.

This book is here to help you get your job done. In general, if example code is offered with this book, you may use it in your programs and documentation. You do not need to contact us for permission unless you're reproducing a significant portion of the code. For example, writing a program that uses several chunks of code from this book does not require permission. Selling or distributing examples from O'Reilly books does require permission. Answering a question by citing this book and quoting example code does not require permission. Incorporating a significant amount of example code from this book into your product's documentation does require permission.

We appreciate, but generally do not require, attribution. An attribution usually includes the title, author, publisher, and ISBN. For example, "*AI-Powered Business Intelligence* by Tobias Zwingmann (O'Reilly). Copyright 2022 Tobias Zwingmann, 978-1-098-11147-2."

If you feel your use of code examples falls outside fair use or the permission given above, feel free to contact us at *permissions@oreilly.com*.

O'Reilly Online Learning

 For more than 40 years, *O'Reilly Media* has provided technology and business training, knowledge, and insight to help companies succeed.

Our unique network of experts and innovators share their knowledge and expertise through books, articles, and our online learning platform. O'Reilly's online learning platform gives you on-demand access to live training courses, in-depth learning paths, interactive coding environments, and a vast collection of text and video from O'Reilly and 200+ other publishers. For more information, visit *https://oreilly.com*.

How to Contact Us

Please address comments and questions concerning this book to the publisher:

O'Reilly Media, Inc.
1005 Gravenstein Highway North
Sebastopol, CA 95472
800-998-9938 (in the United States or Canada)
707-829-0515 (international or local)
707-829-0104 (fax)

We have a web page for this book, where we list errata, examples, and any additional information. You can access this page at *https://oreil.ly/ai-powered-bi*.

Email *bookquestions@oreilly.com* to comment or ask technical questions about this book.

For news and information about our books and courses, visit *https://oreilly.com*.

Find us on LinkedIn: *https://linkedin.com/company/oreilly-media*.

Follow us on Twitter: *https://twitter.com/oreillymedia*.

Watch us on YouTube: *https://youtube.com/oreillymedia*.

Acknowledgments

Writing books is the closest men ever come to childbearing.
　—Norman Mailer

This quote resonates with me. Not only because this book's writing process took almost exactly nine months. But mainly because it reminds me who I have to thank first and foremost for everything: my family.

Writing means sacrificing. You sacrifice a lot of your time, energy, and other things in life for a bunch of words on a screen with a highly uncertain outcome. Thus, it can't be taken for granted to count on your family's support for such a preposterous endeavor. I'm blessed that I could always count on the support of my wonderful wife Çiğdem. Her love, trust, and optimism have made all of this possible and she inspires me every day. The words "thank you" cannot express what I feel. You are the best. I love you.

Both of us wouldn't be anything without our mothers. Therefore, I'd like to thank my mother Anett and especially my mother-in-law Gülten for always being there for us and never letting us down. If it wasn't for them, we wouldn't have the possibility to keep chasing our dreams while raising the three most beautiful kids on earth.

I also want to thank the entire team at O'Reilly for making this book possible. I especially want to thank Michelle Smith for her support and for believing in me. I am so glad she entrusted me with the unique opportunity to work on such a wonderful project! I would also like to give a special thanks to my development editor, Rita Fernando, for her great feedback, comments, and overall support. Without her help and our regular meetings, I would have fallen off the ship many times! Thank you for being an amazing writing coach and guiding me through the book chapter by chapter. And last but not least, Chris Faucher, thank you for your dedication to turning a bunch of wild manuscripts into such a beautiful book, and for breathing life into it! I cannot appreciate your help enough.

Many paths can lead to writing a book. Mine began with George Mount. If we had never met, if he had not mentioned this subject, if he hadn't encouraged me to write—this book would never have happened. This is a beautiful example of how big things start with small steps. I am so grateful to have taken that first step with you, George!

Reviewing a technical book is almost as hard as writing it. So I want to thank George Mount, Donald Farmer, and Michael Norris for critically reviewing the content and providing their valuable feedback with great attention to detail.

This book covers so many topics and concepts that it is impossible for one person to know them all. So many people have worked with me or given me their feedback to make this book what it is today. Among them are Ram Kumar, Alexander Niltop, Franco Arda, Piotr Menclewicz, Felix Urban, Marek Drob, and many others. Thank you very much for that!

And finally, I want to thank everyone who contributes to the open source ecosystem with projects like Python, R, and everything that comes with it. Without your groundwork, it would be simply impossible to put so many concepts into a single practical book.

## CHAPTER 1

Creating Business Value with AI

In this chapter, we are going to explore why AI adoption in business intelligence (BI) is becoming more important than ever and how AI can be utilized by BI teams. For this purpose, we will identify the typical areas in which AI can support BI tasks and processes, and we will look at the underlying machine learning (ML) capabilities. At the end of the chapter, we'll go over a practical framework that will let you map AI/ML capabilities to BI problem domains.

How AI Is Changing the BI Landscape

For the past 30 years, BI has slowly but steadily become the driving force behind data-driven cultures in companies—at least until the attention shifted toward data science, ML, and AI. How did this even happen? And what does this mean for your BI organization?

When we look back to the beginning of the first era of decision support systems in the 1970s, we see technical systems used by IT experts to get insights from small (by today's scale) datasets. These systems evolved and eventually became known as *BI* in the late 1980s. Analyzing data was new, so even the most basic insights seemed jaw-dropping. Suddenly, decisions were no longer based on gut instinct, but on actual data that enabled safer and bolder decisions in complex business scenarios.

The second era of BI started in the mid-2000s and was dominated by self-service analytics. A plethora of new tools and technologies made it easier than ever for a nontechnical audience to slice and dice data, create visualizations, and extract insights from ever-larger data sources. These were primarily offered by large software vendors such as Oracle, SAP, and Microsoft, but also spurred the growth of niche BI companies such as Tableau Software. Spreadsheet software also became increasingly integrated into the overall data analytics ecosystem—e.g., by allowing business users to access online analytical processing (OLAP) cubes on a Microsoft SQL Server system via pivot tables in Microsoft Excel.

Most large companies today are still stuck in this second phase of BI. Why is that? First, many technological efforts in recent years have focused on technically managing the exponential growth of the underlying data that BI systems were designed to process and derive insights from. Second, the increase in the amount of data, driven primarily by the growth of the internet and digital services (see Figure 1-1), has led to an increasing shortage of data-literate people who were skilled in handling high-dimensional datasets and the tools to do so (in this case, not Excel).

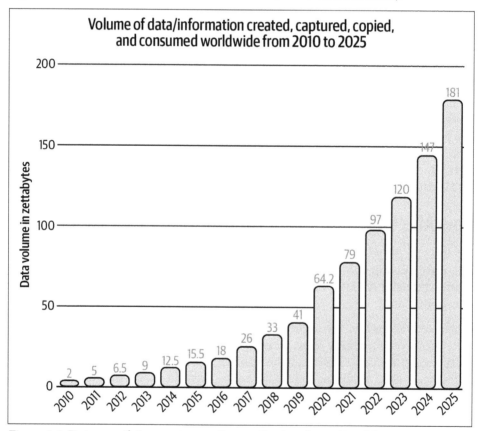

Figure 1-1. Data growth in recent years. Source: Statista (https://oreil.ly/aYY04)

Compared to the consumer market, AI applications are still underserved in the professional BI space. This is probably because AI and BI talent sit in different teams within organizations, and if they ever meet, they have a hard time communicating effectively with each other. This is mainly because both teams typically speak different languages and have different priorities: BI experts usually don't talk much about training and testing data, and data scientists rarely chat about SQL Server Integration Services (SSIS) packages and extract, transform, load (ETL) routines.

The need for AI adoption in BI, however, is going to inevitably increase, based on the following ongoing trends:

The need to get quick answers from data
To remain competitive and grow, organizations demand data-driven insights. Data analysts get overwhelmed with inquiries to explore this or that metric or examine this or that dataset. At the same time, the need for business users to get quick and easy answers from data increases. If they can ask Google or Amazon Alexa about the current stock price of a certain company, why can't they ask their professional BI system about the sales figures from yesterday?

Democratization of insights
Business users have become accustomed to getting insights from data with self-service BI solutions. However, today's data is often too large and too complex to be handed off to the business for pure self-service analytics. Increased data volume, variety, and velocity make it difficult, if not impossible, today for non-technical users to analyze data with familiar tools on their local computers. To continue democratizing insights across an organization, BI systems are needed that are easy to use and that surface insights automatically to end users.

Accessibility of ML services
While use of AI continues to rise within organizations, so does the expectation for better forecasting or better predictions. This applies even more so to BI; low-code or no-code platforms make it easier than ever before to make ML technologies available to non-data-scientists and puts pressure on the BI team members to incorporate predictive insights into their reports. The same advancements in data science are also expected to happen in the field of BI, sooner or later.

To get a better understanding of how BI teams can leverage AI, let's briefly review the analytical insights model published by Gartner (*https://oreil.ly/GGxKR*) (Figure 1-2).

The core functionality of every BI or reporting infrastructure is to deliver hindsight and insight by using *descriptive* and *diagnostic* analytics on historical data. These two methods are paramount for all further analytical processes that layer on top of them.

First, an organization needs to understand what happened in the past and what was driving these events from a data perspective. This is typically called *basic reporting* with some insight features. The technical difficulty and complexity is comparably low, but so is the intrinsic value of this information. Don't get me wrong: reliable and structured reporting is still the most important backbone of data analytics in business, as it lays out the foundation for more advanced concepts and triggers questions or problems that drive further analysis. In fact, every stage of the insights model is inclusive to all previous stages. You can't do predictive analytics until you make sense of your historical data.

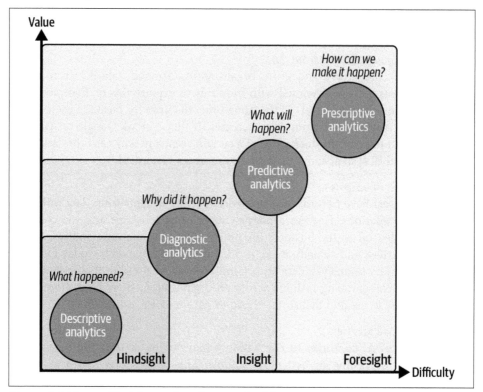

Figure 1-2. Types of insights and analytic methodologies. Source: Gartner (https://oreil.ly/GGxKR)

Consider the following example. A telco company has customers who subscribe to a service on a monthly basis. Each month, a certain number of customers will not renew their service contract and drop out of the business relationship—a phenomenon called *customer churn*.

The most basic requirement for a BI system would be to understand how many customers churned in the past and how this churn has developed over time. *Descriptive analytics* would give us the necessary information to find out how high the churn rate is over time and whether we actually have a problem. Table 1-1 gives an example of what this could look like.

Table 1-1. Churn rate over time (descriptive analytics)

	Q1			Q2		
Month	January 22	February 22	March 22	April 22	May 22	June 22
Churn rate	24%	26%	22%	29%	35%	33%

The intrinsic value of this information is rather low. At this level, the analysis can't really tell why the observed phenomenon happened or what to do about it. But at least it's indicating whether we have a problem at all: from the table, we can see that the churn rate in Q2 appears to be significantly higher than in Q1, so it might be worth looking into this even more.

That's where *diagnostic analytics* come into play. We could now dig deeper and enrich transactional sales data with more information about the customers—for example, customer age groups, as shown in Table 1-2.

Table 1-2. Churn rate over time and customer segments

Customer age	Churn rate Q1	Churn rate Q2
18–29	29%	41%
30–49	28%	30%
50–64	24%	25%
65 and older	20%	19%

This analysis would inform us that churn rates seemed to remain stable across customers who are 50 and older. On the other hand, younger customers seem to be more likely to churn, and this trend has increased in Q2. Classical BI systems would allow us to analyze this data across many variables to find out what's going on.

In many cases, a business would be able to find valuable patterns that lead to manual action or decisions through these kinds of analyses alone. That's why this stage is still so crucial and will always remain very important.

Predictive analytics takes the analysis one step further and answers a single question: what will happen in the future, given that all the patterns we know from the past are repeated? Therefore, predictive analytics adds another level of value and complexity to the data, as you can see in Table 1-3.

Table 1-3. Estimating customer churn probability (predictive analytics)

Customer ID	Age	Plan	Price	Months active	Churn probability
12345	24	A	$9.95	13	87%
12346	23	B	$19.95	1	95%
12347	45	B	$19.95	54	30%

Complexity is added as we leave the realm of historical data. Instead of providing insights in binary terms of true or false, we are now introducing probabilities of certain events happening (churn probability). At the same time, we add value because we incorporate everything we know from the past into assumptions about how this will influence future behavior.

For example, based on the future churn probability and historical sales data, we can calculate a forecasted sales risk for the company in the coming quarters, which is incorporated into our financial planning. Or, we could select those customers with high churn probability to take targeted actions that mitigate the churn risk.

But which actions should we take? Welcome to *prescriptive analytics*! Table 1-4 shows how this might look in practice. In this case, we add another dimension, *next best offer*, which includes a recommended action such as a specific discount or product upgrade, depending on the customer's individual profile and historical purchase behavior.

Table 1-4. Suggesting actions (prescriptive analytics)

Customer ID	Age	Plan	Price	Months elapsed	Churn probability	Next best offer
12345	24	A	$9.95	13	87%	Yearly contract offer
12346	23	B	$19.95	1	95%	Upgrade
12347	45	B	$19.95	54	30%	None

As we look into organizations with thousands or more customers, it becomes clear that to optimize these tasks from a macro perspective, we need to rely on automation on a micro level. It is simply impossible to go through all these mini decisions manually and monitor the effectiveness of our actions for each customer. The return on investment (ROI) of these mini decisions is just too low to justify the manual effort.

And this is where AI and BI go perfectly together. Consider that AI can indicate churn likelihood together with a suggested next best action for each customer. We can now blend this information with classical BI metrics such as the customer's historical revenues or the customer's loyalty, allowing us to make an informed decision about these actions that have the highest business impact and best chances for success.

The relationship between AI and BI can therefore be summed up nicely in the following formula:

Artificial Intelligence + Business Intelligence = Decision Intelligence

The most effective AI-powered BI application is one that blends automated and human decision making. We will explore this practically in Part 2. Now, let's take a concrete look at how AI can systematically help us to improve our BI.

Common AI Use Cases for BI

AI can typically add value to BI in three ways:

- Automating insights and making the analytical process more user-friendly
- Calculating better forecasts and predictions
- Enabling BI systems to drive insights even from unstructured data sources

Figure 1-3 gives a high-level overview of how these application areas map to the various analytical methods.

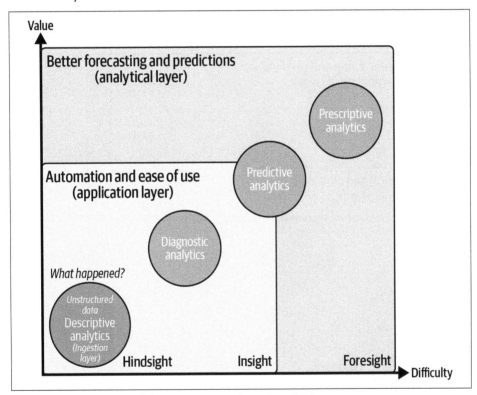

Figure 1-3. How AI capabilities support analytical methods

Let's explore these areas in a bit more detail.

Automation and Ease of Use

Making the BI tool itself more intelligent and easy to use will make it even more accessible to nontechnical users, reducing the workload of analysts. This ease of use is usually achieved through under-the-hood automation.

Intelligent algorithms make it possible to sift through mountains of data in seconds and provide business users or analysts with interesting patterns or insights. As Figure 1-4 shows, these routines are particularly well suited for the descriptive and diagnostic analysis phases.

AI can help discover interesting correlations or unusual observations among many variables that humans might otherwise miss. In many cases, AI is also better able to look at combinations of metrics than humans, who can focus on one metric at a time. But automation and usability also touch the predictive analytics phase—for example, by making it even easier for users to train and deploy custom ML models.

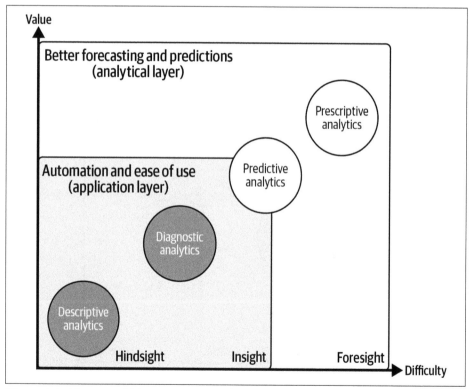

Figure 1-4. AI-powered BI: automation and ease of use (application layer)

There is one important thing to note here: the AI capabilities at this stage are typically built into the application layer, which is your BI software. So you can't typically add these capabilities to a BI platform with a few lines of Python code (in contrast to AI-powered predictions and unlocking unstructured data, which we discuss in Chapters 7, 8, and 9.) If you are using modern BI platforms such as Microsoft Power BI or Tableau, you'll find these AI-enabled features inside these tools. Sometimes they are hidden or happening so seamlessly that you don't even notice that AI is at work here.

The rest of this section describes indicators that AI is working under the hood to make your life as an analyst much easier.

Using natural language processing to interact with data

By using AI-powered natural language processing (NLP) technologies, machines are much better at interpreting and processing textual input from users. For example, let's say you want to know the sales results for last month or the sales in the United States last year as compared to this year. You might type in the following queries:

```
How were my sales in Texas in the last 5 years?
```

or

```
Sales $ in Texas last year vs Sales $ in Texas this year
```

No complicated code or query language needed. This layer of Q&A–like input makes BI much more accessible to nontechnical users as well as more convenient for analysts who really can't anticipate every question a business user might ask with a premade report. Most users will be quite familiar with this approach because it is similar to using a search engine such as Google.

Whether or not Q&A tools are built into your BI tool, not all of these implementations work equally well. In fact, a huge complexity needs to be solved behind the scenes to make these features work reliably in production environments. Analysts have to track the kinds of questions business users ask and validate that the generated output is correct. Synonyms and domain-specific lingo need to be defined to make sure systems can interpret user prompts correctly. And as with all IT systems, these things need constant maintenance. The hope is that the systems will improve and the manual effort needed in the background will decrease over time.

Summarizing analytical results

Even if a chart seems self-explanatory, it is good practice to summarize key insights in one or two lines of natural language, reducing the risk of misinterpretation. But who really enjoys writing seemingly all-obvious descriptions below plots in reports or presentations? Most people don't, and that's where AI can help.

AI-powered NLP cannot only help you to interpret natural language input, but also generate summary text for you based on data. These autogenerated texts will include descriptive characteristics about the data as well as noteworthy changes or streaks. Here's an example of an autogenerated plot caption from Power BI:

```
Sales $ for Texas increased for the last 5 years on record and it experienced
the longest period of growth in Sales between 2010 and 2014.
```

As you can see, these small AI-generated text snippets can make your life as an analyst much easier and save you a bulk of time when it comes to communicating insights to other stakeholders. Besides that, they can help cover accessibility requirements for screen readers.

Using automation to find patterns in data

You've seen how NLP capabilities can help you get descriptive insights from your data efficiently. The next logical step is to find out why certain observations happened in the past, such as why exactly did sales in Texas increase so much?

With diagnostic analytics, you would normally need to comb through your dataset to explore meaningful changes in underlying data distributions. In this example, you might want to find out whether a certain product or a certain event was driving the overall change. This process can quickly become tedious and cumbersome. AI can help you decrease the *time to insight* (TTI).

Algorithms are great at recognizing underlying patterns in data and bringing them to the surface. For example, with AI-powered tools such as decomposition trees or key influencer analysis, you can quickly find out which characteristic(s) in your data led to the overall observed effect—on the fly. In Chapters 5 and 6, we'll look at three concrete examples of using AI-powered capabilities in Power BI to make your life as a data analyst or business user easier.

Better Forecasting and Predictions

While descriptive and diagnostic analytics have been at the heart of every BI system, the imminent desire has always been to not only understand the past but also foresee the future. As you can see in Figure 1-5, AI-enhanced capabilities can support end users to apply powerful predictive and prescriptive analytical methods for better *forecasting* and *predictions* based on historical data.

This will add complexity since we leave the realms of binary data from the past and introduce probabilistic guesses about the future, which naturally contain many uncertainties. At the same time, the prospected value rises: if we are about to predict the future, we can make much better decisions in the present.

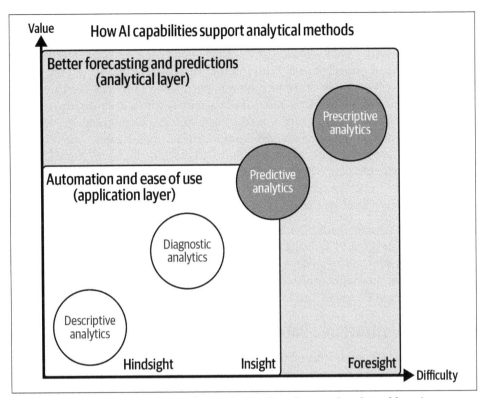

Figure 1-5. AI-powered BI: better forecasting and predictions (analytical layer)

Now, maybe you've heard about statistical methods like regression or autoregressive integrated moving average (ARIMA) before (perhaps in high school or basic college courses), and are wondering what's the big deal with AI. Take note of the two following aspects:

AI can produce better forecasts with more data and less human supervision.
AI leverages old-school techniques such as linear regression at its core. But at the same time, AI can apply these techniques to complex datasets by using stochastic approaches to quickly find an optimal solution without the need for extensive human supervision. Specialized algorithms for time-series predictions are designed to recognize patterns in larger amounts of time-series data. AI tries to optimize the forecast based on feature selection and minimizing loss functions. This can lead to better or more accurate predictions using a short time horizon, or trying to predict more accurately over a longer period of time. More complex, nonlinear models can lead to more granular and, eventually, better predictive results.

AI can calculate predictions at scale for optimized decision making.

Forecasting the total number of customers over the next quarter is nice. But what's even better is to calculate a churn likelihood for every customer in your database, based on recent data. With this information, we not only can tell which customers will probably churn next month, but also optimize our decision making. For example, we can determine, of all customers who will churn next month, which should be targeted with a marketing campaign. Combining ML with BI creates a potentially huge value proposition for an organization. And with the advance of novel techniques such as automated machine learning (AutoML) and AI as a service (AIaaS), which we will explore further in Chapter 3, organizations can reduce the bottlenecks caused by not having enough data scientists or ML practitioners to leverage these AI potentials.

AI capabilities for enhanced forecasting or better predictions can be found as an integral part of existing BI software (application layer). These capabilities also can be applied independently, directly on a database level (analytical layer). This makes them always available, no matter which BI tool you are using. We explore how to apply these techniques in Chapters 7 and 8.

Leveraging Unstructured Data

BI systems typically work with tabular data from relational databases such as enterprise data warehouses. And yet, with rising digitalization across all channels, we see a dramatic increase in the use of unstructured data in the form of text, images, or audio files. Historically, these forms are difficult to analyze at scale for BI users. AI is here to change that.

AI can increase the breadth and depth of available and machine-readable data by using technologies such as computer vision or NLP to access new, previously untapped data sources. *Unstructured data* such as raw text files, PDF documents, images, and audio files can be turned into structured formats that match a given schema, such as a table or CSV file, and can then be consumed and analyzed through a BI system. As this is something that happens at the data-ingestion level, this process will ultimately affect all stages of the BI platform (see Figure 1-6).

By incorporating these files into our analysis, we can get even more information that can potentially lead to better predictions or a better understanding of key drivers. Chapter 8 will walk you through examples of how this works in practice.

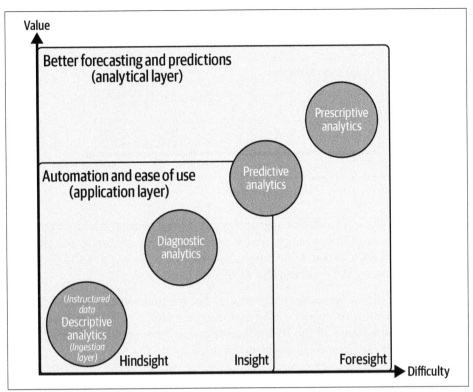

Figure 1-6. AI-powered BI: unlocking unstructured data in the ingestion layer

Getting an Intuition for AI and Machine Learning

We've talked a lot about how AI can be used with BI. But to actually build AI-powered products or services, we need to dig deeper and understand what AI is and what it is capable (and not capable) of achieving.

So what is AI, really? If you ask 10 people, you will probably get 11 answers. For the course of this book, it is important to have a common understanding of what this term actually means.

Let's first acknowledge that the term *artificial intelligence* is not new. In fact, the term dates back to military research labs in the 1950s. Since then, researchers have tried many approaches to accomplish the goal of having computers or machines replicate human intelligence. As Figure 1-7 shows, two broad fields of AI have emerged since its inception: general AI and narrow AI.

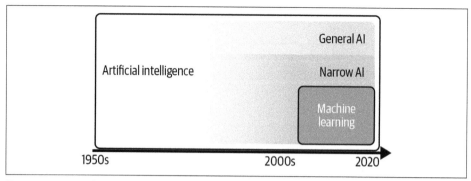

Figure 1-7. Development of artificial intelligence

General AI, or *strong AI*, refers to a technology that aims to solve any given problem that the system has never seen or been exposed to before, similar to the way the human brain works. General AI remains a hot research topic, but it is still pretty far away; researchers are still uncertain that it will ever be reached.

Narrow AI, on the other hand, refers to a rather specific solution that is capable of solving a single, well-defined problem it has been designed for and trained on. Narrow AI has powered all the AI breakthroughs we have seen in the recent past, both in research and in practical or business-related fields.

At the core of narrow AI, one approach has stood out in terms of business impact and development advancements: machine learning. In fact, whenever I talk about AI in this book, we look at solutions that have been made possible through ML. That is why I will use *AI* and *ML* interchangeably in this book and consider AI as a rather broad term with a quite literal meaning: AI is a tool to build (seemingly) intelligent entities that are capable of solving specific tasks, mainly through ML.

Now that the relationship between AI and ML is hopefully a bit clearer, let's discuss what ML actually is about. *ML is a programming paradigm that aims to find patterns in data for a specific purpose.* ML typically has two phases: *learning* (training) and *inference* (also called *testing* or *prediction*).

The core idea behind ML is that we find patterns in historical data to solve a specific task, such as putting observations into categories, scoring probabilities, or finding similarities between items. A typical use case for ML is to analyze historical customer transaction data to calculate individual probabilities of customer churn. With inference, our goal is to calculate a prediction for a new data point given everything that we learned from the historical data.

To foster your understanding of ML, let's unpack the core components of our definition:

A programming paradigm

> Traditional software is built by coding up rules to write a specific program. If you develop a customer support system, you come up with all the logic that should happen after a customer files a support ticket (e.g., notify support agents via email). You document all the rules, put them into your program, and ship the software.

> ML, however, inverts this paradigm. Instead of hardcoding rules into a system, you present enough examples of inputs and desired outputs (labels) and let the ML algorithm come up with the rule set for you. While this setup is ineffective for building a customer support system, it works great for certain scenarios where the rules are not known or are hard to describe. For example, if you want to prioritize customer support tickets based on a variety of features such as the ticket text, customer type, and ticket creation date, an ML algorithm could come up with a prioritization model for you just by looking at how past tickets have been prioritized. Instead of handcrafting a complicated if-then-else logic, the ML algorithm will figure it out, given a certain amount of computation time and computational resources.

Pattern finding in data

> To find useful patterns in data, three important concepts play together: algorithm, training, and model. An ML *model* is the set of rules or the mathematical function that will calculate an output value given a specific data input. Think of it as a big stack of weighted if-then-else statements. The ML *algorithm* describes the computational process a machine has to follow to get to this model. And the term *training* means iterating many times over an existing dataset to find the best possible model for this particular dataset, which yields both a low prediction error and a good generalization on new, unseen data inputs so that the model can be used for a specific purpose.

A specific purpose

> ML tasks are typically categorized by the problem they are trying to solve. Major areas are supervised and unsupervised learning. Although this isn't a book on ML fundamentals, we cover them in a bit more detail in Chapter 3.

If we consider all of the components, the task of an ML practitioner in a real-world situation is to gather as much data about the situation of interest as is feasible, choose and fine-tune an algorithm to create a model of the situation, and then train the model so that it's accurate enough to be useful.

One of the biggest misconceptions about AI and ML that business leaders often have is that AI and ML are super hard to implement. While designing and maintaining specific, high-performing ML systems is a sophisticated task, we also have to acknowledge that AI has become commoditized and commercialized so that even non-ML experts can build well-performing ML solutions using existing code libraries, or no-code or low-code solutions. In Chapter 4, you will learn more about these techniques so you can implement ML solutions by yourself without the help of data scientists or ML engineers.

AI as a term can be scary and intimidating for people who don't really know what it means. The truth is, we are far off from *The Terminator* and general AI. If you want to get broader acceptance and adoption of AI solutions inside your organization, you need to communicate what AI is in friendly and nontechnical language. Thinking about AI as automation or being able to implement better decisions based on past learning should make you comfortable enough to spot potentially good use cases and share that spirit with fellow coworkers.

Mapping AI Use Case Ideas to Business Impact

Now that you have learned more about AI and how it can be applied to BI, you might already have some ideas in mind for applying AI to your own use cases. To figure out which of those have the most potential and are worth fleshing out, we will take a look at a story-mapping framework you can use for exactly this purpose. The framework is inspired by Agile project management techniques and should help you structure your thinking process.

The core idea of this AI story-mapping framework is to contrast the present implementation of a process with an AI-enabled implementation of that process. This technique will give you a high-level, end-to-end overview of what would be different, which things you would need to change, and, above all, help you structure your thinking process.

The creation of a storyboard is straightforward. Take a blank piece of paper and divide it into a table with four columns and two rows. The four upper boxes will map your current process, and the lower boxes will describe the future, anticipated implementation. Name the columns from left to right: Setup, Actions, Outcomes, Results. Figure 1-8 shows how your piece of paper should look.

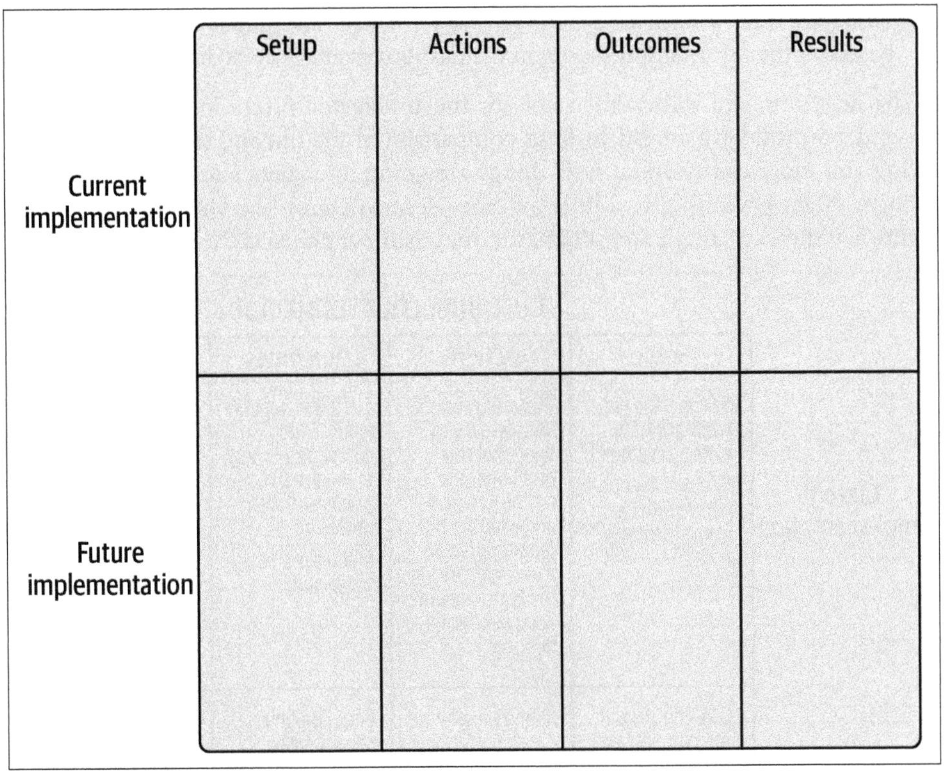

	Setup	Actions	Outcomes	Results
Current implementation				
Future implementation				

Figure 1-8. Storyboard template

To create your storyboard, you need to populate the columns from left to right. You start with the first row, outlining how the current implementation of a given process works along the following dimensions:

Setup
> Describes how the process starts and lists your assumptions, resources, or starting criteria.

Actions
> Holds all tasks and action items that are executed by or on the resource outlined in the setup.

Outcomes
> Describes the actual artifacts of the process. What exactly is being generated, created, or modified?

Results
> Holds the impacts the outcomes have on the business, and/or subsequent next steps for the outcomes. For example, displaying a report in a dashboard is an

outcome, but by itself does not have any impact. The impact is what happens based on the information shown in the dashboard and who is doing this.

In the next step, you will do the same for the anticipated future implementation. In the end, you will have a head-to-head comparison of the old and the new approach, giving you more clarity about how things are going to change and the impact these changes might have. To give a little bit more context about how this exercise works, Figure 1-9 shows a sample storyboard for our customer churn use case.

Customer chum predictor				
	Setup	**Actions**	**Outcomes**	**Results**
Current implementation	• Salespeople get feedback from existing customers. • Customer support gets feedback from customers.	• Customer support and sales try to figure out the problems customers have and whether the problems can be fixed (e.g., pricing too high, customers need onboarding help, etc.).	• Customer support works with customers, trying to resolve pain points and solve problems. • Manual reports of complaints.	• Customer will hopefully stay with the current service after the issue is resolved.
Future implementation	• Collect historical customer data on product usage and if churn happened (yes/no). • Bring in sales and customer support expertise together with data analyst.	• Analyze historical data to determine if key drivers for churn can be identified. • Develop predictive model that calculates churn risk for every customer. • Explainable model providing insights for churn reasons.	• Each customer record will be scored for an individual churn probability and explainable factors. • Chum scores will be displayed in BI and CRM system so they're accessible for both sales and customer support.	• Customer support will reach out proactively to customers with a high churn likelihood and high revenue in order to help with problem solutions before the customer raises a support ticket. • Total churn rates should decrease over time.

Figure 1-9. Storyboard example

Let's walk through our storyboard example. We'll start at the top-left corner, laying out the current setup for the existing process.

Currently, customer churn is detected by salespeople who get feedback from existing customers when talking to them in their regular meetings, or by customer support employees who receive feedback from customers that some things are not working out as they hoped or that they face other issues. In the next step, customer support or sales staff try to solve the problem directly with the customer—for example, providing onboarding help.

The main outcome of this process is that customer support (hopefully) resolves existing pain points and problems for the customer. Pain points might be reported to a management level or complaint management system. As a result, the customer will hopefully stay with the current service after the issue has been resolved.

Let's contrast this with an AI-enabled implementation, starting with the bottom-left corner and proceeding right. In our setup, we would collect historical data about the ways customers use various products and services and would flag customers who churned and did not churn. We would also bring in staff from sales and customer service to share their domain expertise with the analyst in the loop.

Our next action would be to analyze the historical data to determine whether key drivers of customer churn can be identified in the dataset. If so, we would develop a predictive model to calculate an individual churn risk for each customer in our database as well as provide insights for why the churn might be likely to happen.

As an outcome, these churn risk scores and churn reasons would be presented to the business. The information could be blended with other metrics, such as customer revenue, and presented in a report in the customer relationship management (CRM) or BI system.

With this information, customer support could now reach out proactively to customers with a high churn risk and try to solve the problem or remove roadblocks before the customer actually flags a support ticket or churns without opening a ticket at all. As a result, the overall churn rate should reduce over time because the organization can better address reasons for customer churn at scale.

With both story maps—the existing and the new process—you should feel more confident about describing what a possible AI solution might look like, the benefits it could bring, and whether it is even reasonable to go for the new approach by either replacing or blending it with the existing process. As an exercise, use the storyboard template and map two or three AI use case ideas. Which of these ideas seem to be the most promising to you?

As a conclusion, the purpose of a storyboard is to provide a simple one-pager for each use case that intuitively contrasts the differences between, and benefits of, the existing and the new solution. A storyboard will help you to structure your thinking process and is a solid starting point when it comes to prioritizing AI use cases.

Summary

In this chapter, you learned how AI is changing the BI landscape, driven by the needs of business users to get quicker answers from data, the growing demand for democratized insights, and an overall higher availability of commoditized ML tools. We explored how exactly AI can support BI through automation and better usability, improved forecasting, and access to new data sources, thus empowering people to make better decisions. By now, you should have a basic understanding of how AI and ML work and their capabilities today. You also learned to use a framework that can help structure your thinking process and craft ideas for ML use cases.

In the next chapter, we will take a deeper look at how AI systems are designed and which factors you need to consider before implementing these technologies in your BI services.

## CHAPTER 2

From BI to Decision Intelligence: Assessing Feasibility for AI Projects

In the preceding chapter, you learned how ML capabilities could drive business impact. But to create a roadmap of prioritized use cases and make an informed decision about which use cases to pursue as a priority, we need to consider another dimension of criteria: feasibility.

This chapter dives much deeper into the fundamentals of ML to enable you to assess the complexity and overall feasibility of a given AI use case. We will explore feasibility based on three main topics: data, infrastructure/architecture, and ethics. As a result, you will be able to create the first version of your AI-powered BI use case roadmap.

Putting Data First

AI projects require a different mindset than classic BI projects. Most BI projects are done in a relatively straightforward manner, often following the traditional waterfall model: define the metric you want to show, design the data model, integrate the data, and make sure it works (which is often hard enough). Iterate if necessary. Job done.

The main difference in AI projects is that—even under ideal circumstances—the outcome is highly uncertain. We simply do not know whether an AI model will work with our data and be good enough to deliver value until we test it with real data.

For this reason, AI projects typically require multiple, shorter iteration cycles in an Agile-like project framework such as the cross-industry standard process for data mining (CRISP-DM), as shown in Figure 2-1. For example, CRISP-DM suggests iterating between the Business Understanding and Data Understanding phases until you find a business problem that is both worth solving and likely to be solved, given the data you have. Similarly, it might happen that the data looks good at first, but it's not possible to develop a sufficiently good model, which you realize only in the Evaluation phase. That's when you want to go back to the Business Understanding phase to try to reformulate your problem statement.

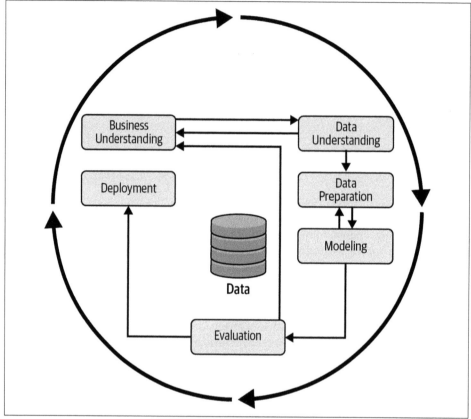

Figure 2-1. CRISP-DM model. Source: Wikimedia Commons (https://oreil.ly/qBdhY)

A common way to approach AI projects and deliver ROI is first to develop a mini-mum viable solution or prototype and, only after validating the prototype, launch a large-scale project. We discuss this topic in more detail in Chapter 4.

Nevertheless, you can do certain things even before you build a prototype. Think about the problem you want to solve and which data you will use to do it. At this stage, you do not need to worry about technical complexities like databases or data formats yet. Instead, I recommend you look at the data from a high level and use simple words to describe what you are trying to achieve.

In our previous customer churn example, the description of your goal may look like the following:

We want to use historical data mainly from the CRM and enterprise resource planning (ERP) system to predict customer churn for the next month.

Your *essential data questions* about this use case might be as follows:

- What data do you need for your use case?
- Is this data available? If so, what exactly do you have (tables, media files, text)?
- Do you have access to this data?
- Who can access it?
- Does your company own it, or do you have to buy it?
- Do you have legal authority to use this data?

All these questions still have nothing to do with concerns like "this is not in the data warehouse" or "we cannot stage PNG files." If you cannot answer these essential questions about the data, it is advisable not to proceed further with the data assessment. Instead, it would be better to focus on answering these questions: How could you get the data? Who would you need to talk to? And so on.

But let's assume you could answer these essential questions and the data seems to be available (at least in theory). In that case, it's worth exploring some of the data features in more detail before creating your prototype.

No gold standard exists for doing this systematically. However, one popular framework is the 4V framework, which I like for its simplicity. We'll explore this framework in more detail in the next section.

Assessing Data Readiness with the 4V Framework

The *4V framework* helps you better understand the characteristics of your data without getting too technical about the four dimensions of volume, variety, velocity, and veracity. This approach should enable you to consider which use cases are more or less realistic at a given stage. Again, you should perform this analysis only after you have answered more fundamental questions, such as do you actually have the data, and are you allowed to use it?

Volume indicates how much data is available at any given time. You can interpret this in at least two ways: first, as the number of observations (examples, rows), and second, as the depth of information contained in the data (attributes, columns).

Different types of ML require different amounts of data, so making a reasonable estimate of what "enough" data is can be difficult. However, to give you at least a rough idea, Table 2-1 lists data requirements for various ML techniques.

In most cases, models get better as more data is added. Therefore, more data volume is almost always desirable. However, volume alone does not automatically add value.

Table 2-1. Data requirements for ML techniques

ML capability	Rule-of-thumb volume needed
Regression	~ 100 examples
Classification	~ 1,000 examples per category for modest feature dimensionality (10 variables)
Image classification/detection	~ 100 examples per category for clearly different categories (e.g., cats versus dogs) ~ 1,000–10,000 examples for more similar categories (e.g., dog breeds)
Text/NLP	~ 500 examples per class for tasks like sentiment or entity detection

Now, let's discuss *variety*. Most of the data in your organization is not even stored in tabular form. Raw text, images, or log files, for example, fall into a category often referred to as *unstructured data*. This data does not have a reliable schema suitable for your purpose. This is problematic for a downstream analysis process. BI systems typically require data stored in relational schemas. Even most ML algorithms expect your data to be in structured (tabular) form. Therefore, unstructured data may require extensive preprocessing—or an AI service—to convert it into structured data (as you will see in later chapters).

Variety, however, can also be interpreted in the context of tabular data and refers to how well your data represents the real world, including edge cases, and whether it's generally representative. For example, do you have observations on all class labels in your dataset? Depending on how you view this term, variety may be something to aim for or avoid. Either way, you need to choose a coherent approach that fits your organization and an evaluation framework to assess different use cases in the same way.

Velocity is the rate at which data is produced and flows through your systems. Are you dealing with batch data that is updated perhaps once a day? Or are you dealing with streaming data that is constantly being updated? The velocity of the data affects two things: technology requirements and data drift. Streaming data tends to place higher demands on your infrastructure. And high-velocity data needs to be monitored more closely for data variance. High-velocity data that remains consistent can help train an ML system quickly because it helps accumulate volume. However, if this data changes rapidly over time because of its velocity, it can be difficult to maintain a consistent view of ground truth at any point in time.

Veracity refers to the data's accuracy, as a representation of the real world. Does the data exhibit inconsistencies, incompleteness, or ambiguity? Veracity is about whether your data is good enough for its intended use. And in the case of ML, this means first and foremost, does the data contain ground truth—do you have data labels? If your data does not contain labels, the only way to get them over time is to buy a labeling service or wait for a business process to produce labeled data as output.

Combining 4Vs to Assess Data Readiness

By looking critically at all 4Vs together, you can begin to see some of the relative strengths and weaknesses of your data for a particular use case. Table 2-2 summarizes some of the key questions you should ask yourself for each category and the scale you might use to evaluate them.

Table 2-2. Key questions for assessing data along the 4V model

Dimension	Questions	Possible scores from...to...	
Volume	How much data do you have available? How much data will be produced?	Small amount (1)	Large amount (5)
Variety	Does the data contain enough variety to capture even rare events? Does the data contain so much variety that it holds too much noise and requires heavy data cleaning?	Undesired variety (1) Poorly representative data (1)	Desired variety (5) Highly representative data (5)
Velocity	How often are relevant data sources produced or updated? Are data sources updated often enough to retrain the model soon enough to mitigate the risk of data drift?	Low velocity (1) High risk of data drift (1)	High velocity (5) Low risk of data drift (5)
Veracity	How accurate is the data? How complete is the data? How consistent is the data? Do you have labels?	Poor data quality (1) No labels (1) Poor fit for use (1)	High data quality (5) All examples correctly labeled (5) Good fit for use (5)

With these scores, you could, for example, create net charts. Figure 2-2 shows a possible net chart for the churn example.

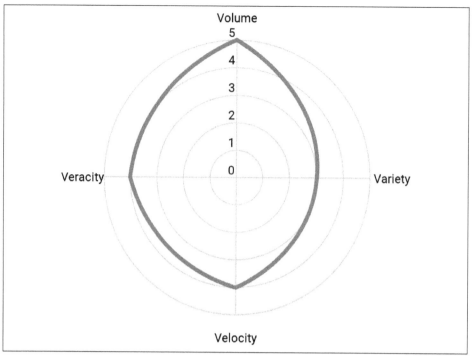

Figure 2-2. Example net chart for the customer churn use case

The chart can be interpreted as follows:

Volume score, 5 out of 5
> We have a large customer base with many attributes regarding the purchase behavior, and we think the volume of data will be enough for training ML models.

Variety score, 3 out of 5
> While all of our data is tabular and should be easy for an ML model to digest, we expect that we will have only a few examples of long-term, high-value customers. On the other hand, we might have lots of new customers for which we don't have much information available, such as buying preference, because this data might not be in the CRM system nor captured elsewhere.

Velocity score, 4 out of 5
> Data in our CRM and ERP system should be up-to-date and updated at least daily. We assume that this is frequent enough to avoid data drift.

Veracity score, 4 out of 5

We can obtain the true labels (Churned) from the data itself, so no labeling service is needed. Furthermore, we expect data in the CRM system to be mostly correct because a data governance process is in place.

This net chart indicates a feasible use case from a data perspective at this stage and allows us to compare this approach with other use cases as well.

Choosing to Make or Buy AI Services

Building an AI solution is a time-consuming process that requires a significant amount of ongoing maintenance. Figure 2-3 shows an example process with all the steps required to build an end-to-end AI solution by yourself.

When you think about this and the complexity involved, sometimes the best AI solution is not to develop an AI solution at all. The good thing is that you do not necessarily have to do all of these steps yourself. One option might be to develop only some components on your own, another to rely entirely on off-the-shelf AI services. Ultimately, like any other business decision, AI solutions are a make-or-buy choice.

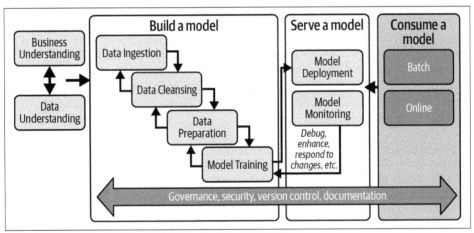

Figure 2-3. High-level architecture of an AI system

To give you an overview of the possible stages of AI-related make-or-buy patterns, let's look at the various stages you could choose as a business (see Figure 2-4) and briefly review their relative pros and cons.

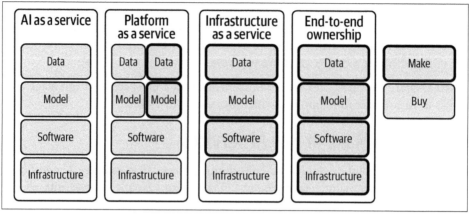

Figure 2-4. Make-or-buy patterns for AI systems

AI as a Service

With *AI as a service* (*AIaaS*), you rent a fully managed AI service and typically pay per use (e.g., API calls). For example, you might send an image to an API and receive back a JSON document with the labels recognized in the image.

The advantage is that you do not have to develop or maintain anything. You pay for only what you use, and often you can use a free tier to try out the AI service before spending money, to see how well the service works with your data. Also, AIaaS offerings do not require training data from you. The provider has trained the AI service on specific use cases, such as facial recognition or sentiment detection, and you can go straight into inference mode.

Since a variety of AI services are available for different common use cases, switching services is relatively easy, so you can try multiple services without risk. In addition, AI services do not require ML expertise or knowledge. If a graphical user interface (GUI) is provided, business users can use the service without intensive training.

The biggest drawback of AIaaS offerings is that they are usually closed boxes: you do not know what's happening inside the service. You get only input and output, nothing more. Also, you cannot modify the AI yourself. So if you want to specialize in your own data or use different labels than the ones provided by the service, there's usually not much you can do. For this reason, off-the-shelf AI services like Microsoft Azure Cognitive Services, Google Cloud Vision AI, and Amazon Rekognition usually work well for general use cases (e.g., detecting sentiment in user reviews), but they quickly deteriorate for more specific use cases. For example, you typically cannot use an AI service to extract specific things like product names from text data.

Last but not least, you need to trust the company providing the service. Deleting data for every API query may not be in that company's best interest, so you generally lack flexibility and control over your data.

The following is a summary of the pros and cons for AIaaS:

Pros
- Speed: Rapid implementation
- Cost: Pay-as-you-go model
- Instant scalability: Grow to (almost) any scale
- Services are always improving
- No or little ML knowledge required

Cons
- Always requires online connectivity
- Usually requires a cloud setup/project
- No control over model (closed box)
- Poor performance on specific data
- Expensive at scale
- Privacy concerns

Platform as a Service

Platform as a service (PaaS) is the way to go for most enterprises. With PaaS, you get access to a managed ML platform where you can train your own models or access already pretrained models through marketplaces. Typically, you pay per license, per use, or a combination of both.

If you want to build models from scratch, most ML platforms support you with tools like AutoML. AutoML uses ML itself to find the best-fitting model for a given dataset, so even less experienced practitioners can quickly create a good initial ML model with the click of a mouse. We will explore this approach a bit later in this book. Of course, with concepts like AutoML, you'll need to bring your own training data.

If you have no or very little training data, most ML platforms provide marketplaces where you can buy ready-made AI models for various use cases. These are called *pretrained models*. In some cases, you can fine-tune these models to your data, which requires much less training data than training a model from scratch. For example, instead of requiring thousands of images to build a computer vision model from scratch, fine-tuning would require perhaps only a dozen images of each category to produce good results, depending on the use case.

Many PaaS offerings also support you with more advanced features such as a custom labeling service or support for deploying and monitoring your models. In most cases, ML platforms run in the cloud (examples include Azure Machine Learning Studio, Amazon SageMaker, and Google Vertex AI), but many vendors support on-premises environments, such as DataRobot or H2O.

The following are the main advantages and disadvantages of PaaS:

Pros
- Ease of use: In most cases, you won't have to worry about infrastructure, as it is provided by the PaaS vendor.
- Speed: Not having to do infrastructure setup and maintenance is a big time-saver, resulting in faster onboarding for non-ML experts.

Cons
- Expensive at scale: If you need to train many models or use cases, it can get very expensive quickly.
- Vendor lock-in: You are locked into one platform for training your models and deploying them. What if you need to swap?

I would say that for most companies that want to experiment with ML, this is the perfect way to start. PaaS gives you a well-maintained and easy-to-use infrastructure that is still flexible enough to adapt to your unique needs. You can experiment quickly without having to deal with too much overhead.

Infrastructure as a Service

With *infrastructure as a service (IaaS)*, you rent storage, compute, and network services from a cloud provider on a pay-per-use basis. You can deploy any ML frameworks you want. The IaaS approach makes sense for companies that are willing to invest heavily in ML and software talent, but do not want the burden of dealing with infrastructure hardware. This approach is typically recommended when your organization has reached a certain level of maturity in developing and maintaining ML models.

Examples of IaaS offerings include the big cloud vendors such as Amazon Web Services (AWS), Microsoft Azure, and Google Cloud Platform (GCP), where you can provision huge infrastructure resources with just a few lines of code or a simple shell script. A broad range of modern digital services rely on these capabilities, ranging from consumer video-streaming services up to business-to-business (B2B) fleet management systems for commercial vehicles.

Here are the pros and cons of IaaS in a nutshell:

Pros
- High flexibility: Easy to scale up and down. This allows for quick adjustments of your resources according to business needs.
- Avoiding lock-in: If you're just using infrastructure, you can switch providers relatively easily when necessary to reduce costs or improve quality of service.
- Focus on data science: In IaaS scenarios, you have full control over your data and software. Therefore, you can focus on the development of your ML algorithms without being distracted by infrastructure-related issues, while having full customizability.

Cons
- Cloud experts needed: Managing cloud infrastructures needs expertise. If you don't have the talent, this will be a critical bottleneck.
- ML experts needed: Since you are not relying on a prebuilt ML platform, you need to do the software integration yourself, which is time-consuming and requires expertise.

IaaS is well suited for companies that want to focus on their data science and software development while having the ability to scale up and down quickly.

End-to-End Ownership

With *end-to-end ownership*, you are responsible for everything— infrastructure hardware, networking, software frameworks, and databases. Fun fact: many companies unknowingly start here because they already run an on-prem infrastructure and have their data scientists doing things in Jupyter Notebook on their computers. This approach will soon run into bottlenecks if you try to implement it at scale without proper platform management.

End-to-end ownership is usually the most complex scenario, and also the most resource intensive if you are doing it for more than a handful of use cases. To justify the overhead, your company needs at least one very strong AI use case that will make or break the business (think autonomous driving at Tesla). End-to-end ownership is mandatory if you want to create an initial proof of concept (PoC) but are not allowed to move data to the cloud or your company policies do not allow you to adopt an ML platform.

Here are the pros and cons of end-to-end ownership:

Pros
- Complete control
- Full flexibility

Cons
- Needs up-front investment
- Complex setup and launch
- Resource intensive
- Experts needed

 When choosing your AI infrastructure approach, remember that not every company needs to own the entire process from the ground up. The level you need depends on your use case, your budget, and most importantly, the talent available.

ML solutions are not a one-time process but require continuous development and maintenance. Think twice about which of these pieces you want to focus on and how you will benefit from them.

In our customer churn analysis example, we would likely choose a managed ML platform because we need to build our own model for this use case (no AI can perform customer churn analysis as a service without training) and the data from our source systems can likely be easily uploaded to the ML platform.

Basic Architectures of AI Systems

Now that we have covered the feasibility aspect of AI use cases in terms of data and infrastructure setup, let's briefly cover the general architecture of modern AI systems. I promise we will not get too technical here. But if you understand how AI use cases are built, you will be in an even better position to assess the technical feasibility of a particular AI use case.

At the top level, we can typically identify three layers on which AI solutions are built: the data layer, the analysis layer, and the user layer, as shown in Figure 2-5.

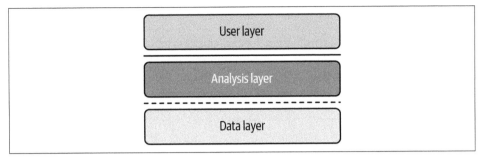

Figure 2-5. High-level layers of AI solutions

This high-level framework will be enough for us to understand the following:

- The problem we want to solve for the user and what the outcome should look like (user layer)
- The ML capabilities we are going to use for this (analysis layer)
- The data we need, and with which processing (data layer)

The underlying technical architectures are, of course, much more complex, but this high abstraction will get you very far. Later in this book, you'll find these high-level architectures for the use cases we cover, so you can quickly see how the solution works. Let me briefly explain each layer and what it means, followed by two example architectures.

User Layer

The first layer is the *user layer*, and it is usually a good step to start here. This is where we determine what problem we want to solve and, more importantly, what our solution should look like. Are we going to host a web service that users can access? Or is our end result a dashboard that displays a specific forecast in our BI? Being clear about our end result will give us the scope we need for our AI use case, even though the desired outcome may change during the development process. Here are some popular elements that can be used in the user layer:

- API
- Web application
- Dashboard or other BI integration
- Files (e.g., Excel, CSV)
- Legacy connector (e.g., SAP, custom enterprise software)

Data Layer

Following closely on the introduction to this chapter, let's first look at the data we want to use to achieve the proposed outcomes in the user layer before we get into the technical details of the analysis. The *data layer* contains components that describe the sources or source systems of the data we want to use. Some example components are as follows:

- Databases
- Media files
- Data warehouses
- APIs
- Files (e.g., CSV)
- User inputs
- Legacy connectors (e.g., SAP, custom enterprise software)

In addition, we can use the data layer to describe at a high level what we intend to do with the data before applying an ML service. The steps include, but are not limited to, the following:

- Labeling data
- Merging data
- Aggregating data
- Reshaping data
- Simulating data

How far this goes depends on your use case. For some use cases, reasoning about the data sources and their manipulation will be the main part, whereas for others, the focus might be more shifted toward the user or analysis layer.

Analysis Layer

Now that we have scoped the problem and our data, it's time to move on to the middle part of our architecture, where the magic happens with our ML capabilities: the *analysis layer*. Note that incorporating ML capabilities is not necessarily required here. Instead, you can also consider filling the middle layer entirely without ML to get a first baseline. Are there any business rules or heuristics you can apply? Are there other existing models? If so, integrate them and put them together as your base architecture.

Once you have created this, you can start replacing your baseline components with the ML-supported functions. This way, you will have a clear indication of where your ML-supported approach is likely to add value.

Be aware that your architecture is not necessarily one-way, which means that data can flow back and forth between the layers. You'll see what this means if we briefly look at two examples. The first architecture example, shown in Figure 2-6, illustrates a possible setup for the customer churn use case.

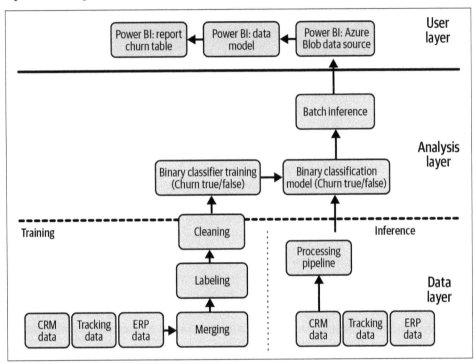

Figure 2-6. Example architecture for the customer churn use case

Let's go through this architecture in reverse order, starting with the user layer. From the box in the upper-left corner, Power BI: Report Churn Table, we can see that the end result should be a report in Microsoft Power BI showing the predicted churn table. To do this, we will provide a data model (different tables and their relations) that the user can see in Power BI (hence, this is still at the user layer). Power BI accesses the data from Azure Blob Storage.

Moving down to the analysis layer, the data from Azure Blob Storage comes from a batch inference job that uses a binary classifier to create the churn true/false labels for the data that has gone through a preprocessing pipeline from the CRM, ERP, and web tracking systems. To obtain the model, we used the same data sources for training; merged, labeled, and cleaned them; and used this data to train the binary classifier that performs the predictions.

Without having written a single line of code or even touched a single data source, we can use this architecture to discuss it with business stakeholders and ask questions like these:

- Is this the way the solution was intended to be?
- How complex do we think this will be?
- What is the minimum viable product or prototype we could ship?
- Does that fit the story mapping we did?

Let's take a look at another architecture. Figure 2-7 shows an example of a chatbot use case, where the data moves back and forth between the layers. At the upper left, you can see that the final user interaction should be a chat application on a website, which typically starts the conversation with a prompt like "How can I help you today?" The user responds with a question, which we store in a database along with some metadata (timestamp, user information, if allowed).

In parallel with storing the data, we feed the user text into a real-time NLP model for entity recognition that extracts entities from the user input. These entities can be general topics such as billing or technical issues, or more detailed entities such as product names. For this simple chatbot, the entities are used to trigger a business rule. This could be a response with pre-written answers related to the entity mentioned by the customer or asking a clarifying question.

The user responds with another input, and the process continues until the user leaves the chat. When the user leaves the chat, they are invited to a survey and asked for feedback. This feedback is stored in our database and combined with previous chat histories that we have collected. We clean this data and assign labels; i.e., we label entities in the historical conversations. We can then use these labels to retrain the NLP entity-recognition model and improve the existing solution.

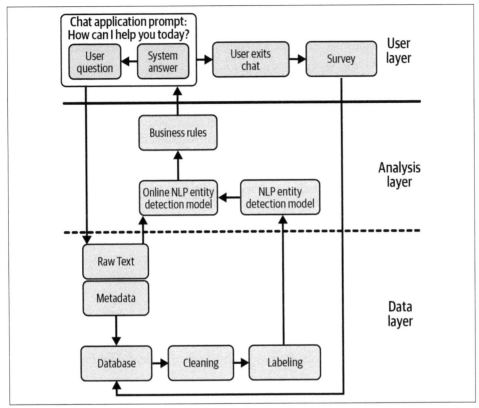

Figure 2-7. Example architecture of a chatbot use case

As you can see from this use case, the architecture can be bidirectional, and data can flow back and forth between the layers. This high-level framework has helped me a lot in scoping AI projects and discussing use case ideas with technical and nontechnical stakeholders. I hope this framework will also be helpful to you as you think about your next AI use case.

Ethical Considerations

The final topic we will address to assess the feasibility of our AI use case is ethics. *AI ethics* is an immensely growing field. Even if you intuitively would not think about it ("I do not want to hurt anyone!" I hear you say), considering ethics is still important, at least in principle. In this section, I provide you with a concise framework to help you identify areas for which certain AI use cases might be critical or less critical.

Let's get this out of the way right away: when we talk about AI ethics, we are talking about AI services that are highly specialized tools, not self-aware entities that think about the consequences of their actions (and are thus exempt from responsibility for themselves). Rather than assessing the AI service itself, therefore, we need to assess the use case or application for which AI technologies are being adapted. And it is the people who are responsible for them who ultimately bear the responsibility and must be held accountable.

In almost every AI use case, potential ethical considerations must be addressed both before and after the solution is implemented. In some cases, these issues are so serious that the use case cannot proceed. In other cases, you need to make changes to the use cases to be morally safe. And in still other use cases, the risk of discriminating against people on a large scale is very low. The point is that as a business leader or someone trying to think about developing AI solutions, you are responsible for going through this thought process before you try your first prototype in the wild.

Critical in this case has two dimensions:

Ethical criticality
> Ranges from applications that have no impact on other humans to those that involve the life and death of one or more humans

Privacy criticality
> Ranges from nonpersonal machine data, to personally relatable data, to highly sensitive personal data based on privacy categories

Figure 2-8 shows the framework. Some applications are presented and classified here as examples.

The applications in the lower-left corner of this diagram seem to be the most harmless, since data without personal reference is sufficient and the results have little or no impact on others. Many Internet of Things (IoT) applications are in this category, for example. Think of quality control in a factory, where an AI-based system determines whether a workpiece meets quality criteria. When dealing with items that pose little risk to humans (think computer keyboards), the manufacturer's quality requirements for AI can be enforced without extensive ethical considerations.

However, when the products have a significant impact on people's lives, the use case is ethically critical, even if no personal data is used. Take medical drug testing, for example. At some point in a medical experiment, the data is so highly anonymized that it is impossible to associate data points with specific individuals. Now imagine you are evaluating the development of a new AI service that predicts whether a drug will be successful in a particular cohort of patients, rather than performing a manual statistical analysis. While the data required for this does not include personal data, the entire use case is ethically critical, as the end result (produced using AI) can make the difference between life and death for people.

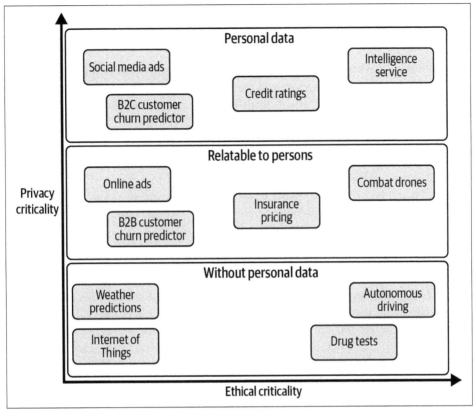

Figure 2-8. A framework for assessing ethical and privacy-related criticality for AI use cases (source: "AI Ethics," by Tobias Zwingmann and Tobias Gärtner [Springer])

Let's look at the other extreme at the top right of the diagram. These are the highest-risk areas that require the most careful ethical consideration. They include use cases that directly tailor or build on personal data and directly impact people's lives—on a large scale. Intelligence services fall into this category, but so do credit ratings. If your algorithm goes wrong in production and you serve millions of customers, you are potentially preventing many people from accessing financial resources or other services like housing and shopping, based on that rating data. Or, at the other extreme, you are giving many people access to resources they should not have and burdening them without the ability to ever pay them back—leading to personal and corporate losses in the long run.

We could position our customer churn use case in the middle-left portion of the chart if it is a B2B churn predictor. In this case, we would calculate the churn probability for accounts (companies) rather than individual customers (people). This makes the data related to individuals, but not as immediate as, say, a business-to-consumer (B2C) churn example for which we calculate churn scores at the individual level. In any case, the impact of our churn predictor on individuals is rather small. In the worst case, some individuals would receive a bad-performing (or no) personal offer with an incentive to stay.

When developing AI use cases, you should be aware of both—the amount of personal data needed to realize the use case, and the impact your solution will have on people. Both categories should help you prioritize which use cases require deeper ethical engagement and which seem less critical.

Whether you take this approach or another, I strongly recommend that you develop and implement a consistent ethical framework for evaluating ML use cases. This framework does not have to be super complex and lead to a result with double-digit accuracy. It can be broad and highly customized to your needs. Most importantly, it must be consistent and comprehensive. Both your customers and your business will thank you for it.

Creating a Prioritized Use Case Roadmap

By the end of this section, you should be able to assess the feasibility of your use case based on the three themes of data, infrastructure/architecture, and ethics. This will give you the second-dimension you need to complement the impact score we determined with the story mapping exercise from Chapter 1. We can now create a simple diagram for each use case that shows impact and feasibility, as shown in Figure 2-9.

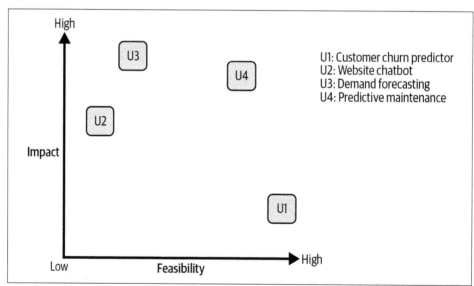

Figure 2-9. Feasibility versus impact matrix with use case examples

As you may have noticed, I have not used a formal scoring metric in this chapter to calculate actual numerical values for each use case. You can do that, and more sophisticated approaches do just that, but my advice is to start simple and compare all your ideas or use cases on a relative scale to one another. Which use case is likely to have the greatest impact, and which the least? Which use case do you think will be relatively easy to implement, and which will be more challenging?

Following this system will give you four types of use cases to map to your diagram, as shown in Figure 2-10.

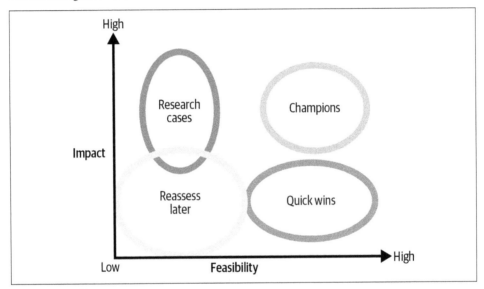

Figure 2-10. Use case segments

These use case areas are as follows:

Champions
    Use cases that have high impact and high feasibility. These should be your first priority and drive your ML roadmap.

Quick wins
    Use cases that have similar high feasibility to champions, but lower business impact. Because these use cases are often less complex, they are easier to implement. However, they can be a good showcase and demonstrate the value of ML and AI applications. Think of this as an area where off-the-shelf AI services can be used, for example.

Research cases
    These areas have a high impact but are generally not feasible in the short term. Either you do not have the data or you are not allowed to use it (yet), or certain

technical limitations exist. However, because these use cases potentially have such a big impact on your business, do not neglect them; keep them on your radar.

Reassess later

These use cases have the potential to consume enormous resources without contributing much business value. They should be put on the back burner and reevaluated later. Use cases with low impact and low feasibility can turn into quick wins as technology changes. For example, some time ago, creating an automated priority ranking for customer support tickets was complex. However, with new developments in AI services, this could suddenly be feasible overnight, making it a potentially interesting quick win for your business.

How would we evaluate our churn use case? It's hard to say, because we do not have much information yet. Stop for a moment and think: in which cluster would you place it?

Based on what we know so far, I would rate the technical feasibility as relatively high, which makes the churn use case a good candidate for a quick win or a champion. From the storyboard in Chapter 1 as well as from my experience with other churn use cases, I estimate the impact to be high if done correctly. Therefore, I would lean more toward champion. Would you agree with that?

In conclusion, the following are some guidelines and best practices for translating your diagram into a prioritized use case roadmap.

Mix Champions and Quick Wins

Setting ambitious goals is good, but it is even better to achieve them from time to time. Again, AI projects are often open-ended, and you never know if things will go as expected. Therefore, it's always good to have some use cases in your pipeline that have a relatively short development time and a high probability of successful implementation, even if the impact is not that big.

Identify Common Data Sources

If you have to choose between use cases, take the ones that use the same data sources instead of mixing too many data domains at once. For example, I would rather run three use cases based on CRM data than look at CRM and sensor data from a production facility. With each new data source, you will most likely identify new problem areas that you would not have expected before. Once you thoroughly understand a data source, you should try to exploit it as much as possible.

Build a Compelling Vision

Do you think your company has a killer use case but is still far from technically feasible? Do you see a competitive advantage for your company in an AI area but cannot capitalize on it yet? Put it on your roadmap, but make it clear that there could still be a long way to go. Crafting a compelling story and pursuing a moonshot goal will give you a strong narrative to align other (less complex, less impactful) use cases until you finally get there. As the saying goes, Rome was not built in a day. But you could start now with the Circus Maximus.

Summary

In this chapter, you learned how to evaluate the feasibility of AI use cases by considering data, infrastructure/architecture, and ethics. You should know how to perform an initial data assessment using the 4V framework and understand your options when choosing an ML infrastructure such as AIaaS or PaaS. We also looked at a high-level architecture you can use to describe your AI use cases.

We covered a lot, but you have laid the perfect foundation for developing successful AI-powered prototypes on your own. Before we get into the practical application of AI use cases in various BI scenarios, the next chapter will revisit some fundamental ML concepts that you'll need in order to build your own AI applications from this book.

## CHAPTER 3

Machine Learning Fundamentals

This chapter contains everything you need to know about machine learning—at least for this book. And it's a great primer for the rest of your learning. The following sections should give you enough knowledge to follow along with the use cases in this book and help you build your own first prototypes. We'll cover supervised machine learning, popular ML algorithms, and key terms, and you will learn how to evaluate ML models.

If you're already familiar with these topics, feel free to consider this chapter a refresher. Let's get started with supervised machine learning!

The Supervised Machine Learning Process

Let's consider a simple example: imagine you want to sell your house and are wondering how to come up with a listing price. To get a realistic price, you would most likely look at other similar houses and the prices they were sold for. To come up with a good estimate, you would probably also compare your house to other houses in terms of some key features, such as overall size, bedrooms, location, and age. Without knowing it, you would have just acted like a supervised machine learning system.

Supervised machine learning is a process of training an ML model based on historical data when the ground truth is known. For example, if you want to estimate (or predict) the real estate price as in our example, a supervised learning algorithm would look at historical house prices (the label) and other information that describes the houses (the features). Supervised machine learning is in contrast to *unsupervised machine learning*, where this ground truth isn't known and the computer has to group data points into similar categories. *Clustering* is a popular example of unsupervised machine learning.

Most enterprise ML problems fall into the realm of supervised learning. I'll walk you through the basic process of supervised machine learning by showing you the key steps so you can apply them later when we build our first ML model starting in Chapter 7.

Step 1: Collect Historical Data

In order for an ML algorithm to learn, it must have historical data. As such, you need to collect data and provide it in a form that the computer can process efficiently.

Most algorithms expect your data to be tidy. *Tidy data* has three characteristics:

- Every observation is in its own row.
- Every variable is in its own column.
- Every measurement is a cell.

Figure 3-1 shows an example of tidy data. Bringing your data into tidy form might be the most cumbersome process of the entire ML workflow, depending on where you got the data from.

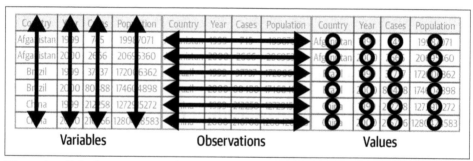

Figure 3-1. Tidy data. Source: R for Data Science by Hadley Wickham and Garrett Grolemund (O'Reilly)

Step 2: Identify Features and Labels

All that your algorithm is trying to do is to build a model that will predict some output *y* given inputs *x*. Let's unpack this concept briefly.

Labels (also called *targets, outputs,* or *dependent variables*) are the variables that you want to predict based on other variables. These other variables are called *features* (or *attributes, inputs,* or *independent variables*) in ML jargon. For example, if you want to predict house prices, the house price would be your label, and variables such as bedrooms, size, and location would be your features. In a supervised learning setting, you have historical data that contains features and labels for a given number of observations, also called *training examples.*

If your label is numeric, this process is called a *regression* problem. If your label is categorical, this process is called a *classification* problem.

Different algorithms are used for classification and regression problems. In "Popular Machine Learning Algorithms" on page 49, I will introduce three popular algorithms that will be enough for our prototyping purposes.

Step 3: Split Your Data into Training and Test Sets

When you have your data organized in tidy form and have defined your features and labels, you usually have to split your dataset into a training set and a test set. The *training set* is the part of the historical dataset that will be used to train the ML model (usually between 70% to 80% of the data). The *test set* (or *holdout set*) is the part of your data that will be used for the final evaluation of your ML model.

In most AutoML scenarios, you don't need to take care of this split manually, as it will be handled automatically by the AutoML tool. Sometimes, however, AutoML services will not be able to guess the best split for your dataset and you'll need to adjust manually (for example, in the case of time-series data). That's why it is important to understand what data splits are, why you need them, and why you can evaluate your model only once on the test set.

You split the data because you want to make sure that the model will perform well not only on the data it knows, but also on new, unseen data from the same distribution. That's why it's essential to keep some data aside for final evaluation purposes. The performance that your model has on the test set will be your performance indicator for new, unseen data.

Step 4: Use Algorithms to Find the Best Model

In this step, you try to find the model that represents your data best and that has the highest predictive power. You do that by trying out various ML algorithms with multiple parameters. Again, let's quickly go through this concept.

The *model* is the final deliverable of your ML training process. It is an arbitrarily complex function that calculates an output value for any given set of input values.

Let's consider a simple example. Your model could be the following:

```
y = 200x + 1000
```

This is an equation of a simple linear regression model. Given any input value for x (for example, house size), this formula would calculate the final price y by multiplying the size by 200 and then adding 1,000 to it. Of course, ML models are usually much more complex than that, but the idea stays the same.

So, how can a computer, given some historical input and output data, come up with such a formula? Two components are needed. First, we need to provide the computer with the *algorithm* (in this case, a linear regression algorithm). The computer will know that the output must look something like the regression equation:

```
y = b1x + b0
```

The computer will then use the historical training data to find out the best parameters b1 and b0 for this problem. This process of parameter estimation is called *learning*, or *training*, in ML. We can achieve and accelerate this learning process for big datasets in various ways, but they are beyond the scope of this book and unnecessary for our purposes.

The only thing you need to know is that you need to define an ML algorithm in order to train a model on training data. This is the place where experts like data scientists or ML experts can ace. In our case, we will rely mostly on AutoML solutions to find the best model for us.

Step 5: Evaluate the Final Model

Once our training process is complete, one model will show the best performance on the test set. Different evaluation criteria are used for different ML problems, which we explore further in "Machine Learning Model Evaluation" on page 55.

It is important to understand how these metrics work, as you will need to specify these metrics to the AutoML service to find the best model. Again, don't worry; your AutoML service will suggest a good first-shot evaluation metric.

Step 6: Deploy

Once you decide on a model, you usually want to deploy it somewhere so users or applications can use it. The technical term for this part of the ML process is *inference*, *prediction*, or *scoring*. At this stage, your model doesn't learn anymore but is only calculating the outputs as it receives new input values.

The way this works depends on your setup. Often the model is hosted as an HTTP API that takes input data and returns the predictions (*online prediction*). Alternatively, the model can be used to score a lot of data at once, which is called *batch prediction*.

Step 7: Perform Maintenance

Although the development process of the ML model has finished after deployment, the process never actually ends. As data patterns change, models need to be retrained, and we need to look at whether the initial performance of the ML model can be kept high over time.

We don't have to deal with these things during the prototyping phase, but it's important to note that ML models need a considerable amount of maintenance after deployment, which you should consider in your feasibility analysis. We will explore this topic further in Chapter 11.

Now that you understand on a high level how the process for supervised machine learning looks in general, let's look at the most popular ML algorithms used to train a model for both classification and regression problems.

Popular Machine Learning Algorithms

In this section, I will introduce you to three popular families of ML algorithms: linear regression, decision trees, and ensemble methods. If you know these three classes, you'll be able to tackle probably 90% of all supervised ML problems in business.

Table 3-1 gives an overview of these classes of algorithms, and then we'll look at them in a little more detail.

Table 3-1. Popular machine learning algorithms

Algorithm class	Used for	Performance	Interpretability
Linear regression	Regression problems	Low to high	High
Decision trees		Average	High
Ensemble methods (bagging and boosting)	Regression and classification problems	High	Low
		High	Low

Linear Regression

Linear regression is one of the most essential algorithms to understand in ML because it powers so many concepts. Logistic regression, regression trees, time-series analysis, and even neural networks use linear regression at their core.

The way linear regression works is simple to explain, but hard to master. Given some numeric input data, the regression algorithm will fit a linear function that calculates (predicts) corresponding numeric output data.

Two main assumptions are important for regression:

- The features should be independent from one another (we should have low correlation among features).
- The relationship between the features and the outcome variable should be linear (e.g., when one variable increases, the output variable should also increase or decrease with a fixed pattern).

Figure 3-2 shows an example of a simple linear regression: the input variable on the x-axis predicts the variable on the y-axis. The dots in the plot are the actual data points (labels) that were observed for each value of x in the historical dataset. The prediction from the regression would be the y value on the straight line for each value of x. Of course, this is just a basic example for illustration purposes. Linear regression also works with many more than just one input variable and can also model different shapes than just straight lines (for example, in polynomial regression).

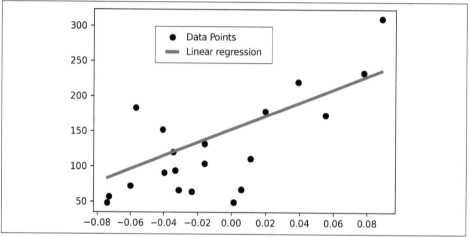

Figure 3-2. Simple linear regression

As you can see in the first row of Table 3-1, the model performance of linear regression can range anywhere from very low to very high. That's because the performance of the linear regression algorithm depends heavily on the data and how well the data meets the assumptions of linear regression. If the input variables are really independent and have a linear relationship to the output variables, regression can beat any neural network.

That said, regression is not a good choice if your data contains nonlinear patterns. For example, if a certain value is met, then suddenly the relationship to the target variable changes. These sort of if-then-else rules can be better modeled with other algorithms, such as decision trees.

Decision Trees

In contrast to a regression model, tree-based models can work with both categorical and numerical data (regression trees), as you can see in Table 3-1. *Decision trees* split the data at various levels, variable after variable, until the data slices become so small that you can make a prediction. Imagine decision trees as a hierarchical order of if-then rules.

Decision trees are usually good all-round algorithms that can be used on almost any tabular dataset as a first baseline model. Decision trees can be easily shared and explained even to nontechnical stakeholders. On the downside, single decision trees often don't deliver the best results in all cases because the algorithm is "greedy." That means it will do those splits first at the point where the data shows the highest discrepancy. This process isn't ideal in all situations.

Figure 3-3 shows an example decision tree that predicts the survival of passengers on the *Titanic*, a popular research dataset. You read the tree from the top to the bottom, and each node represents a decision step.

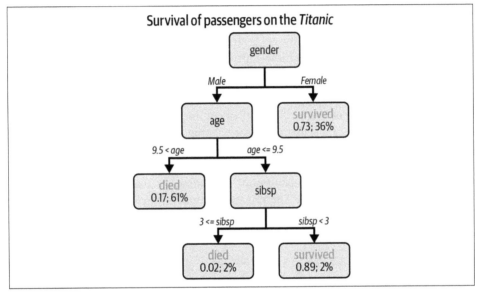

Figure 3-3. Decision tree

Because the decision tree is greedy, it will make the first split on gender. If you pick a random female passenger from the Titanic dataset, the chances that this person survived are 73%. Not bad for a first guess. For men, the tree looks a little more complicated. The prediction will be died or survived, considering multiple factors such as the person's age and the number of siblings or spouses (sibsp).

We don't go much more into detail here. It's important only that you understand how decision trees work conceptually, because we will build on them in the next concept: ensemble learning.

Ensemble Learning Methods

Linear regression and decision trees are pretty straightforward, and the way they work is rather easy to explain. *Ensemble methods* sit pretty much at the other end of the spectrum. As you can see in Table 3-1, ensemble methods provide generally high predictive power. However, interpreting the way they make a decision is not so easy.

Both linear regression and decision trees are typically considered *weak learners,* which means that they struggle if data relationships become more complex. For example, regression can't work with nonlinear data, and decision trees can make a split only once for each variable in your dataset.

To combat these issues, ensemble methods allow you to combine several weak learners into a strong learner that shows a strong performance on complex datasets. The two typical methods of ensemble learning are bagging and boosting, which are differentiated by the way they combine weak learners.

Bagging (from *bootstrap aggregating*) tries to combine multiple weak learners by training various models individually and then combining them by using an averaging process. Figure 3-4 shows a schema of how bagging works. In the middle layer, you can see four models that are all trained on the same training dataset. This could be four decision trees, for example, with different parameters for the tree depths or the minimum node sizes. For each data point, each of these four models will make an individual prediction (top layer). The final prediction will be an aggregation of these four results (for example, a majority vote in the case of a classification example, or an average value for a regression problem).

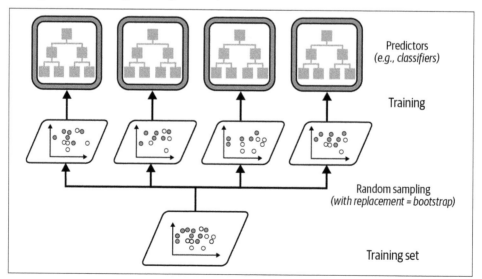

Figure 3-4. Bagging

A popular bagging ensemble method is called *random forest*. This method splits the decision trees into multiple subtrees so we have less correlation between them.

Boosting, on the other hand, sequentially adds models to an ensemble, each one correcting the errors of its predecessor. It's a popular and powerful technique. Two popular boosting methods are AdaBoost (adaptive boosting) and gradient boosting.

Figure 3-5 shows a conceptual overview of how bagging works. The training process starts at the bottom left as the first model (for example, a decision tree) is trained and gives a first prediction with relatively high errors (top left). Next, another decision tree is trained that tries to correct the errors that the preceding model made (the second model from the left in the bottom row). This process is repeated several times until the errors become smaller and smaller and a well-performing model has been found. Figure 3-5 has three iterations, which then result in the final model at the bottom right.

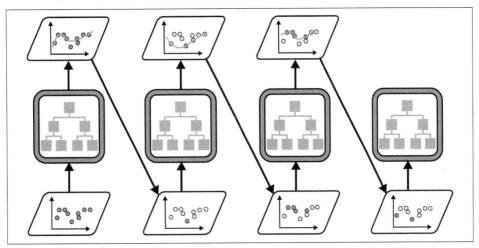

Figure 3-5. Boosting

As you might see from this example, ensemble methods are much harder to interpret than linear regression or decision trees. However, in most cases they provide better performance.

The approach you should take depends on your goals. If explainability is not as important as accuracy for your projects, choosing a strong learner such as adaptive boosting is typically the better choice. On the other hand, if your ML model needs to be well understood and interpreted by users or other stakeholders, choosing a slightly less-accurate model such as a decision tree or linear regression might be the better choice. When in doubt, choose the simpler model if it provides similar performance.

Deep Learning

The algorithms we have covered so far work well on structured, tabular data typically found in spreadsheets or data warehouses. For other data types, such as images or text, you need different algorithms. This area is often referred to as *deep learning*.

We won't go into much detail about that here. The AI services we will later use from Azure Cognitive Services are based on deep learning techniques, but we are not going to build them out ourselves. For our purposes, it's enough to have a general idea of what these deep learning concepts mean and how they work.

Deep learning refers to a variety of ML approaches and techniques that are specialized to work with *high-dimensional datasets*—data with many features. No formal definition explicitly details where "shallow" ML ends and "deep" learning starts, but it mostly comes down to the data types.

Consider the following example: even if you build an ultra-high-dimensional sales predictor, you will probably not create more than a few dozen, maybe even hundreds, of features from your tabular CRM data. Now imagine you're analyzing images for object detection. Even for rather small images with a resolution of 300 × 300 pixels, you would get 90,000 dimensions (one dimension for each pixel). With colored red, green, and blue (RGB) pictures, this amount triples.

You can see that a considerable difference still remains between a high-dimensional table of maybe 1,000 columns (dimensions) and a small image representation of 90,000 dimensions—for every picture. And that's why deep learning is often considered for nontabular data such as images, videos, and unstructured text files.

Two broad categories have emerged in deep learning: computer vision (dealing with picture or video data) and natural language processing (dealing with text data).

Natural Language Processing

You have probably already heard about AI services that are able to interpret human language, do translations more accurately than ever before, or even generate new texts completely automatically. Large language models that have been trained on billions of human text examples combined with a breakthrough technology called transformers (*https://oreil.ly/kDnMj*) has catapulted the NLP field from a small research domain to one of the hottest areas in AI development.

We won't train NLP models ourselves in this book, but you will be exposed to using state-of-the-art language models to analyze language data at scale. This doesn't apply to just written text. NLP technologies are also excellent for analyzing spoken words. This area is often referred to as *speech to text*.

Computer Vision

Computer vision is a technology that enables machines to "see" and interpret image and video files. A technology called *convolutional neural networks* (*CNNs*) has led to incredible breakthroughs in this field in recent years. Applications range from identifying commodity entities in images such as cars, bicycles, street signs, animals, and people, to face recognition and extracting text structures from images.

It's a diverse field with lots of things happening. In Chapter 9, we will use a computer vision AI service to detect and count cars in image files.

Reinforcement Learning

The last deep learning category I want to highlight is *reinforcement learning*. We will see a reinforcement learning service in action in Chapter 8. Reinforcement learning works differently than supervised or unsupervised learning and has become a separate field of its own.

The reason lies in the way reinforcement learning models learn. Instead of relying on historical data, reinforcement learning approaches require a constant stream of new data coming in so the model can learn the best strategies, given the current state of a system and policies the model is allowed to act in.

Reinforcement learning has seen major breakthroughs by being able to beat world-class human players in games like Go and *StarCraft*. But as you will find out later, it is also a great way to personalize user experiences and learn over time what users want and how to interact with them.

Machine Learning Model Evaluation

With the knowledge you've gained from this book so far, you should be confident enough to build and apply ML models from a prototyping stage to real-world use cases. One component is still missing, though. And that is how to assess how well your model is actually working.

Being able to measure the performance of an ML model is critical not only during prototyping but also later in production. The evaluation metric we choose should not differ, only the value of the metric. So how do we evaluate the performance of an ML model?

Welcome to the world of evaluation metrics! Evaluation metrics are calculated for two reasons:

- To compare models to one another in order to find the best predictive model
- To continuously measure the model's true performance on new, unseen data

The basic idea behind model evaluation is always the same: we compare the values that our model predicts to the values that the model should have predicted according to our ground truth (e.g., the labels in our dataset). What sounds intuitively simple carries a good amount of complexity. In fact, you could write a book on evaluation metrics alone.

In our case, we'll keep it short and focus on the most important concepts you will most likely encounter when working with ML algorithms. We use different evaluation metrics for classification and regression problems.

Evaluating Regression Models

Remember that regression models predict continuous numeric variables such as revenues, quantities, and sizes. The most popular metric to evaluate regression models is the *root-mean-square error* (RMSE). It is the square root of the average squared error in the regression's predicted values ($\hat{y}$). The RMSE can be defined as follows:

$$RMSE = \sqrt{\frac{\Sigma_{i=1}^{n}(y_i - \widehat{y}_i)^2}{n}}$$

RMSE measures the model's overall accuracy and can be used to compare regression models to one another. The smaller the value, the better the model seems to perform. The RMSE comes in the original scale of the predicted values. For example, if your model predicts a house price in US dollars and you see an RMSE of 256.6, this translates to "the model predictions are wrong by 256.6 dollars on average."

Another popular metric that you will see in the context of regression evaluation is the *coefficient of determination*, also called the *R-squared* statistic. R-squared ranges from 0 to 1 and measures the proportion of variation in the data accounted for in the model. It is useful when you want to assess how well the model fits the data. The formula for R-squared is as follows:

$$R^2 = 1 - \frac{\Sigma_{i=1}^{n}(y_i - \widehat{y}_i)^2}{\Sigma_{i=1}^{n}(y_i - \overline{y})^2}$$

You can interpret this as 1 minus the explained variance of the model divided by the total variance of the target variable. Generally, the higher R-squared, the better. An R-squared value of 1 would mean that the model could explain all variance in the data.

While summary statistics are a great way to compare models to one another at scale, figuring out whether our regression is working as expected from these metrics alone is still difficult. Therefore, a good approach in regression modeling is to also look

---

at the distribution of the regression errors, called the *residuals* of our model. The distribution of the residuals gives us good visual feedback on how the regression model is performing.

A residual diagram plots the predicted values against the residuals as a simple scatterplot. Ideally, a residual plot should look like Figure 3-6 to back up the following assumptions:

Linearity
> The points in the residual plot should be randomly scattered without exposing too much curvature.

Heteroscedasticity
> The spread of the points across predicted values should be more or less the same for all predicted values.

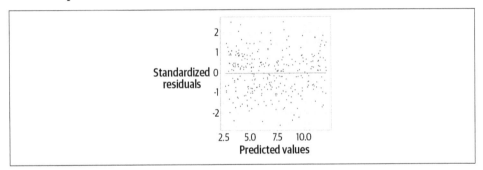

Figure 3-6. Residual analysis

Residual plots will show you on which parts of your data the regression model works well and on which parts it doesn't. Depending on your use case, you can decide whether this is problematic or still acceptable, given all other factors. Looking at the summary statistics alone would not give you these insights. Keeping an eye on the residuals is always a good idea when evaluating regression models.

Evaluating Classification Models

How do we evaluate the performance of a predictive model if the predicted values are not numeric but categorical? We can't just apply the metrics we learned from the regression model. To understand why, let's take a look at the data in Table 3-2.

The table shows the true labels of a classification problem (in the column Targets) as well as the corresponding outputs (in the Predicted and "Probabilistic output" columns) of a classification model.

Table 3-2. Example classification outputs

Targets	Predicted	Probabilistic output
1	1	0.954
1	0	0.456
0	0	0.012
0	1	0.567
0	0	0.234
...	...	...

If you look at the first four rows, you'll see four things that could happen here:

- The true label is 1, and our prediction is 1 (correct prediction).
- The true label is 0, and our prediction is 0 (correct prediction).
- The true label is 1, and our prediction is not 1 (incorrect prediction).
- The true label is 0, and our prediction is not 0 (incorrect prediction).

These four outcomes would also happen if we had more than two categories. We could simply observe these four outcomes for each category in our dataset.

The most popular way to measure the performance of a classification model is to display these four outcomes in a *confusion table*, or *confusion matrix*, as shown in Table 3-3.

Table 3-3. Confusion matrix

		Predicted class	
		Negative	Positive
Actual class	Negative	2,388 true negative (TN)	558 false positive (FP)
	Positive	415 false negative (FN)	2,954 true positive (TP)

This confusion table tells us that for our example classification problem, there were 2,388 observations where the actual label was 0 and our model labeled them correctly. These observations are called *true negatives*, because the model correctly predicted the negative class label. Likewise, 2,954 observations were identified by our model as *true positives*, as both the actual and the predicted outcome had the positive class label (in this case, the number 1).

But our model also made two kinds of errors. First, it wrongly predicted negative classes to be positive (558 cases), also known as a *type I error*. Second, the model incorrectly predicted 415 cases to be negative that were, in fact, positive. These errors are known as *type II errors*. Statisticians were rather less creative in naming these things.

Now, we can calculate various metrics from this confusion table. The most popular metric that you will see and hear often is accuracy. *Accuracy* describes how often our model was correct, based on all predictions. We can easily calculate the model's accuracy by dividing the number of correct predictions by the number of all predictions:

$$\text{ACC} = \frac{\text{TP+TN}}{\text{TP+TN + FP + FN}}$$

For the confusion matrix in Table 3-3, the accuracy is (2,388 + 2,954) / (2,954 + 2,388 + 558 + 415) = 0.8459, meaning that the predictions of our model were correct in 84.59% of all cases.

While accuracy is a widely used and popular metric, it has one big caveat: accuracy works only for balanced classification problems. Imagine the following example: we want to predict credit card fraud, which happens in only 0.1% of all credit card transactions. If our model consistently predicts no fraud, it would yield an astonishing accuracy score of 99.9%, because it would be correct in most cases.

While this model has an excellent accuracy metric, it's clear that this model isn't useful at all. That's why the confusion matrix allows us to calculate even more metrics that are more balanced toward correctly identifying positive or negative class labels.

The first metric we could look at is *precision*. This measures the proportion of true positives (predicted true labels that were actually true). Precision, also called the *positive predictive value* (*PPV*) is defined as follows:

$$\text{PPV} = \frac{\text{TP}}{\text{TP+FP}}$$

In our example, the precision is 2,954 / (2,954 + 558) = 0.8411. This value can be interpreted to mean that when the model labeled a data point as positive (1), it was correct in 84% of all cases. We will pick this metric if the costs of a false positive are very high and the costs of a false negative are rather low (for example, when we want to decide whether we are going to show an expensive ad to an online user).

Another metric that looks at the positive classes but has a slightly different focus is *recall*, sometimes also called *sensitivity*, or *true positive rate* (*TPR*). It gives the percentage of all positive classes that were correctly classified as positive. Recall is defined as follows:

$$TPR = \frac{TP}{TP+FN}$$

In our example, this would be 2,954 / (2,954 + 415) = 0.8768. The value means that the model could identify 87.68% of all positive classes in the dataset. We would pick this metric to optimize our model for finding the positive classes in our dataset (e.g., for fraud detection). Using recall as an evaluation metric makes sense when the costs of missing these positive classes (false negatives) are very high.

If you don't want to lean toward precision or recall, and accuracy seems to be not capturing your problem well enough, you could consider another commonly used metric called the *F-score*. Despite its technical name, this metric is relatively intuitive as it combines precision and recall. The most popular F-score is the F1-score, which is simply the harmonic mean of precision and recall.

We can thus easily calculate the F1-score if we already know the precision and the recall:

$$F_1 = 2 \times \frac{PPV \times TPR}{PPV+TPR} = \frac{2TP}{2TP + FP + FN}$$

In our case, the F1-score would thus be 2 × (0.8411 × 0.8768) / (0.8411 + 0.8768) = 0.8586.

A higher F1-score indicates a better-performing model, but what does it tell us exactly? Well, the F1-score isn't as easily explained in one sentence as the preceding metrics, but it is usually a good go-to metric to assess the quality of a model. Since the F1-score uses the harmonic of precision and recall instead of the arithmetic mean, it will tend to be lower if one of these would be very bad.

Imagine an extreme example with a precision of 0 and recall of 1. The arithmetic mean would return a score of 0.5, which roughly translates to "If one is great, but the other one is poor, then the average is OK." The harmonic mean, however, would be 0 in this case. Instead of averaging out high and low numbers, the F1-score will raise a flag if either recall or precision is extremely low. And that is much closer to what you would expect from a combined performance metric.

Evaluating Multiclassification Models

The metrics we used for binary classification problems also apply to *multiclassification problems* (which have more than two classes to predict). For example, consider the following targets and predicted values:

```
targets = [1, 3, 2, 0, 2, 2]
predicted = [1, 2, 2, 0, 2, 0]
```

The only difference between a binary and a multiclassification problem is that you would calculate the evaluation metrics for each class (0, 1, 2, 3) and compare it against all other classes. The way you do that can follow different approaches, usually referred to as the *micro* and *macro* value.

Micro scores typically calculate metrics globally by counting all the total true positives, false negatives, and false positives together and only then dividing them by each other. *Macro scores*, on the other hand, calculate precision, recall, and so forth for each label first and then calculate the average of all of them. These approaches produce similar, but still different, results.

For example, our dummy series for the four classification labels has a micro F1-score of 0.667 and a macro F1-score of 0.583. If you like, try it out and calculate the numbers by hand to foster your understanding of these metrics.

Neither of the micro or macro metrics is better or worse. These are just different ways to calculate the same summary statistic based on different approaches. These nuances will become more critical after you work on more complex multiclass problems.

There are even more performance metrics to look at, but these are beyond the scope of this book. For example, so far we haven't even looked at performance metrics that consider the probabilistic outputs of the models, such as the area under the ROC curve (*AUC*).

There's no silver bullet when it comes to evaluation metrics. It is important that you at least understand on a high level what these metrics are trying to capture and identify which metric is practical for your use case. And you need to know which performance is good enough to stop training more and more complex and (seemingly) accurate ML models. We will dive deeper into that in the next section.

Common Pitfalls of Machine Learning

ML is a powerful tool for solving many modern problems, but like any other tool, it is easy to misuse and can lead to poor results. This section outlines some beginner's mistakes you should avoid.

Pitfall 1: Using Machine Learning When You Don't Need It

If you have a hammer, everything looks like a nail. The worst thing you could do is take your newly acquired knowledge of ML and look for business problems that seem like a good fit. Instead, look at it from the opposite angle: once you have identified a relevant business problem, consider whether ML could help solve it.

And even then, it's important to start with a simple baseline first. This baseline is important to get a performance benchmark that the ML algorithm needs to outperform. If you have never done churn analysis before, you should not start with an ML-based approach, but rather use simple heuristics or hardcoded rules. These have low complexity and are easy for business stakeholders to understand. Switch to ML models as soon as you find that they perform significantly better than your baseline solution.

Pitfall 2: Being Too Greedy

Don't be too greedy in maximizing the performance metrics of your training set. This can cause your model to perform poorly on new data that it has never seen before. It may sound counterintuitive, but you should be more conservative in your training, especially on smaller datasets, as this can lead to better generalization of your model to unseen data. This concept is also known as *Occam's razor*: when in doubt, a simple solution is better than a complex one.

Pitfall 3: Building Overly Complex Models

Building models that are too complex goes hand in hand with the previous point: to achieve high accuracy, inexperienced people tend to create overly complex models such as neural networks. In many cases, a less accurate model with lower complexity is preferred to a highly complex, highly accurate model.

Complex models have two disadvantages:

- They can be difficult to maintain and debug in production. If something goes wrong or your model predictions are off (which they certainly will be from time to time), highly complex models are harder to correct than simpler models.

- Complex models can lead to *overfitting*: your model performs well on your training data but poorly on new data. Predictive analysis is about finding a sweet spot (see Figure 3-7) where the prediction errors in training (historical data) and testing (new data) are approximately equal. To avoid overfitting, you should always monitor the performance of your model on new data as well as the complexity of your model.

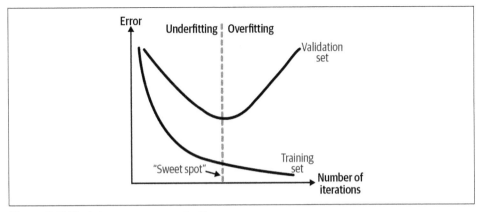

Figure 3-7. Training error versus testing error

Pitfall 4: Not Stopping When You Have Enough Data

Rarely will you have perfectly labeled ML data lying around in your organization. As you have already learned, usually the more examples (observations) we have, the better. However, experience shows that ML algorithms reach a plateau at a certain point, where additional training examples no longer significantly increase accuracy. This effect is illustrated in Figure 3-8.

When you reach this point, it is simply no longer cost-effective to spend more money on data labeling. For this reason, it is important to have a clear goal in mind. How accurate does your model need to be for you to use it? The threshold can range from "anything better than baseline" to "99.99 accuracy required," such as in medical cases. Knowing your goal and what you want to achieve can help you avoid high costs.

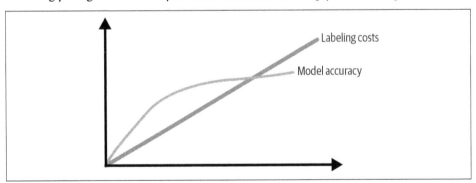

Figure 3-8. Model accuracy versus labeling costs

Pitfall 5: Falling for the Curse of Dimensionality

While the "the more data, the better" principle works for observations (rows), it can be counterproductive for features (columns). Imagine the following example.

You want to predict US home prices based on the variables size, bedrooms, and location (zip code). Size and bedrooms can be modeled as two individual features (columns), which increases the dimensionality of your dataset by only an order of two, as shown in Figure 3-9.

However, once you start using zip codes, most ML algorithms require that you encode this categorical variable into a single-column feature that is exactly as wide as the number of unique values. This increases the dimensionality of the data not just by an order of 1, but by an order of 41,692 (possible US zip codes), since it would be single columns containing either the value 0 or 1 for each example.

Most ML algorithms will struggle to find actual patterns in the data because the data is too sparse. No absolute rules can help you avoid the curse of dimensionality, but here are some tips:

- Be careful when adding new features to your dataset and do not hesitate to delete redundant or irrelevant features. This can sometimes be difficult, as you may need solid domain expertise for this step.

- Try to reduce the number of relations between attributes by coding these dependencies as a single attribute. For example, instead of having two attributes, price and size, you could calculate a new attribute, price per square foot. The fewer dependencies you have between variables in your dataset, the easier it will be for your ML algorithm to understand them.

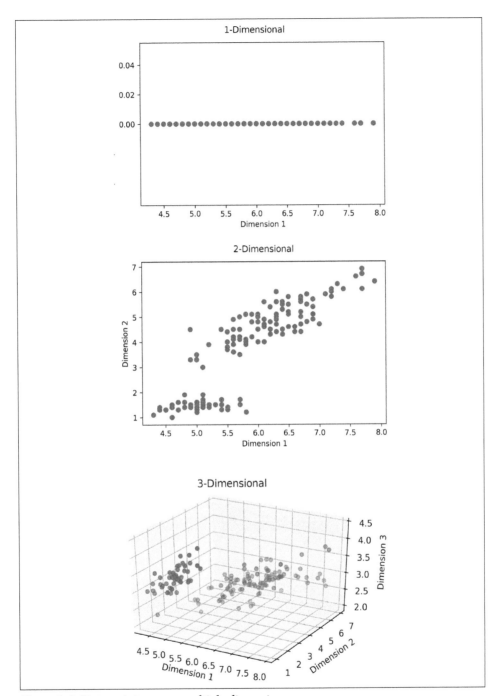

Figure 3-9. Data points across multiple dimensions

Pitfall 6: Ignoring Outliers

Outliers are data points that are far above the average value of your dataset. For example, imagine a dataset that contains people's salaries and net worth. If you plot the data, it might look like the chart at the top in Figure 3-10.

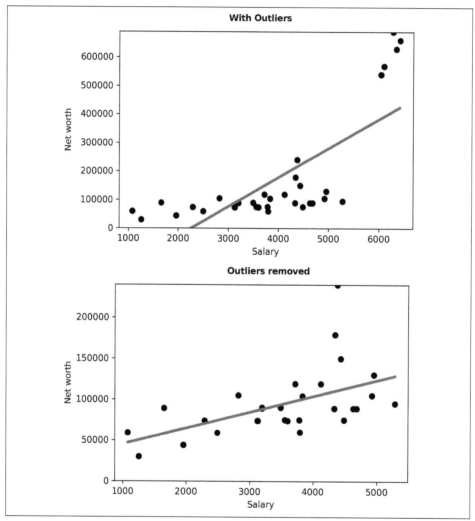

Figure 3-10. Sample data with outliers (top) and without (bottom)

You can see that a strong correlation seems to exist between the two variables *salary* and *net worth*. But a few data points are very far away from all others. These represent people who have a high salary, but even higher net worth. The regression line (dashed) in this case is skewed toward these outliers, resulting in a poor fit for all other data points. Once we remove this group of high-net-worth individuals (on the bottom in Figure 3-10), the regression line seems to fit the remaining points much better.

The impact of outliers can be huge for many algorithms, especially those that work with regression tasks. This means that you should pay close attention to detecting outliers in your dataset.

Pitfall 7: Taking Cloud Infrastructure for Granted

In this book, I make the bold assumption that you have access to cloud computing for both model training and model inference. But let's face it: in many companies that may not be the case (yet). Although cloud computing adoption is growing rapidly, most companies are still largely using on-premises solutions. The reasons for this are many, but one important reason is the fear of losing control of data.

I strongly recommend that you try cloud computing (AIaaS or ML platforms) at least for prototyping with noncritical data, as described in the next chapter. While this may not yet be a lived practice in your organization, it will give you a quick head start and put you in touch with cutting-edge ML workflows and tools. This will also enable you to discuss with your team how cloud computing could be an investment that benefits your overall AI/ML strategy.

Summary

In this chapter, you learned the basic concepts of supervised machine learning and got an idea of which algorithms are important for ML. We also touched on deep learning, computer vision, and NLP.

Of course, you have much more to learn about ML, but these pages will give you everything you need to build your own ML-powered prototypes. I hope you feel a little more confident to do this by now. If not, don't worry!

Later, as we approach practical use cases, the concepts from this chapter will probably seem much more accessible to you, as they'll be connected to some practice. If you want to dig deeper into ML, I recommend any of the following books:

- *Machine Learning Design Patterns* by Valliappa Lakshmanan et al. (O'Reilly)
- *Introduction to Machine Learning with Python* by Andreas C. Müller and Sarah Guido (O'Reilly)
- *Building Machine Learning Powered Applications* by Emmanuel Ameisen (O'Reilly)

I also recommend bookmarking this chapter and coming back here anytime you need a refresher on ML fundamentals.

## CHAPTER 4

Prototyping

By now, you should finally have enough theoretical background knowledge to get hands-on with some AI use cases. In this chapter, you'll learn how to use a prototyping technique borrowed from product management to quickly create and put ML use cases into practice and validate your assumptions about feasibility and impact.

Remember, our goal is to find out quickly whether our AI-powered idea creates value and whether we are able to build a first version of the solution without wasting too much time or other resources. This chapter will introduce you not only to the theoretical concepts about prototyping, but also to the concrete tools we are going to use in the examples throughout this book.

What Is a Prototype, and Why Is It Important?

Let's face the hard truth: most ML projects fail. And that's not because most projects are underfunded or lack talent (although those are common problems too).

The main reason ML projects fail is because of the incredible uncertainty surrounding them: requirements, solution scope, user acceptance, infrastructure, legal considerations, and most importantly, the quality of the outcome are all very difficult to predict in advance of a new initiative. Especially when it comes to the result, you never really know whether your data has enough signals in it until you go through the process of data collection, preparation, and cleansing and build the actual model.

Many companies start their first AI/ML projects with a lot of enthusiasm. Then they find that the projects turn out to be a bottomless pit. Months of work and thousands of dollars are spent just to get to a simple result: it doesn't work.

Prototyping is a way to minimize risk and evaluate the impact and feasibility of your ML use case before scaling it. With prototyping, your ML projects will be faster, cheaper, and deliver a higher return on investment.

For this book, a *prototype* is an unfinished product with a simple purpose: validation. Concepts such as a PoC or a minimum viable product (MVP) serve the same purpose, but these concepts have a different background and involve more than just validation. The idea of validation is so important because you don't need to build a prototype if you don't have anything to validate.

In the context of AI or ML projects, you want to validate your use case in two dimensions: impact and feasibility. That's why it's so essential that you have a rough idea of these categories before you go ahead and build something.

Here are some examples of things you can validate in the context of ML and AI:

- Does your solution provide value to the user?
- Is your solution being used as it was intended?
- Is your solution being accepted by users?
- Does your data contain enough signals to build a useful model?
- Does an AI service work well enough with your data to provide sufficient value?

To be an effective validation tool, ML prototypes must be end-to-end. Creating an accurate model is good. Creating a useful model is better. And the only way to get that information is to get your ML solution in front of real users. You can build the best customer churn predictor in the world, but if the marketing and sales staff aren't ready to put the predictions into action, your project is dead. That's why you need quick user feedback.

When you prototype your ML-powered solution, don't compromise on data. Don't use data that wouldn't be available in production. Don't do manual cleanups that don't scale. You can fix a model; you can fix the UI. But you can't fix the data. Treat it the way you'd treat it in a production scenario.

A prototype should usually have a well-defined scope that includes the following:

Clear goal
> For example, "Can we build a model that is better than our baseline B in predicting y, given some data x?"

Strict time frame
> For example, "We will build the best model we can in a maximum of two weeks."

Acceptance criteria

For example, "Our prototype passed the user acceptance test if feedback F happened."

When it comes to technology, a prototype should leave it up to you to decide which technology stack is the best to achieve the goals within the time frame. Prototypes give you valuable insight into potential problem areas (e.g., data-quality issues) while engaging business stakeholders from the start and managing their expectations.

Prototyping in Business Intelligence

For decades, the typical development process for BI systems was the classic waterfall method: projects were planned as a linear process that began with requirements gathering, then moved to design, followed by data engineering, testing, and deployment of the reports or metrics desired by the business.

Even without AI or ML, the waterfall method is reaching its limits. That's because several factors are working together. Business requirements are becoming increasingly fuzzy as the business itself becomes more complex. In addition, the technology is also becoming more complex. Whereas 10 years ago you'd have to integrate a handful of data sources, today even small companies have to manage dozens of systems.

When your project plan for a large-scale BI initiative is ready, it's often already overtaken by reality. With AI/ML and its associated uncertainties, things aren't going to get much easier.

To launch a successful AI-driven solution as part of a BI system, you must essentially treat your BI system as a data product. That means acknowledging the facts that you don't know whether your idea will ultimately work out as planned, what the final solution will look like, and whether your users are interacting with it as expected. Product management techniques, such as prototyping, will help you mitigate these risks and allow for more flexible development. But how exactly can you apply prototyping in the realms of BI?

Reports in BI production systems are expected by default to be reliable and available, and the information they contain is accurate. So your production system isn't the best choice for testing something among users. What else do we have?

Companies typically work with test systems to try out new features before putting them into production. However, the problem with test systems is that they often involve the same technical effort and challenges as the production system. Usually, the entire production environment is replicated for testing purposes: a test data warehouse, a test frontend BI, and a test area for ETL processes, because you want to make sure that what works on the test system also works in production.

In the sense of our definition, a prototype takes place before testing, as shown in Figure 4-1. For the prototype, you need deep vertical integration from data ingestion, over the analytical services, to the user interface, while keeping the overall technical complexity low.

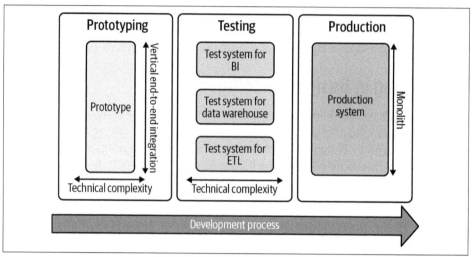

Figure 4-1. Prototyping in the software development process

In most cases, especially with monolithic BI systems, your production and test stack aren't suitable for prototyping in just a few days or weeks. For our purposes, we need something less complex and lightweight.

Whatever tech stack you use for this, you should make sure of the following:

- The tech stack supports all three layers of the AI use case architecture (data, analytics, and user interface) to ensure that data is available and fit for use, your models perform well enough on your data, and users accept and see value in your solution.

- Your stack should be open and provide high connectivity to allow future integration into the test and perhaps even the production system. This aspect is essential because, if testing is successful, you want to enable a smooth transition from the prototyping phase to the testing phase. If you prototype on your local machine, it'll be complicated to transfer the workflow from your computer to a remote server and expect it to work as smoothly. Tools like Docker will help you ease the transition, adding technical friction that no longer has anything to do with your original validation hypothesis.

Therefore, the perfect prototyping platform for AI-powered BI use cases offers high connectivity, many available integration services, and low initial investment costs. Cloud platforms have proven to meet these requirements quite well.

In addition, you should use a platform that gives you easy access to the various AI/ML services covered in Chapter 2. If you have the data available, prototyping the ML model should take no more than a maximum of two to four weeks, sometimes only a few days. Use AutoML for regression/classification tasks, AIaaS for commodity services like character recognition, and pretrained models for custom deep learning applications rather than training them from scratch.

To avoid wasting time and money unnecessarily on your next ML project, build a prototype first before going all in.

The AI Prototyping Toolkit for This Book

We'll use Microsoft Azure as our platform for prototyping in this book. You could use many other tools, including AWS or GCP. These platforms are comparable in their features, and what we do here with Azure, you can basically do with any other platform.

I chose Azure for the following two reasons:

- Many businesses are running on a Microsoft stack, and Azure will be the most familiar cloud platform to them.
- Azure integrates smoothly with Power BI, a BI tool that is popular in many enterprises.

You may be wondering how a full-fledged cloud platform like Azure can ever be lightweight enough for prototyping. The main reason is that we don't use the entire Azure platform, but only parts of it that are provided "as a service," so we don't have to worry about the technical details under the hood. The main services we'll use are Azure Machine Learning Studio, Azure Blob Storage, an Azure compute resource, and a set of Azure Cognitive Services, Microsoft's AIaaS offering.

The good thing is that although we're still prototyping, the infrastructure would stand up to a production scenario as well. We would need to change the solution's processes, maintenance, integrations, and management, but the technical foundation would be the same. We'll go into this in more detail in Chapter 11.

I'll try not to rely too much on features that work exclusively with Azure and Power BI, but keep it open enough so you can connect your own AI models to your own BI. Also, most Azure integrations into Power BI require a Pro license, which I don't want to put you through. Let's start with the setup for Microsoft Azure.

Working with Microsoft Azure

This section gives you a quick introduction to Microsoft Azure and lets you activate all the tools you'll need for the use cases starting in Chapter 7. While you may not need all of these services right away, I recommend that you set them up in advance so you can focus on the actual use cases later instead of dealing with the technical overhead.

Sign Up for Microsoft Azure

To create and use the AI services from Chapter 7 onward, you need a Microsoft Azure account. If you are new to the platform, Azure gives you free access to all the services we cover in this book for the first 12 months (at the time of writing). You also get a free $200 credit for services that are billed based on usage, such as compute resources or AI model deployments.

To explore the free access and to sign up, visit *https://azure.microsoft.com/free* and start the sign-up process.

 If you already have an Azure account, you can skip ahead to "Create an Azure Compute Resource" on page 83. Be aware that you might be billed for these services if you are not on a free trial. If you are unsure, contact your Azure administrator before you move ahead.

To sign up, you will be prompted to create a Microsoft account. I recommend you create a new account for testing purposes (and take advantage of the free credit bonus!). If you have a corporate account, you can try to continue with that, but your company might have restrictions. Therefore, it may be best to start from scratch, play around a bit, and once you have everything figured out, continue with your company's account.

On the following page, click "Create one!" (Figure 4-2).

Figure 4-2. Creating a new Microsoft account

Next, enter your email address and click Next. Create a password and continue. After confirming that you are not a robot, you should see the screen in Figure 4-3.

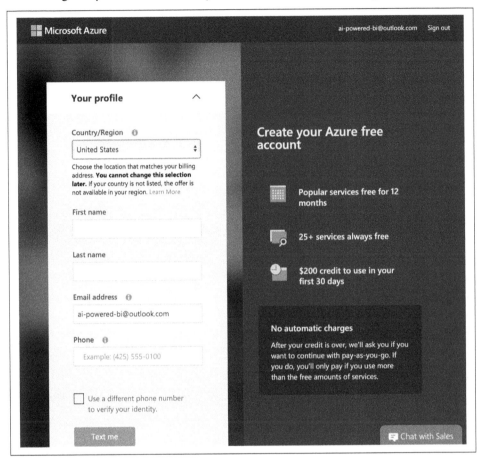

Figure 4-3. Azure sign-up prompt

You must confirm your account with a valid phone number. Enter your information and click "Text me" or "Call me." Enter the verification code and click "Verify code." After successful verification, check the terms and click Next.

You are almost there! The last prompt will require you to provide your credit card information. Why? It's the same with all major cloud platforms. Once your free credit is used up or the free period expires, you will be charged for using these services. However, the good thing about Microsoft for beginners is that you will not be charged automatically. When your free period ends, you'll have to opt for pay-as-you-go billing.

After successfully signing up, you should see the Azure portal screen shown in Figure 4-4.

Figure 4-4. Azure portal dashboard

Welcome to Microsoft Azure! You can access this home page at any time by visiting *portal.azure.com*. Let's quickly explore the Azure portal home page:

Navigation bar (1)
> You can open the portal menu on the left or navigate to your account settings at the top right.

Azure services (2)
> These are the recommended services for you. These may look different for you, especially if you are newly signed up.

Create a resource (3)
> This will be one of the most commonly used buttons. You use it to create new resources like services on Azure.

Navigate (4)
> This section contains tools and all the other items that take you to various settings. You will not need them for now.

When you see this screen, you are all set with the setup for Microsoft Azure. If you are having trouble setting up your Azure account, I recommend the following resources:

- Azure videos (*https://oreil.ly/dWMDM*)
- Azure Lessons website (*https://oreil.ly/dmaaH*)

Create an Azure Machine Learning Studio Workspace

Azure Machine Learning Studio will be our workbench in Microsoft Azure to build and deploy custom ML models and manage datasets. The first thing you need to do is create an Azure Machine Learning workspace. The workspace is a basic resource in your Azure account that contains all of your experiments, training, and deployed ML models.

The workspace resource is associated with your Azure subscription. While you can programmatically create and manage these services, we will use the Azure portal to navigate through the process. Remember, everything you do here with your mouse and keyboard can also be done through automated scripts if you wish later.

Log in to the Microsoft account you used for the Azure subscription and visit *portal.azure.com*. Click the "Create a resource" button (Figure 4-5).

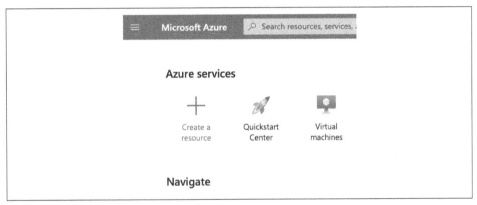

Figure 4-5. Creating a new resource in Azure

Now use the search bar to find **machine learning** and select it (Figure 4-6).

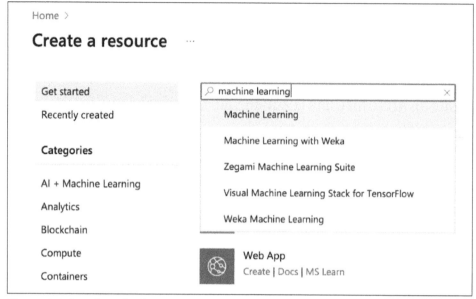

Figure 4-6. Searching for the ML resource

In the Machine Learning section, click Create (Figure 4-7).

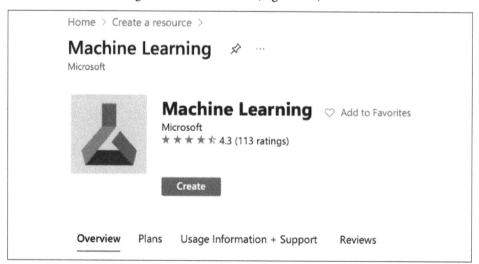

Figure 4-7. Creating a new ML resource

You need to provide some information for your new workspace, as shown in Figure 4-8:

Workspace name

Choose a unique name for your workspace that differentiates it from other workspaces you create. Project names are typically good candidates for workspace names. This example uses `auto-ml`. The name must be unique within the selected resource group.

Subscription

Select the Azure subscription you want to use.

Resource group

A resource group bundles resources in your Azure subscription and could, for example, be tied to your department. I strongly advise you to create a new resource group at this stage and assign any service you are going to set up for this book to this resource group. This will make the cleanup much easier later. Click "Create new" and give your new resource group a name. This example uses `ai-powered-bi`. Whenever you see this reference anywhere, you need to replace it with the name of your own resource group.

Location

Select the physical location closest to your users and your data resources. Be careful when transferring data outside of protected geographical areas such as the European Union (EU). Most services are typically available first in US regions.

Once you've entered everything, click "Review + create." After the initial validation has passed, click Create again.

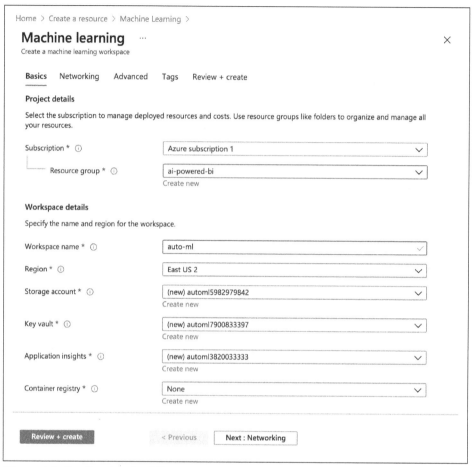

Figure 4-8. Configuring the ML resource

Creating your workspace in the Azure cloud can take several minutes. When the process is finished, you will see a success message, as in Figure 4-9.

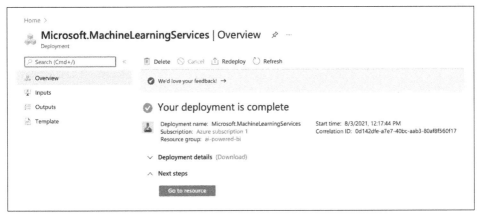

Figure 4-9. ML resource successfully created

To view your new workspace, click "Go to resource." This will take you to the ML resource page (Figure 4-10).

Figure 4-10. ML resource overview

You have now selected the previously created workspace. Verify your subscription and your resource group here. If you were to train and deploy your ML models via code programmatically, you could now also head over to your favorite code editor and continue from there.

But since we want to continue our no-code journey, click "Launch studio" to train and deploy ML models without writing a single line of code. This will take you to the welcome screen of the Machine Learning Studio (Figure 4-11). You also can access this directly via *ml.azure.com*.

Figure 4-11. Azure Machine Learning Studio home

The Machine Learning Studio is a web interface that includes a variety of ML tools to perform data science scenarios for data science practitioners of all skill levels. The studio is supported across all modern web browsers (no, this does not include Internet Explorer).

The welcome screen is divided into three main areas:

- On the left, you will find the menu bar with access to all services within ML Studio.

- On the top, you will find suggested services and can directly create more services by clicking "Create new."

- On the bottom, you will see an overview of recently launched services or resources within ML Studio (which should still be empty by now, since you just set up your account).

Create an Azure Compute Resource

You have created an Azure subscription and a workspace for Machine Learning Studio. You can consider these things still as "overhead." So far, you haven't launched any service or resource that actually does something.

That's about to change now. In the following steps, you will create a *compute resource*. You can imagine a compute resource as a virtual machine (or a cluster of virtual machines) where the actual workload of your jobs is running. On modern cloud platforms such as Microsoft Azure, compute resources can be created and deleted with a few clicks (or prompts from the command line) and will be provisioned or shut down in a matter of seconds. You can choose from a variety of machine setups—from small, cheap computers to heavy machines with graphics processing unit (GPU) support.

 Once you create a compute resource and this resource is online, you will be charged according to the price mentioned in the compute resources list (e.g., $0.6/hour). If you are still using free Azure credits, this will be deducted from them. If not, your credit card will be charged accordingly. To avoid unnecessary charges, make sure to stop or delete any compute resource that you don't need any more.

You'll create a compute resource that you can use for all the examples in this book. In practice, you may want to set up different compute resources for different projects, as well as to have more transparency about which project incurs which costs. However, in our prototyping example, one resource is sufficient, and you can easily track whether the resource is running so that it doesn't eat up your free trial budget.

You can create a compute resource directly in Azure ML Studio. Click the Compute option in the left navigation bar.

Then click "Create new compute," and a screen like the one in Figure 4-12 will appear. To select the machine type, select the "Select from all options" radio button.

Figure 4-12. Creating a new compute instance

Here you can see all available machine types (Figure 4-13). The more performance you allocate, the faster an ML training usually will be. The cheapest resource available is a Standard_DS1_v2 machine with one core, 3.5 GB RAM, and 7 GB storage— which costs about $0.06 per hour in the US East region.

Type **Standard_DS1** in the "Search by VM name" option and select the machine with the lowest price, as shown in Figure 4-13. You can really choose any type of machine here; just make sure that the price is reasonable, because we don't need high performance at the moment.

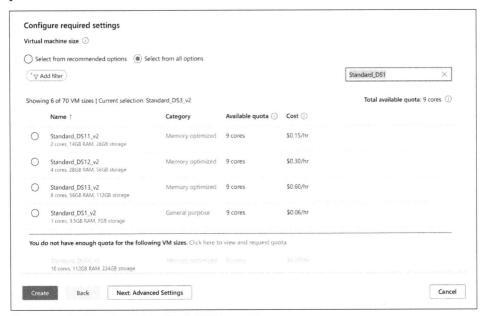

Figure 4-13. Choosing a Standard_DS11 machine

Click the Create button. This should take you back to the overview page of your computing resources. Wait for the resource to be created, which usually takes two to five minutes. The compute resource will start automatically once it's provisioned (see Figure 4-14).

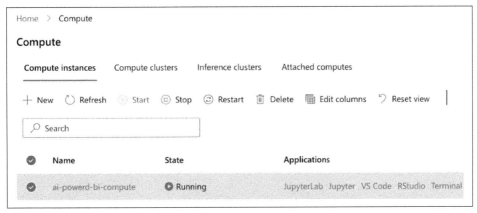

Figure 4-14. Compute resource running

Since you won't need this resource until Chapter 7, select the resource and click Stop to prevent it from being encumbered. In the end, your compute resource summary page should look similar to Figure 4-15. Your compute resource should appear in the list, but its state should be Stopped.

Figure 4-15. Compute resource stopped

Create Azure Blob Storage

The last building block you need for our prototyping setup is a place to store and upload files such as CSV tables or images. The typical place for these binary files is Azure Blob Storage; *blob* stands for *binary large object*—basically, file storage for almost everything with almost unlimited scale. We will use this storage mainly for writing outputs from our AI models or staging image files for the use cases in Chapter 7 onward.

To create blob storage in Azure, visit *portal.azure.com* and search for **storage accounts**. Click Create and create a new storage account in the same region where your ML Studio resource is located. Give this account a unique name, and then select standard performance and locally redundant storage, as shown in Figure 4-16. As this is only test data, you don't need to pay more for higher data availability standards. Again, you will save data here only temporarily, and the expenses will be more than covered by your free trial budget.

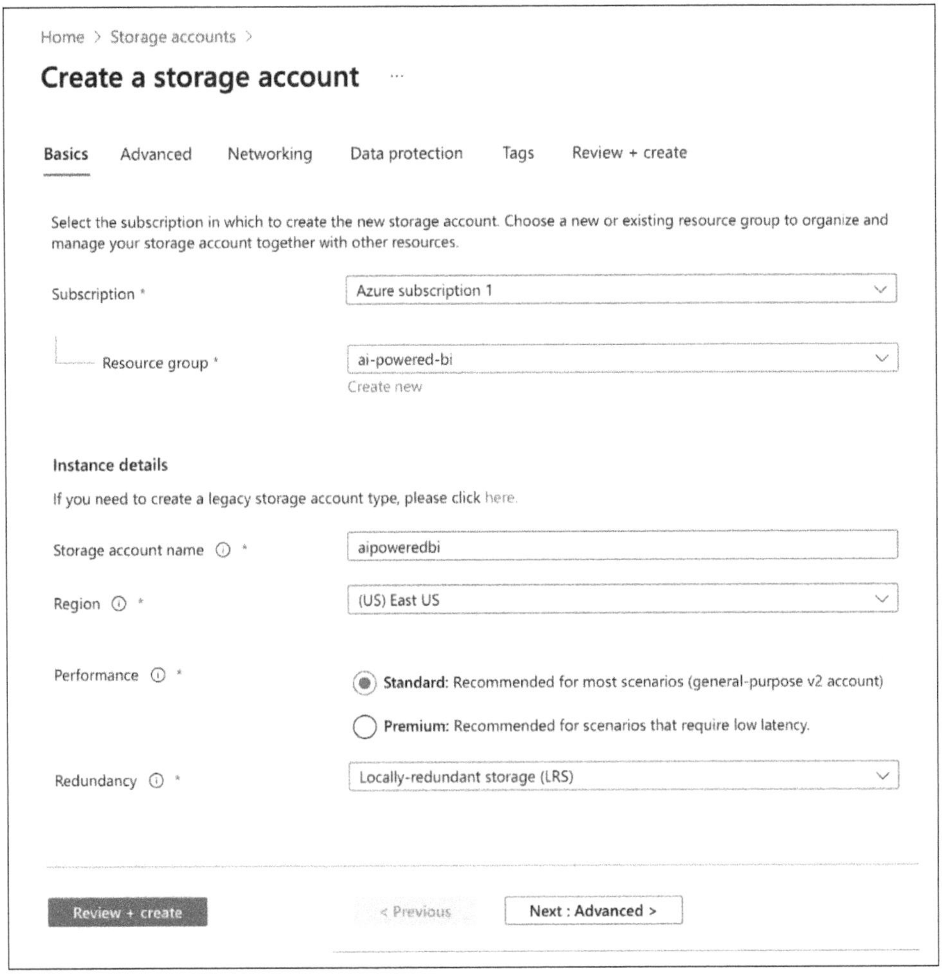

Figure 4-16. Creating a storage account

Once the deployment is complete, click "Go to resource." You will see the interface shown in Figure 4-17.

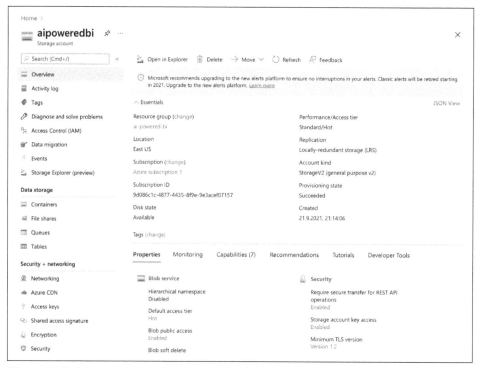

Figure 4-17. Azure storage account overview

Click "Access keys" on the left to open the screen shown in Figure 4-18. You will need these access keys when you want to access objects in that storage programmatically.

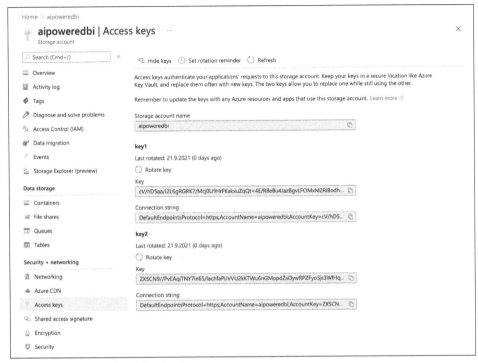

Figure 4-18. Access keys for the Azure storage account

Now that you have a storage account and keys to manipulate data here, you have to create a *container*, which is something like a file folder that helps organize files. Click the Containers option on the left-side menu and then click "+ Container" at the top of the screen, as highlighted in Figure 4-19.

Figure 4-19. Creating an Azure Blob Storage container

Create a container called **tables**. Set the access level to Container, which will make it easier to access the files later through external tools such as Power BI. Create another Container called **simulation** with the same settings.

If you deal with sensitive or production data, you would of course choose Private here to make sure that authorization is needed before the data can be accessed. Voilá, the new container should appear in the list and is now ready to host some files.

Working with Microsoft Power BI

For the user layer, we will rely on Microsoft Power BI as our tool to display reports, dashboards, and the results from our AI models. Power BI comes in two versions: Power BI Desktop and Power BI Service.

Power BI Desktop is currently available only for Windows. This offline application is installed on your computer and has all the features you can expect from Power BI. If you have a Microsoft Office subscription, Power BI is most likely part of that. You can download Power BI from the Microsoft Power BI downloads page (*https://oreil.ly/9LpZX*).

Power BI Service is an online version of Power BI that runs across all platforms, including Macs. It doesn't currently have all the features of the desktop version, but new features are added regularly. I can't give you a guarantee that all things we cover in this book will work on Power BI service, but it's worth a try if you can't or don't want to install Power BI on your computer. You can get started with Power BI service at its Getting Started page (*https://oreil.ly/9SyDY*).

If you've never worked with Power BI before, it might be useful to watch Microsoft's 45-minute introductory course (*https://oreil.ly/ySgML*), which gives you a high-level introduction on how the tool works.

 Unfortunately, Power BI does not always give exactly reproducible results. As you follow along with the use cases in this book, you may notice that some of your visuals and automated suggestions may not match the screenshots in this book. Don't get confused by it too much, as the overall picture should still be the same, even if little variations appear here and there.

In case you don't like using Power BI or want to use your own BI tool, you should be able to re-create everything in the case studies (except for Chapters 5 and 6) in any other BI tool as well, as long as it supports code execution of either Python or R scripts.

To run the Python or R scripts inside Power BI, you need to have one of these languages installed on your computer and Power BI pointed to the respective kernel. Check the following resources to make sure that Power BI and R, or Power BI and Python, are set up correctly:

- Run R scripts in Power BI Desktop (*https://oreil.ly/mY33x*).
- Run Python scripts in Power BI Desktop (*https://oreil.ly/Ineut*).

Besides the clean Python or R engines, you need a few packages for working on the use cases later. For R, these packages are the following:

- *httr* (for making HTTP request)
- *rjson* (for handling the API response)
- *dplyr* (for data preparation)

For the Python scripts, the equivalents are as follows:

- *requests*
- *json*
- *pandas*

Make sure that these packages are installed for either the R or Python engine that Power BI is using in your case. If you don't know how to install packages in R or Python, check out these YouTube videos:

- "Installing Packages in R" (*https://oreil.ly/Z8g56*)
- "Python workshop—Installing Packages" (*https://oreil.ly/WT1pF*)

Summary

I hope that this chapter has given you a solid understanding of a prototype in the context of data product development, and why it is highly recommended to start any AI/ML projects with a prototype first. By now, you should also have your personal prototyping toolkit ready so that you can tackle the practical use cases in the next chapters. Let's go!

## CHAPTER 5

AI-Powered Descriptive Analytics

In this chapter, we will explore two use cases that illustrate how AI can help us perform descriptive analytics faster and provide a more intuitive and seamless way to interact with large datasets—even for nontechnical people. We will also see how the natural language capabilities of modern BI tools (in this example, Power BI) can take away some of the mundane tasks from us.

Use Case: Querying Data with Natural Language

The typical analytical thinking process of a business user often starts with a simple question, such as one of these:

- How were my sales last month?
- Did we sell more this year than last year?
- What's the top selling product?

These questions are mostly descriptive in nature. Users first need to understand the status quo before they can dive deeper into analysis or even anticipate future events.

The classic way to solve this problem would be for an analyst to create a set of static reports for the most common questions for specific business units or departments. However, it's extremely difficult for business analysts or BI designers to anticipate all of the most common questions by using static reports or visualizations. Depending on which problem you look at and which people you ask, the exact area of interest can be fundamentally different. In organizations, this usually leads to long, exhaustive meetings with different stakeholders discussing which charts to display in a dashboard.

This is where self-service BI systems typically come in, allowing individuals to create their own content. Instead of generating all the important dashboards and visualizations in advance, business users can slice and dice data themselves and create the visualizations they need.

However, self-service BI systems have their problems as well. First, it's simply not possible to enable all possible thinking pathways through customizable drill-downs or additional dimensions. One issue often leads to another, and anticipating all the possible thinking pathways in the data model leads to complex data structures and unintuitive report builders—just to show some descriptive analytics from the past. And second, not all business users understand how to properly slice and dice data, leading to incorrect dashboards and flawed insights. Pulling together various metrics and dimensions into a custom dashboard still means a lot of friction for nontechnical users who are not trained data analysts.

As a conclusion, none of the static and self-service approaches in BI systems are able to answer all possible questions from individuals, and individuals usually can't always sift through the data themselves because it's not one of their primary tasks. What business users want instead is to ask questions and have them answered. At this point, they would typically call a data analyst for help to solve the problem. Of course, this approach does not scale well, as organizations typically have more business users than data analysts. And even if you could afford to have a lot of analytical expertise in house, you don't want to keep your analysts busy with repetitive, easy-to-solve tasks. Let's now lay out the scenario for our example use case.

Problem Statement

We are looking at sales data in Power BI. Sales management has approached the BI team after recognizing a positive revenue trend and wants to get a deeper understanding of what's currently going on. As BI analysts, we have been tasked to provide support to sales staff and help them get insights with regards to revenue development in their particular areas of interest. In the same sense of self-service BI, we want to provide "help for self-help" and enable salespeople to interact with the dataset seamlessly and without any technical friction.

Solution Overview

Rather than team up business users with data analysts to get answers for simple descriptive statistics, a more efficient approach is to simply let users ask questions against the data by using natural language and have them answered automatically without any, or with very little, human assistance. Most people don't even realize that they've been trained in this method for years (or for however long they have been using an internet search engine like Google).

For example, if a business user wants to compare sales figures for a certain country with the numbers from last year, they might want to shoot off a query such as this:

`Show me sales in the USA last year versus this year`

In fact, AI-powered natural language features let users do just that. What is happening under the hood is that an AI-powered natural language model is interpreting the user input and tries to map it to available data in the dataset and come up with an appropriate visualization for it. The experience should be quick, interactive, and frictionless. Figure 5-1 shows the conceptual architecture of our solution.

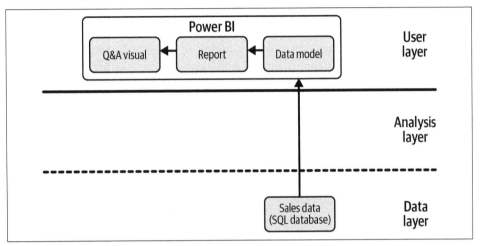

Figure 5-1. Natural language use case architecture

As you can see in Figure 5-1, we are using Power BI as our BI tool and will leverage its built-in AI capabilities for our purposes. The analysis layer is therefore empty because we are not using any external analytical service. Everything is built into Power BI and happening in the user layer. Other BI tools such as Tableau offer similar functionalities, but the details might be different. In any case, choosing a good BI frontend for this task is key, since you cannot add NLP capabilities to BI software if it offers no native support (or add-ons that are offering this).

In Power BI, the NLP feature is called the *Q&A visual*. The Q&A visual lets you use natural language to explore your data in your own words. Q&A is interactive and can even be fun. It seems like a good candidate for our problem statement.

The Q&A visual can be dragged onto a report just like any other visual so the user can perform custom queries against the data. The Q&A visual can also be added as a button in the ribbon, independent from a report, and be integrated into dashboards. It works with the following data sources: imported data, live connection to Azure

Analysis Services, and SQL Server Analysis Services (via a gateway) as well as Power BI datasets.

Power BI Walk-Through

To follow along with this example, you will first need to download the *Sales & Marketing sample PBIX.pbix* file from the book's website (*https://oreil.ly/jgjFu*). The dataset contains various sales and marketing data from a fictitious manufacturing company.

The dataset comes pre-populated with some reports to keep track of the company's market share, product volume, sales figures, and sentiment scores. For our case study, we assume that all manufacturers in this dataset belong to one holding group so that we can analyze the total revenue as a metric of interest. In return, we are not so interested in the individual manufacturers' market share as highlighted in the original scenario. You can learn more about the dataset from the Power BI website (*https://oreil.ly/S6rOE*).

Let's start by opening Power BI Desktop. In the upper-left section of Power BI, choose File → Open report → Browse reports. Then, select the *Sales & Marketing sample PBIX.pbix* file from the folder where you downloaded it. You should see the intro screen of this report file (Figure 5-2).

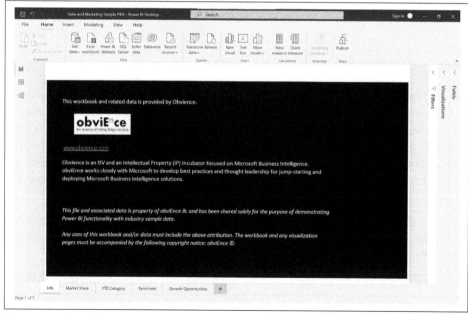

Figure 5-2. Sample Power BI report

For now, we won't bother with the pre-written reports and dashboards. Our goal is to provide a high-level overview on sales data plus an ability for our users to query our data interactively.

If this is the first time you're using Power BI, I recommend spending four minutes reading the Microsoft article "Tour the Report Editor in Power BI" (*https://oreil.ly/2jBnn*). It will familiarize you with the most basic terms and concepts, such as the Report canvas and the Filters, Visualizations, and the Fields panes.

You first need to add a new blank page to the report by clicking the plus sign at the bottom of the screen. On an empty report page, open the Visualizations pane on the right. Select the Q&A visual icon from the Visualizations pane (Figure 5-3) and double-click to add it to the canvas.

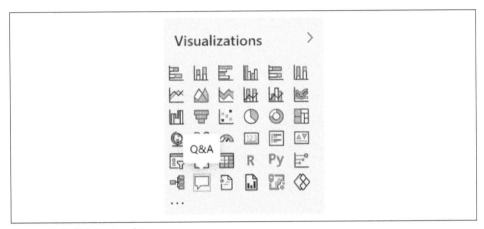

Figure 5-3. Q&A visual icon

Drag the border so the visual fills the whole width of your report. Increase the height so that it covers roughly half of your Report canvas. Your report screen should now look similar to Figure 5-4.

Figure 5-4. Q&A visual default screen

Now, let's explore this visual in a bit more detail. The Q&A visual consists of four core components:

Text box (1)

> This is where users type their questions or queries and where they will see autocomplete and autosuggest features.

List of suggested questions (2)

> This pre-populated list contains sample questions the user can run with a single click.

Convert icon (3)

> This converts the output from the Q&A tool into a standard Power BI visual.

Q&A cog icon (4)

> This opens a Settings menu that allows designers to configure the underlying natural language engine.

Let's give this visual a try by selecting the first suggested question. Click the first sample expression: "top geo states by sum of score." (If Power BI makes a different suggestion, just follow along with that.)

Power BI will respond with the visual that seems most appropriate for this analysis. In this case, it presents a map visual, showing the top states (Figure 5-5).

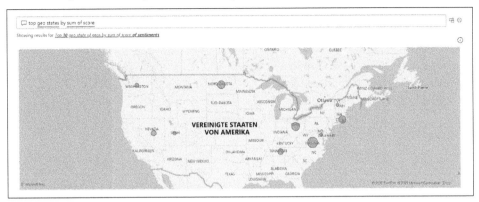

Figure 5-5. Q&A map output

We can change this to almost any other type of visual by making that part of our query. Try changing the text in the text box as follows: **top geo states by sum of score as bar chart**. This query will present a horizontal bar chart instead of a map (Figure 5-6).

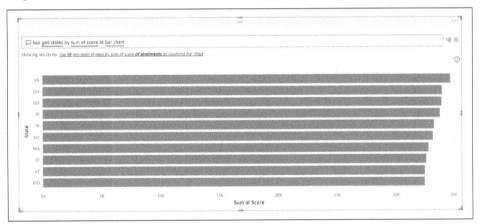

Figure 5-6. Q&A bar chart output

Now, let's head back to the text box and explore how users would input questions here. The Q&A tool can answer a variety of queries, including but not limited to, those listed in Table 5-1.

Since we are interested in revenue trends, we want to create a simple line chart showing the total revenue over time, ideally broken down by year. To achieve this, let's ask Power BI a simple query: **Show me revenue over time**.

Table 5-1. Example commands for the Power BI Q&A visual

Type	Example
Ask natural questions	Which sales have the highest revenue?
Relative date filtering	Sales in the last year
Filter by variables	Sales in the US
Filter by conditions	Sales for product Category A or Category B
Show a specific visual	Sales by product as pie chart
Show aggregations	Median sales by product
Sorting	Top 10 countries by sales ordered by country code
Comparisons	Date by total sales versus total cost
Time	Sales over time

The result we see in Figure 5-7 isn't quite what we expected. The output simply shows some dates from 1999. What's going on here?

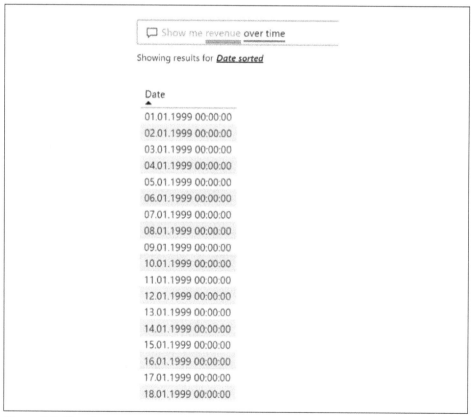

Figure 5-7. Showing revenue over time

We can find out more by looking at the text box, where Power BI helps us identify problematic phrases in our query. The red line below "revenue" tells us that Power BI could not interpret this variable. In fact, the underlining here follows a distinct color code:

- A solid blue underline indicates that the system successfully matched the word to a field or value in the data model.

- An orange underline indicates that the expression was matched with low confidence. This happens if the expression is ambiguous—for example, because multiple fields contain an expression like "sales."

- A red underline means that the Q&A tool could not match the word at all with anything in the data model.

If you click an underlined word, you will see suggestions for how Power BI would solve the conflict. In the case of the "revenue" expression, Power BI can't assign it to a measure. Let's be more explicit and adjust the query as follows: **Show me sum of revenue over time**.

As you can see, you have to be specific with the query if you rely on the default values. We'll fix this later, but for now, let's accept the suggestion and see what happens (Figure 5-8).

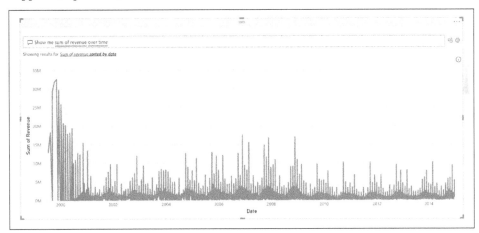

Figure 5-8. Showing sum of revenue over time

This looks more like what we expect. Power BI shows a line chart listing the total revenue over time, split up by day. Although this is not bad, it is hard for us to see the big trends. So let's be even more specific and ask, **Show me sum of revenue over time by year**.

The addition of by year indicates to Power BI that we are looking for a yearly aggregation. As a result, Power BI shows us a clean line chart, where we can instantly see that the revenue spiked in 2006 and then followed a negative trend afterward (Figure 5-9). Since 2010, the trend seems to be positive again.

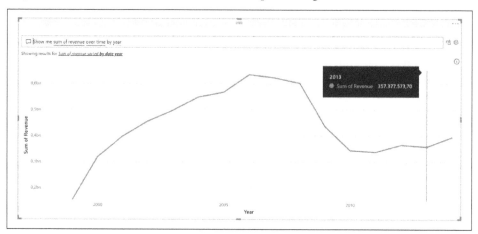

Figure 5-9. Showing sum of revenue over time by year

Let's say we want to keep this visual to provide a high-level overview about sales for our report consumers. By default, the query isn't saved or persisted on the report. So if the report gets shared and opened by another user, they would see the empty Q&A visual with the initial suggestions, just as we did previously.

If you want to share the output of the Q&A visual, you have to convert it into a static visual first. To do so, click the Convert visual icon, shown previously in Figure 5-4. Power BI will convert the Q&A visual into a plain line chart.

So far, we've created a static high-level visual. Now, we can work on adding a self-service area enabling business users to query the data with custom questions.

Resize the revenue visual horizontally to make a little more space below it. Choose Insert → Text Box to insert a headline on top of the visual, reading **Self-Service Revenue Analysis**. Rename this report sheet from "Page 1" to **Total Revenue by Year**.

Let's add a second visual. Double-click the Q&A visual from the Visualizations pane so it appears below the total revenue line chart. Your report should now look similar to Figure 5-10.

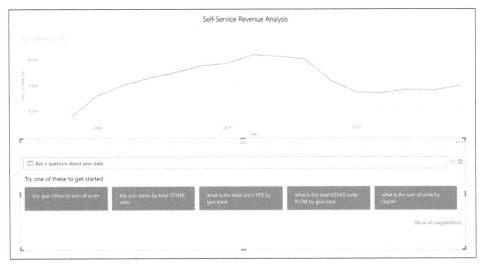

Figure 5-10. Q&A report layout

To make the Q&A visual more helpful and more intuitive for business users, we want to adjust the default suggestions as well as the wording used inside the Q&A tool. Click the Q&A cog icon to the right of the text box to edit the settings of the Q&A visual. You will see various options. Over the next few paragraphs, I will walk you through several options that will be enough to customize the Q&A visual in a way that business users (and not just data analysts) can use it.

Let's start with *field synonyms*, shown in Figure 5-11. In the Q&A tool, every *field* (e.g., a measure, dimension, or table) can have one or multiple synonyms. For example, let's say your data model has the measure "sales" but you want your users to refer to this metric as "revenue." In this case, "revenue" would be a field synonym for "sales."

Power BI will present you with a list of your data dimensions and allow you to add synonyms to the various fields in the business lingo that your users speak. For this example, open the SalesFact list, as shown in Figure 5-11.

Figure 5-11. Field synonyms in the Q&A tool

You will see all measures in this list along with autosuggestions for synonyms and a toggle button enabling you to choose whether this field should be included in the Q&A widget. Scroll down to Sum of Revenue. Click the Add button and include "total revenue" here as a synonym, as shown in Figure 5-12. Also add "total of revenue," "revenue," "total income," "total of sales," and "total sales" to the synonyms. We could go through the other fields as well, but for now let's end this exercise.

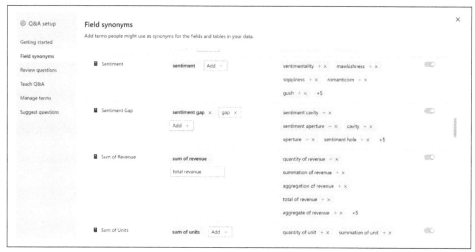

Figure 5-12. Q&A field synonyms

Click "Manage terms" in the left menu, and you will see a list of all the terms and definitions that were added to the Q&A visual (Figure 5-13). This way, you can easily keep track of any changes you made and delete terms that are not appropriate.

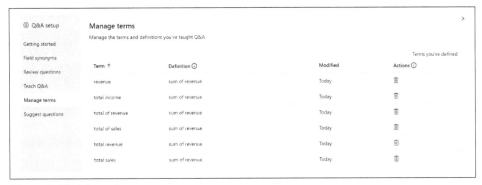

Figure 5-13. Managing terms

Head over to "Suggest questions" in the left menu now. This section allows you to edit the questions that are suggested to users by default, which you can see in Figure 5-14.

Let's start with a revenue breakdown by region. Type in `Show me revenue by region`. This should yield a plot in the preview window (Figure 5-14).

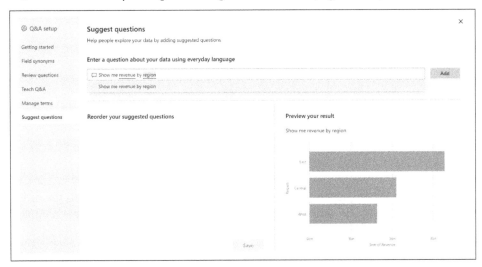

Figure 5-14. Suggesting questions

Fine, let's add that to our suggestions by clicking the Add button.

Business users are usually very good at learning by example. To give users more intuition on how they can use the Q&A tool, let's add a variation to the previous question. Business users should later be comfortable replacing things like "region" with "product" or whatever it is that is on their mind.

Add the following suggestion: `Show me revenue by region by year`. This produces three line charts, which leads us to the idea of comparing data points. So let's add an example of how business users can compare sales performance among products. Let's add this slightly more complex suggested question: `Show me revenue of Maximus UM-01 vs. Maximus UM-02 by year`.

This results in a very insightful chart, showing us that Maximus UM-01 had decreasing revenues since its peak in 2005, and the new product Maximus UM-02 seems to be slowly taking off after its initial release in 2007. By 2012, the new product contributed more revenue than its predecessor, as you can see in Figure 5-15.

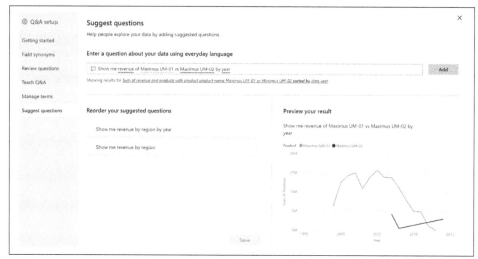

Figure 5-15. Q&A revenue comparison

To organize the list of suggested questions, you can drag the questions into the order you want. Let's move the simplest query to the first position and the most complex one to the last. Save the suggestions. Close the Q&A setup window.

Taking a look again at our report, we can see that the three suggestions we just created now show up in the Q&A visual. Business users can start their data exploration by simply clicking a suggestion and then modifying the query as they like—for example, by replacing "region" with "geo state." You can see the final example in Figure 5-16.

Figure 5-16. Final report with Q&A visual

This basic setup would be sufficient enough for shipping an early prototype of this report to a sample of beta business users. You have the chance to collect valuable feedback, see whether it is accepted, and discover areas for improvement.

To access the user query data, click the Q&A cog icon on the right side of the text box to access the tool's settings. Here, you will find the menu option "Review questions." This will list all queries submitted over the last 28 days so you can see exactly how people used your report and which synonyms, suggestions, or fields might be still missing. This is a great place to start iterating over your product and scaling it to more users. If you want to share this report, you will need a Power BI Pro or Premium license.

If you'd like to read more about how the Q&A tool and its administration work in detail, you might find the following resources useful from the Microsoft documentation:

- "Best Practices to Optimize Q&A in Power BI" (*https://oreil.ly/DMRFN*)
- "Intro to Q&A Tooling to Train Power BI Q&A" (*https://oreil.ly/anFXF*)
- "Edit Q&A Linguistic Schema and Add Phrasings in Power BI Desktop" (*https://oreil.ly/pSVXM*)

Use Case: Summarizing Data with Natural Language

Business analysts often have to craft data stories to communicate insights to business stakeholders. While most of their time is typically spent on creating compelling visuals, the process of annotating with conclusions can be cumbersome and tedious. Too often, analysts therefore skip the step of adding verbal comments to their visuals since the charts speak for themselves, don't they? No, in fact, many charts can be misinterpreted, especially when it comes to more complex visualizations. Let's imagine the following scenario.

Problem Statement

Building off the visuals we created in "Use Case: Querying Data with Natural Language" on page 93, we now want to add captions to assist nontechnical stakeholders in interpreting the data. We want to provide captions to make insights clear, but we don't want to spend much time writing them out manually.

Solution Overview

Natural language capabilities let us use machines to not only analyze and interpret human language, but also generate text based on defined inputs. In this example, we can use AI technology to create captions or annotations for a given plot and its underlying data.

The annotations should address key takeaways, point out trends, and allow editing the language and format tailored to a specific audience. And they are a great way of making our reports more accessible to the visually impaired as well! Figure 5-17 shows the high-level use case architecture.

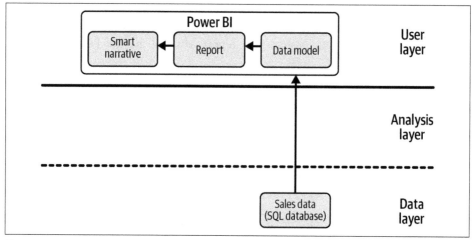

Figure 5-17. Smart narrative use case architecture

Again, we are solely using built-in Power BI functionalities for this example. The feature in Power BI, called *smart narrative*, is available in both Power BI Desktop and Power BI Service for designers and developers. The feature is available for all license types and does not require a Pro or Premium license. We will explore how to use these autogenerated captions to generate a data story for the visuals we created in "Use Case: Querying Data with Natural Language" on page 93.

Power BI Walk-Through

Open *Sales & Marketing sample PBIX.pbix* from "Use Case: Querying Data with Natural Language". Create a new report page and call it Story.

We want to create the following four visualizations:

- Revenue by year
- Revenue by state
- Revenue by segment
- Revenue by year and segment

You can use the Q&A tool to achieve this quickly: double-click the Q&A visual from the Visualizations pane, type the query from the preceding list, and then convert it into a standard visual. Repeat this process for each of the revenue breakdowns. Do you see how fast it is to create these visuals with the AI NLP capabilities in Power BI compared to the traditional approach of manually choosing a visual in combination with mapping data and filtering by hand?

Arrange the visuals on the page in a way that some space remains to the right for the narratives. Your page should look similar to Figure 5-18.

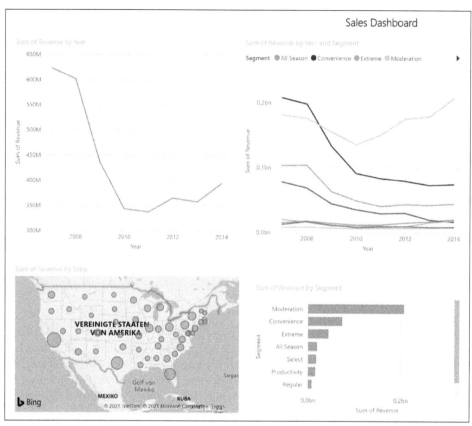

Figure 5-18. Sales dashboard

Open the Visualizations pane. You should see the "Smart narrative" icon (Figure 5-19).

If you don't see the "Smart narrative" icon in the Visualization pane, you may be using an older version of Power BI and will need to turn on the smart narrative option. Choose File → Options and Settings → Options → Preview feature, and make sure the smart narrative visual is turned on.

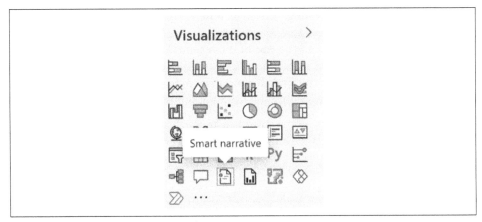

Figure 5-19. Smart narrative visualization

Double-clicking the "Smart narrative" icon should add a text box to the right side of your page. Alternatively, you can drag and drop the visual to a place on the page you like. This text box will contain the description that Power BI suggests for all visualizations on the page. In our case, the description will look like the output in Figure 5-20. If you click the text box, you will see the highlighted values that Power BI calculated here.

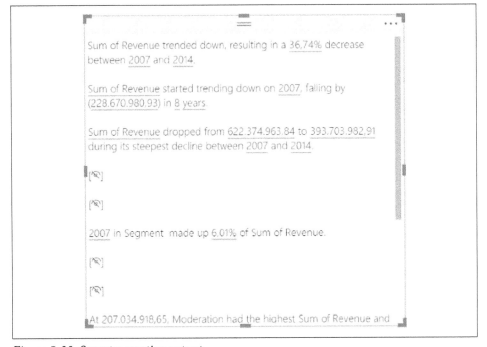

Figure 5-20. Smart narrative output

There are a couple of interesting things to note here. On the first line, you can see that Power BI recognized that the revenue trended down and calculated the percentage of the beginning and the end of the revenue time series (see Figure 5-21). It also suggests that the product segment Moderation accounted for 52.59% of the total revenue in 2014. When you find that a statement is not relevant enough or even redundant, you can simply delete this line from the summary.

You can also explore the calculated values in more detail and apply formatting to them. For example, click the values that calculate the revenue figures. In the context menu, you can choose to display this value as a currency without any decimals after the comma.

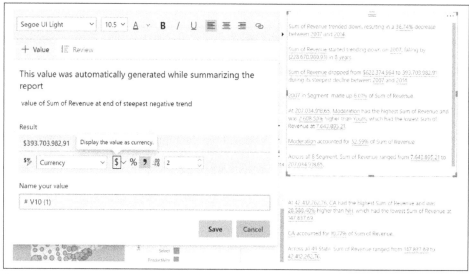

Figure 5-21. Smart narrative formatting

Formatting the automated text output will make it more accessible to the reader and will look much nicer overall. When we look at the summary, however, we realize that no information was given about the regional sales breakdown. Maybe this information was not important enough to Power BI? To add these details manually, right-click the map plot that shows the sales figures by state and choose Summarize from the context menu. Power BI will add another text box that shows descriptions for just the plot that you selected. Again, you can delete or modify the descriptions as you like.

One important thing to note about the automated captions is that they are fully dynamic and respond to changes in the underlying graphs. To demonstrate this, let's add a page filter to our dashboard to show only data from after 2010, as shown in Figure 5-22. Open the Fields pane and then drag and drop the field Year to the "Filters on this page" option pane. Once you apply the filter, notice how the content of the text box changes. Power BI recognizes that the revenue trend is now going upward and updates the corresponding percentages accordingly.

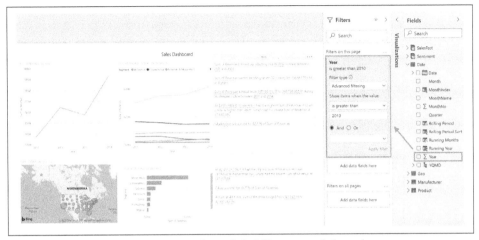

Figure 5-22. Smart narrative responds to global filtering and data changes

What is still missing is an explanation for one of the most important charts on this dashboard: the revenue breakdown by segment. You can clearly see that the segment Moderation is the only segment with a relevant positive trend—this is something that should be easy to recognize by the smart narrative tool, shouldn't it? Right-click the plot and click Summarize. But what happens? Power BI just responds with a single line of text in the smart narrative box, which is very hard to interpret.

We have hit the boundaries of the smart narrative feature here. At the time of this writing, it is not possible to summarize very complex charts that have many categories or underlying trends. In addition, renaming dynamic values or editing automatically generated dynamic values is currently not supported, and summaries cannot be produced for visuals that contain on-the-fly calculations like complex measures or percentages.

Since the smart narrative feature was initially released only in 2021, it will be exciting to see which of these limitations are going to disappear. You can find more details about the smart narrative tool in the Microsoft resource documentation (*https:// oreil.ly/F75ve*).

For now, let's just add the final conclusion for our dashboard by hand. Add a new line to the last text box and type **Conclusion: Sales from product segment Moder ation were the main reason for the positive revenue trend between 2011 and 2014**. Your final sales dashboard should now look similar to Figure 5-23.

While the smart narrative tool has many more customizations and configurations than this book could cover (for example, defining custom values by using the

Q&A–style language queries), we will leave it like this. If you'd like to find out more about the smart narrative tool, check out the YouTube video tutorial "How to Use Smart Narrative with Power BI" (*https://oreil.ly/Z4UJU*) from Microsoft.

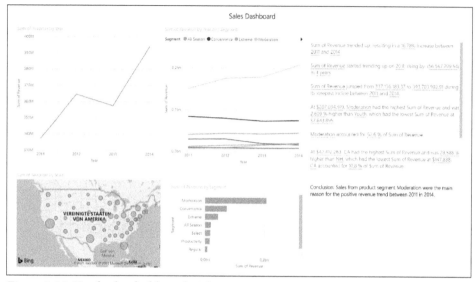

Figure 5-23. Final sales dashboard with annotations

You could now easily export this page to a PDF (File → Export → Export to PDF) or publish it to a Power BI server. While a detailed discussion of the various sharing and publishing features in Power BI would be beyond the scope of this book, I recommend reading the Microsoft documentation "Ways to Collaborate and Share in Power BI" (*https://oreil.ly/9z9A3*) if you want to get started on this topic.

For now, just save the report (File → Save), as we're coming back to this example in the next chapter. You can retrieve the completed file that contains all exercises from this chapter by downloading *Sales & Marketing Sample_AI-Powered.pbix* from this book's website (*https://oreil.ly/jgjFu*).

Summary

In this chapter, you have learned how to use the AI-powered natural language capabilities in the form of the Q&A tool in Power BI to create visualizations faster and give your users a better BI experience. You have also learned how to automate the annotation process of your visualizations and add descriptions on the fly using the smart narrative tool in Power BI.

In the next chapter, we will further explore our data and find out which factors affect the revenue trend. We will use AI-powered tools to reduce our time to insights and comb through the data automatically for interesting patterns.

## CHAPTER 6

AI-Powered Diagnostic Analytics

Finding out *what* happened is only half as interesting as finding out *why* it happened. Although raw data can't tell us the causal reasons why something happened, we can analyze the data for patterns and derive informed conclusions. At the very least, the patterns will point us in the right direction. In this chapter, you will learn how AI can help you reveal those interesting patterns in data automatically so you and your colleagues can concentrate on the interpretation and impacts of this data.

Use Case: Automated Insights

We'll continue with the case study from the preceding chapter: in a fictitious manufacturing company, we support sales management in their decision-making process. In Chapter 5, we found that sales seemed to be slowly recovering after a period of sharp declines. Now we will go deeper and focus on understanding why certain trends have evolved.

Problem Statement

As the business analysts on the team, we want to help sales management find explanations for two of the observed revenue trends: why did sales numbers melt down so dramatically between 2006 and 2010, and what factors explain the slow recovery between 2010 and 2014? On a side note, if this were a real scenario, we probably would not be doing an analysis over an eight-year period because so many things would have changed. If it helps, imagine that we are a manufacturing company with a very long sales cycle.

This process would normally involve going through the data manually, which takes time and is subject to the analyst's availability. Since we don't have the capacity to do one-on-one sessions with each of the business users, we are looking for ways to provide them with insights in a more automated and interactive way.

Solution Overview

Our goal is to find patterns in our dataset automatically by scanning through all available information with as little human assistance as possible. For this purpose, we are leveraging AI-powered techniques to deliver these insights in a fast and interactive manner. This will allow business users to get insights with less, or even without, help from professional data analysts. Figure 6-1 gives you an overview of the use case architecture.

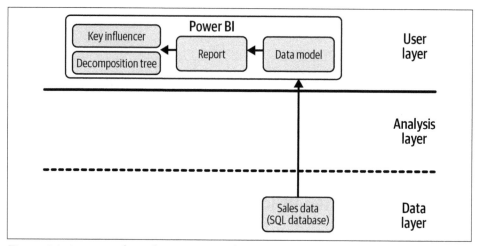

Figure 6-1. Automated insights use case architecture

Just as in the examples from the previous chapter, this architecture is straightforward, as we are doing everything inside Power BI. To deliver this experience, we are using two Power BI tools in particular here: the key influencers and the decomposition tree tools.

The *key influencers visual* helps in comprehending the aspects that influence a metric of interest by showing the top contributors to the selected metric. It examines the information you provide and surfaces the most important aspects to the top by labeling them as key influencers.

Power BI's *decomposition tree visual* allows you to visualize data in numerous dimensions. It aggregates data automatically and allows you to drill down into any dimension in any order. AI will suggest the next most relevant dimension to dive into depending on your particular area of interest. As a result, it's a useful tool for ad hoc investigation and root cause analysis.

We are going to apply these techniques to the sales and marketing example Power BI report to find out which factors were driving both revenue trends and which patterns we can observe from our data. In a corporate scenario, both tools could be provided to the business users in the form of Power BI report pages so they can interact with the data on their own.

Power BI Walk-Through

If you followed along with the use case from the previous chapter, you can continue working in your *Sales & Marketing sample PBIX.pbix* file. If not, feel free to download *Sales & Marketing Sample_AI-Powered.pbix* from the book's website (*https://oreil.ly/ MOYIu*). To quickly recap, this dataset contains various sales and marketing data from a manufacturing company and comes pre-populated with reports for market share, product volume, sales figures, and sentiment scores.

In Chapter 5, we found out that the overall revenue over the last four years has slowly recovered after a hard bounce in the previous year. Figure 6-2 is a snapshot of the sales dashboard we created before.

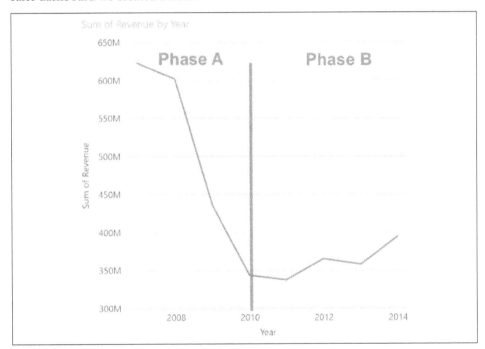

Figure 6-2. Two phases of revenue trends

We are especially interested in what happened during the phase of declining revenues, between 2006 and 2010 (Phase A) and the phase of slowly recovering revenues between 2010 and 2014 (Phase B). For both of these phases, we want to answer the simple but profound question, "What happened?"

We will start by examining Phase A. To re-create the revenue visual, create a new Power BI report page, drag and drop the Q&A visual, and type **Revenue by year between 2006 and 2010**.

Click the Convert icon to turn the Q&A visual into a standard Power BI visual. The chart should look similar to Figure 6-3.

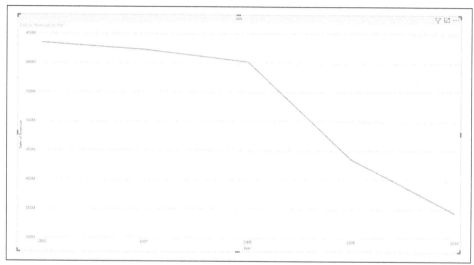

Figure 6-3. Revenue by year from 2006 to 2010

Select this chart and open the Visualizations pane on the right. Click the "Key influencers" icon to convert the line chart into the key influencers visual (Figure 6-4).

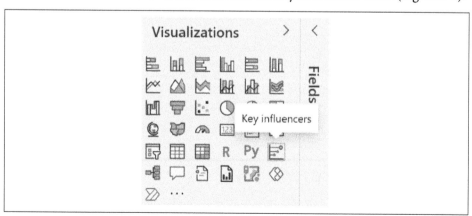

Figure 6-4. "Key influencers" visual icon

Once you select the new visual type, the chart will automatically update to something that should look similar to Figure 6-5. Let's explore the output of this visual in a bit more detail.

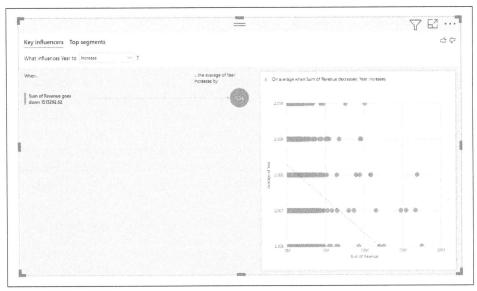

Figure 6-5. Key influencers standard output

Now, this output is probably not what you expected at all and definitely looks a bit weird. What went wrong? Open the Visualizations pane and inspect the properties of the key influencers visual. This should look like Figure 6-6.

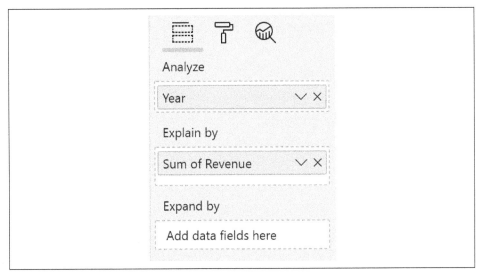

Figure 6-6. Key influencers properties after conversion from the line chart

In the visual properties, you will find two critical fields: Analyze and "Explain by." As the names suggest, Analyze refers to the metric that you want to explore, and "Explain by" refers to the various dimensions you might consider to have an effect on the metric. By default, given our previous line chart, Power BI suggests explaining the dimension Year by the field Sum of Revenue, which absolutely does not make any sense.

Let's fix this by dragging Sum of Revenue from the "Explain by" field to the Analyze field instead of the Year field. Consequently, add additional dimensions into the "Explain by" field by pulling them from the data fields repository on the right. Reasonable candidate fields from a business point of view might be Segment, City, State, Region, Average of Score, Category, and Manufacturer. We will leave out the dimension Product since too many data points are missing. For example, some products were replaced by others, some products were just launched, and some products were deprecated. If we wanted to analyze key influencers down to a product level, we should look at a single year rather than a four-year period.

The updated properties of the key influencers tool should now look like Figure 6-7.

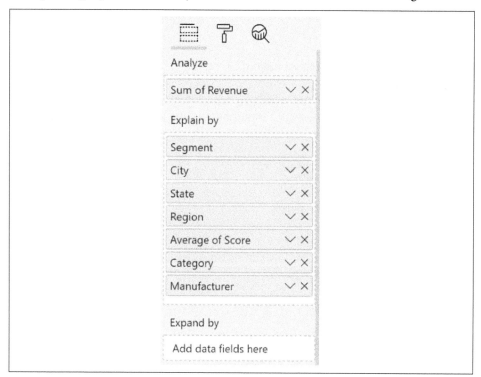

Figure 6-7. Key influencers properties (edited)

Within the key influencers visual, switch the drop-down menu at the top from Increase to Decrease, since we are interested in finding out what made the revenue drop. The updated visual should now look similar to Figure 6-8.

This visual intuitively makes more sense than the previous version. Note that this would be the report page you could share or publish for business users so they can interact with the data on their own. Let's dive into this visual to see how it works in a bit more detail.

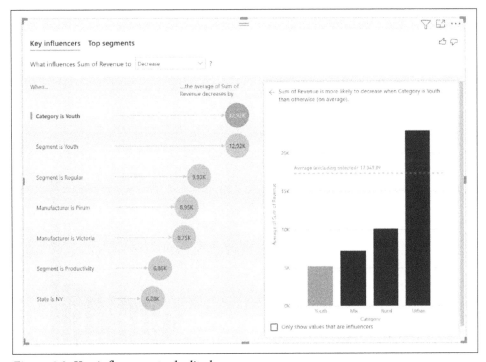

Figure 6-8. Key influencers tool edited

On the left side of the visual, we can see which variables Power BI identified as key influencers for the given metric (in this case, Revenue). We can see that Power BI identified the attribute Youth across the dimensions Category and Segment as the main key drivers that cause the Revenue metric to decrease. On the right side, we are presented with the underlying data distribution for the selected influencer, showing the average of the Revenue metric across all categories from the selected dimension (in this example, the Category dimension). You can read the chart on the right as follows: the average revenue for the Category Youth was just $5,181.98, while the average revenue for all other Categories except Youth was $17,349.89. That means, when the Category is Youth, the average revenue is $12,920 lower compared to all other values of the Category.

It is important to point out that in this case, we are not judging based on the absolute values of a variable but on their averages and number of observations. Depending on the measure you choose to analyze, whether it is categorical or continuous, the key influencers tool will adapt. Instead of averages, it will indicate probabilities such as that the outcome is x times more likely if a certain value is met.

The key influencers tool does not always consider the lowest value of a category as an influencer. Take, for example, the influencer "Manufacturer is Victoria" in our analysis. If you click this influencer, you will see the chart in Figure 6-9. You can see that Victoria is not the manufacturer with the smallest revenue on average, but rather Salvus is. Now why hasn't Salvus been identified as a key influencer?

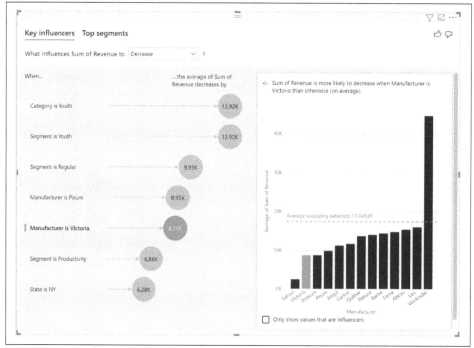

Figure 6-9. Key influencers visual for Phase A (negative revenue trend)

The reasons become clear if we look at the head-to-head comparison of Salvus and Victoria in Figure 6-10, just for the sake of fostering our understanding of how the key influencers tool works.

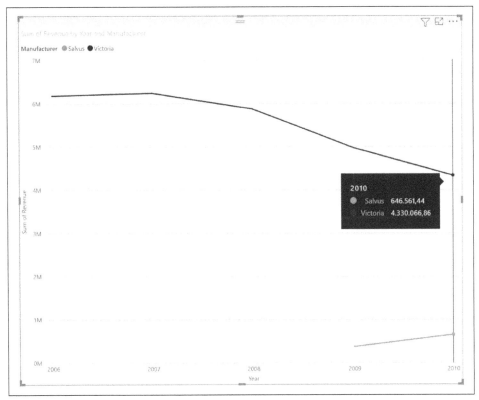

Figure 6-10. Comparing sales of manufacturers Salvus and Victoria

Three factors disqualify Salvus from being a key influencer. First, this manufacturer was introduced in only 2009, so fewer data points exist in total as compared to the other manufacturers. Second, the absolute revenue contribution of Salvus is so little that it probably lacks overall impact. And last but not least, the actual revenue trend of this manufacturer is not negative, but positive. While Victoria dropped from $6.2 million in revenue in 2006 to $4.3 million in revenue in 2010, Salvus actually improved its revenues between 2009 and 2010.

With this background information, it is legitimate to not consider Salvus a key influencer for overall decreasing revenues. The key influencers tool makes it easier for us to find such interesting patterns without combing through all of the data manually.

Let's explore another useful feature of the key influencers tool: the segments. *Segments* can be considered groups in your data combining different values that show a high impact on a metric of interest. Switch over to "Top segments" and select "When is Sum of Revenue more likely to be Low" from the drop-down at the top. You should see the screen in Figure 6-11 as a result.

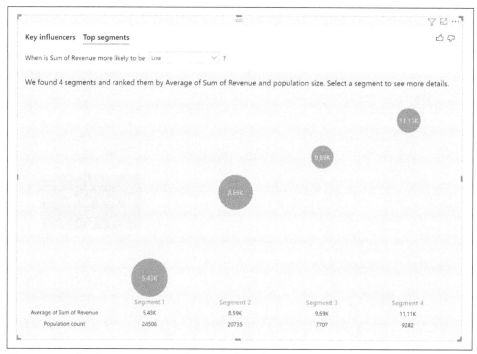

Figure 6-11. Analyzing segments that contributed to negative revenue trend

You can see four segments that Power BI has identified for us. The biggest segment, indicated by the size of the bubble, holds 24,506 observations (sold products) and accounts for an average revenue of just $5.43K per sale. The low-performer segment with the highest (yet below total) average revenue of $11.11K contains 9,282 observations.

To find out more about what is happening here, click on the 5.43K bubble. You will see a detailed view of this segment, which in this case looks like Figure 6-12.

From this chart, we can see that this segment contains almost 16% of all product sales and therefore has a very high relevance for us. The segment contains all sales where the Category was not Urban, the Manufacturer was not VanArsdel, the Region was not West, and the Segment was not Productivity. This segment contributed the largest group of data points and had the lowest average revenue, which makes it an important segment to look at when it comes to explaining the falling revenue trend in Phase A (2006–2010).

To see what this means in detail, let's examine the revenue trend in this segment 1 as compared to the total revenue trend from 2006 to 2010 (Figure 6-13).

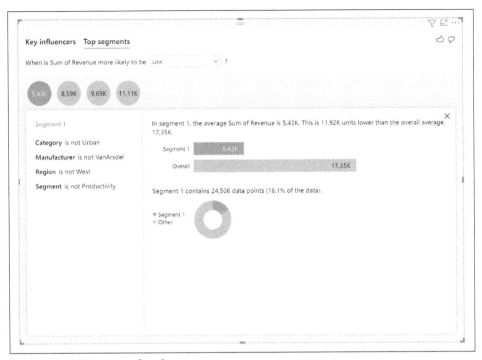

Figure 6-12. Segment 1 details

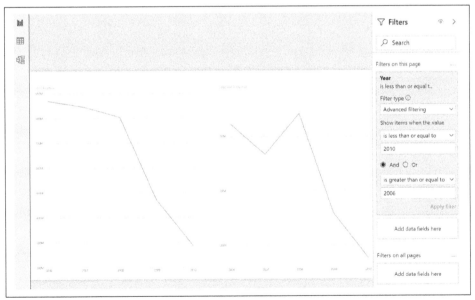

Figure 6-13. Overall revenue trend for total revenue and segment 1 revenue

While the overall revenue was down 46.6% from \$643.28 million to \$343.13 million in the total dataset, segment 1 alone contributed a loss of \$12.3 million, from \$31.10 million in 2006 to \$18.8 million in 2010. These more focused segments should be easier to tackle for business users and identify potential problem areas as opposed to larger trends such as the Category Youth.

We could explore the other segments in a similar way, but let's conclude our analysis for the past revenue drop for now and head over to finding out what happened during the recovery period, between 2010 and 2014, called Phase B. If you are interested in further features and descriptions on how the key influencers tool works, you could check out "Create Key Influencers Visualizations" (*https://oreil.ly/gxgdN*) from Microsoft.

For the analysis of Phase B, we will switch over to the decomposition tree feature in Power BI. The decomposition tree is a great tool for conducting a root cause analysis. You can use it as a smart drill-down, as Power BI suggests the next drill-down level automatically based on a specific metric you want to explore.

For this purpose, start with a blank report page in your Power BI file. Re-create the Revenue by Year chart, this time for the period from 2010 to 2014. Convert this chart into a static visual if you used the Q&A tool for this. The revenue chart should now look similar to Figure 6-14.

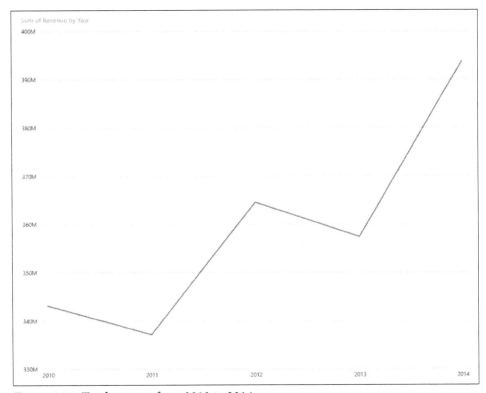

Figure 6-14. Total revenue from 2010 to 2014

Select the line chart and change the visualization type to "Decomposition tree," as shown in Figure 6-15.

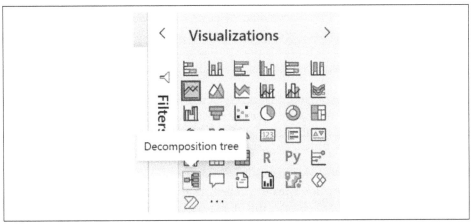

Figure 6-15. "Decomposition tree" icon

Similar to working with the key influencers tool, we have to tell Power BI which variable we want to analyze and which dimensions we consider explanatory factors. Modify the visual properties so that they look like the ones in Figure 6-16.

Figure 6-16. Decomposition tree properties

The initial output of the decomposition tree visual will be a plain summary of our metric of interest on a blank canvas. You can see this output in Figure 6-17.

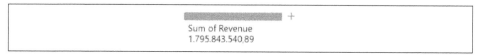

Figure 6-17. Decomposition tree start

The task at hand is to decompose this aggregated metric into smaller chunks, ideally splitting it in such a way that we capture the most important metrics at the top of the tree. When you click the small + icon on the right next to the aggregated revenue, a menu pops up for selecting the next split you want to make.

You could either select the split manually (for example, based on business logic or your own preferences) or use a feature called *AI splits*. We will come back to this concept later, to consider which cases might be reasonable for manually drilling down levels. AI splits are indicated by small light bulbs and will automatically choose the next best drill-down level for you, depending on whether you want to influence your top-level metric to be higher or smaller, as you can see in Figure 6-18.

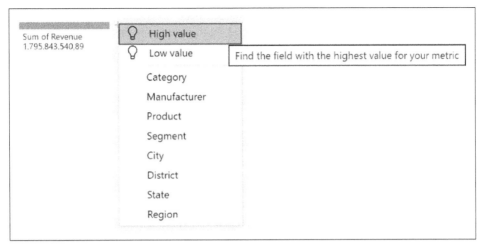

Figure 6-18. Using AI splits in the decomposition tree

Since we are interested in explaining the revenue growth in Phase B, let's choose an AI split for high values. Power BI creates the first split for you on the criteria Category, as shown in Figure 6-19.

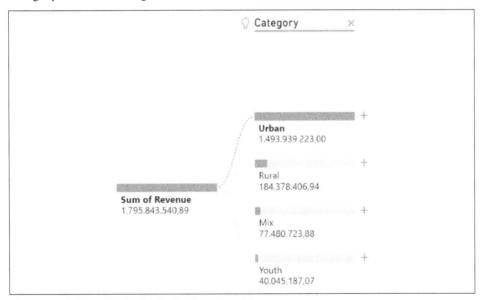

Figure 6-19. First-level split in the decomposition tree

If you hover over the light bulb next to the Category split, you will see a Power BI tooltip explaining the current node of the tree. In this case, this first split tells you that the revenue between 2010 and 2014 was highest when the Category was Urban (see Figure 6-20).

Figure 6-20. AI split explanation

You can now drill down as far as you'd like—for example, to find out which criteria led to the revenue growth within the Urban category. Again, we could select the next drill-down level manually or let Power BI figure it out for us, depending on whether we're interested in high or low values (see Figure 6-21).

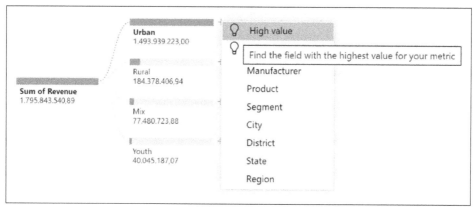

Figure 6-21. Second-level AI split

If you choose "High value" again, you'll see that the next split will be made on the field Manufacturer, as shown in Figure 6-22.

At this point, let's stop for a second and quickly recap why exactly we are seeing these splits in this order. Why isn't the data split first for the Manufacturer and only afterward according to Category? At least we have seen that the manufacturer VanArsdel claims most of the revenue.

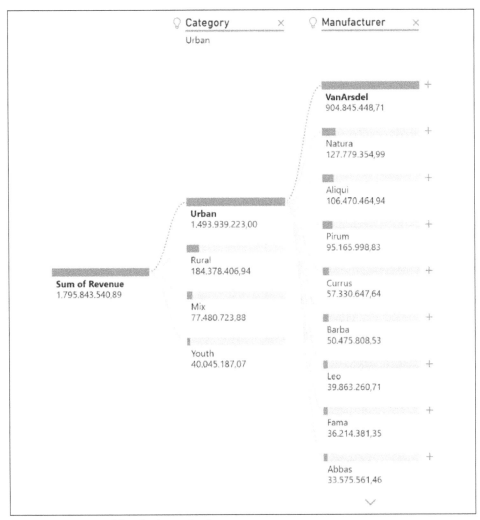

Figure 6-22. Second-level split in the decomposition tree

This happens because the underlying algorithm in Power BI that makes the splits is greedy. It will choose the next drill-down category at the point where the splits will bring the biggest advantage. To demonstrate this phenomenon, let's look at a side-by-side comparison of Revenue by Category and Revenue by Manufacturer, as shown in Figure 6-23.

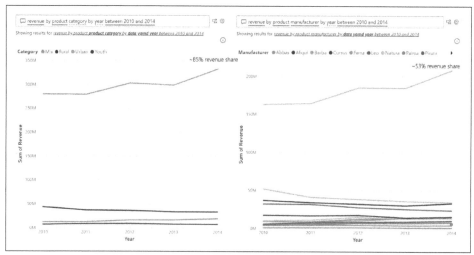

Figure 6-23. Revenue by Manufacturer and by Category

You can clearly see that both Urban and VanArsdel stand out in their classes as main revenue drivers. However, looking more closely, you will note that Urban claims around 85% of the revenue share, and VanArsdel gets only 53%. This is because we have many more manufacturers than categories, which take away plenty of small shares from the leading key driver in this field. And that is why Power BI splits the data first according to Category and only afterward according to Manufacturer.

While this greedy approach works quite well most of the time, you have to be careful in some cases. When you examine data after a certain split, you can analyze only data that actually exists in that split. For example, by splitting for Category first and then exploring the Urban category, you will see only manufacturers in that tree branch that actually produce products in the Urban category. If a manufacturer in the dataset did not produce any goods for the Urban category, that manufacturer would not show up in the downstream splits of that branch of the tree.

On the flip side, this means that Power BI would most likely never (or only at the very end of a tree) suggest to split based on a field in which all observations are equally distributed. We can observe this, for example, in the State dimension of our datasets; the single biggest revenue contributor (California) gains only around 10% of the total revenue, and the smallest contributor counts around 4.8%. The states are pretty much evenly distributed with regard to revenue, so they are not a good candidate for Power BI to create splits on them. If states did play a role for your business (or different business users), you would either select those splits manually at the first level or, alternatively, add a page filter according to the state(s) you are interested in.

Coming back to our decomposition tree example, we want to add two more AI splits for high values. If you add these splits, you should see a tree that looks like Figure 6-24.

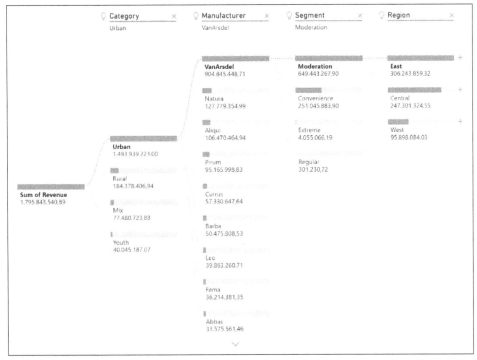

Figure 6-24. Final decomposition tree

When you look at this tree, you can immediately see that sales in the Urban category, from the Manufacturer VanArsdel with the Segment Moderation and within the region East, were the main contributors to the revenue growth in the period 2010–2014. If you create a line chart with exactly this filter criteria and compare it to the overall total revenue, you can clearly see how this plays out in Figure 6-25.

Sales from this segment alone contributed more than $20 million in revenue to our total revenue gain, and grew even stronger on a relative level (+46%) than the absolute revenue trend (+15%).

With the decomposition tree, business users can easily interact with the data and find the relevant contributors on the granularity level that they need. After having combed the data automatically using the AI features of Power BI, it is much easier to loop in a data analyst, if necessary, to verify their conclusions or raise questions that came up during the analysis process.

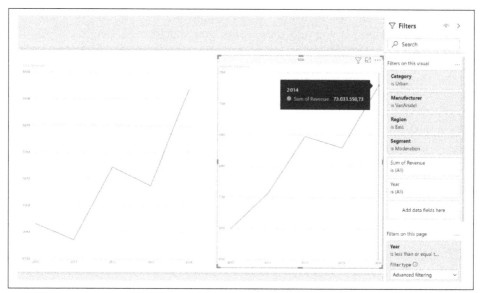

Figure 6-25. Comparing total revenue and the decomposition tree branch

The Power BI report with the decomposition tree can be shared with business users so they can browse through the data on their own. To share reports with other users in your organization, you will need a Power BI Server or a Power BI Pro license.

To find out more about the decomposition tool, check out "Create and View Decomposition Tree Visuals in Power BI" (*https://oreil.ly/ockwx*) in the Microsoft documentation.

Summary

In this chapter, we looked at two powerful AI-backed features in Power BI that help business users and analysts alike reduce their time to insights by automating parts of the data analysis process. The key influencers tool can be used to reveal key drivers of a given metric of interest and identify relevant segments. The decomposition tree in combination with AI splits is very useful for directed drill-downs in any data dimension while keeping an overall business metric fixed. This makes it a great tool for ad hoc data exploration and self-service root cause analysis.

In the next chapter, we will leave the realms of the past and present data and look at how AI can help us anticipate future events or make better predictions about future outcomes. We will start with an automated classification task that helps us categorize future business events based on our past experience.

## CHAPTER 7

AI-Powered Predictive Analytics

Get ready for takeoff! We are entering the space of AI-powered predictive analytics. And we will do that by stepping into the role of a BI analyst at American Airlines. In this chapter, we will look at three use cases from a real-world dataset. First, we will try to classify flights as to whether they will land on time or not. Second, we want to detect bottlenecks in our flight schedule by forecasting actual flight times in contrast to the scheduled flight duration. And finally, we will analyze airports' ability to keep up with the flight schedule by using automatic anomaly detection.

Our goal is to build a prototype of an AI-powered BI solution that proves to solve a specific problem depending on the use case. We want to evaluate how well the AI model works with our data, show it around, and gain support for the new approach in our organization by demonstrating the business value (build fast, show fast, learn fast), as outlined in Chapter 4. To that end, we will start by abstracting away things like setting up data pipelines, handling ETL jobs, and integrating AI services into our enterprise data warehouse. But rest assured—all of these things will be possible, as you will learn in Chapter 11.

What will most likely be the same in the prototyping and production phases is the AI model we will build. Already in our prototype, we will use enterprise-grade AI services from Microsoft Azure that will stand up to production workloads. The only thing that will change later is the way we integrate these services into our overarching system architecture. Once we can prove the business value and build a solid business case for our solution, we can afford the effort to move the prototype into production and build it "properly" there.

Prerequisites

To follow along with the use cases in this chapter, I recommend downloading the following files from the book's website (*https://oreil.ly/X9jmJ*):

Datasets
- *AA_Flights_2021.xlsx*
- *AA_Flights_2021_01.csv*

Use Case: Automating Classification Tasks
- *Arrival_Delay.pbix*
- *AA_Hourly_Batches_2021-02-07_0800-0859.csv*
- *azure-ml-inference-arrdel15.R* or *azure-ml-inference-arrdel15.py*

Use Case: Improving KPI Prediction
- *Elapsed_Time.pbix*
- *azure-ml-inference-elapsedtime.R* or *azure-ml-inference-elapsedtime.py*

Use Case: Automating Anomaly Detection
- *Airports_Anomaly.pbix*
- *azure-anomaly-detection-airports.R* or *azure-anomaly-detection-airports.py*

In addition, you will need an account on Microsoft Azure to train and host the AI model as demonstrated in Chapter 4, some basic knowledge in Python or R to get predictions from the model, and a BI tool capable of executing Python or R scripts to integrate the model predictions into your dashboard.

Although we are using Microsoft Azure to train the model, the same functionality is more or less also available on other cloud platform providers such as GCP or AWS. Once you get a feel for how things work on Azure, getting up and running on the other platforms should be relatively easy and quick.

To build our dashboard, we will use Power BI to achieve consistency with the previous use cases (and because Azure works nicely with Power BI). However, this book is not limited to Power BI users. That is why I will show you how to get inference from your model by using a popular programming language like Python or R. You can integrate Python or R code into Power BI or any other BI tool. Alternatively, you could run the predictions directly on the database (batch predictions) and just display the results in any BI tool such a Tableau or Looker. Chapter 10 offers more details.

About the Dataset

Beware: we will be working on a real-world dataset. This dataset hasn't been tweaked or tuned for ML exercises. So don't expect any jaw-dropping insights or nice-looking charts. But instead, you will get a feel for what a real-world scenario looks like, which gains you can expect from ML, and how you can use this technology to beat your own baselines and automate predictions. The process might get messy, but it's closer to real life than any academic exercise you will find.

The public dataset for this use case has been acquired through the TranStats service of the US Bureau of Transportation Statistics (*https://oreil.ly/y7C8W*). This data source maintains updated information about flight details for flights in the US. Throughout the whole chapter, we will use flight data from January 2021 and February 2021, which I provide as an Excel file through the book's website (*https://oreil.ly/X9jmJ*) for your convenience. The file includes the following processing steps to make it match our case study:

- The dataset has been filtered for American Airlines flights only.
- Canceled flights have been deleted from the dataset.
- Flights without any information on the arrival delay have been removed (< 1%).

If you want to get more data or explore different airlines, feel free to do so by downloading the original files yourself from the TranStats website. If you do, make sure you select the Prezipped File option, as shown in Figure 7-1, before downloading the data.

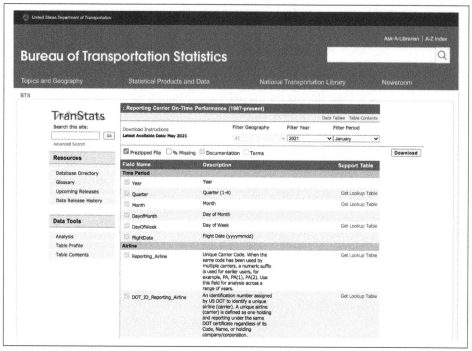

Figure 7-1. Airline On-Time Performance dataset download

Use Case: Automating Classification Tasks

For our first use case, we are tackling a classification problem of predicting whether a given flight will be delayed on arrival. Even if you are not an expert in the aviation industry, you should be familiar with the overall challenge.

Problem Statement

As a member of the BI team of American Airlines, you have been given the task of building a reporting dashboard on a business-critical metric. The metric is the percentage of American Airlines flights that are currently in the air and are expected to be delayed for more than 15 minutes. This metric is important for quality control reasons and for keeping customer satisfaction high, as well as for maintaining the overall flight schedule.

In our example, let's imagine that we receive data every hour containing all flights that departed within the last 60 minutes. These hourly batches contain information as to the flight details (origin, destination, flight number, etc.) and the flight delay upon departure. So, for example, when we look at a batch of data anytime between 9:00 a.m. and 9:59 a.m., the information in this dataset will contain flights that took off between 8:00 a.m. and 8:59 a.m. To make this example less complicated, we're ignoring time zones for now and are assuming that all timestamps are provided in Coordinated Universal Time (UTC).

The metric Proportion of Delayed Flights is currently reported through a BI dashboard, shown in Figure 7-2.

Airline On-Time Dashboard
Estimated Arrival Delay for Departure Time Block:

0800-0859

Flights expected to be late on arrival

Total Flights in Batch

FLIGHT_NUM	Origin	Dest	CRS_DEP_TIME	CRS_ARR_TIME	DepDelay
AA321	SAT	DFW	800	915	23
AA1331	TUL	DFW	820	951	26
AA1163	ORD	LAX	830	1057	20
AA2638	ONT	DFW	830	1327	16
AA456	DFW	CLT	830	1157	88
AA1041	ORD	PHX	835	1136	18
AA1719	DFW	ONT	835	953	30
AA811	ORD	SAN	835	1112	18
AA1939	SNA	DFW	840	1337	21
AA256	DFW	ATL	840	1145	100
AA2870	ORD	RSW	843	1240	34
AA1075	SFO	CLT	844	1640	269

107

Count of FLIGHT_NUM

Expected Delay on Arrival

14

Count of FLIGHT_NUM

Proportion of Delayed Flights

0,1308

Average of DepDel15

Figure 7-2. Reporting dashboard on Proportion of Delayed Flights metric

The dashboard shows the total number of flights (107) in the current batch scheduled for the departure time block 8:00 a.m. to 8:59 a.m. for a given day. Most of these flights will be still in the air before the next data batch comes in.

To estimate whether an arrival delay will occur, we are currently using the departure delay information as a proxy. Up to now, the BI team has used the variable DepDel15, which indicates whether the flight was delayed at least 15 minutes upon departure, to approximate whether the flight will also be late more than 15 minutes upon arrival.

This estimate has been a good first shot, but it is far from perfect. Let's open the Excel workbook *AA_Flights_2021.xlsx* and select the first sheet, AA_Flights_01, as shown in Figure 7-3, to find out how this estimate has performed historically.

Figure 7-3. American Airlines flight data from January 2021

The sheet AA_Flights_01 contains all American Airlines flights from January 2021—almost 38,000 rows of data. Each row is an American Airlines flight that happened during January 2021.

Since this is a historical dataset, we can see the actual arrival delay that happened. Take the first row, for example. The flight Number AA1 from John F. Kennedy International Airport (JFK) to Los Angeles International Airport (LAX) took off on January 1, 2021. The flight didn't have a delay on departure of 15 minutes or more and thus the column DepDelay15 is set to 0. Since the plane landed even ahead of schedule without any delay, the ArrDelay15 column is also set to 0. The first flight that had a departure delay of more than 15 minutes happened in row 21: it is again flight AA1 from JFK to LAX, but this time on January 20, 2021. The DepDelay15 attribute is 1 since the departure delay was 75 minutes, as you can see in Figure 7-4.

	DestCityName	DestState	DestStateFips	DestStateName	DestWac	CRSDepTime	DepTime	DepDelay	DepDelayMinutes	DepDel15
14	Los Angeles, CA	CA	6	California	91	900	900	0	0	0
15	Los Angeles, CA	CA	6	California	91	900	853	-7	0	0
16	Los Angeles, CA	CA	6	California	91	900	855	-5	0	0
17	Los Angeles, CA	CA	6	California	91	900	900	0	0	0
18	Los Angeles, CA	CA	6	California	91	900	855	-5	0	0
19	Los Angeles, CA	CA	6	California	91	900	849	-11	0	0
20	Los Angeles, CA	CA	6	California	91	900	851	-9	0	0
21	Los Angeles, CA	CA	6	California	91	900	1015	75	75	1
22	Los Angeles, CA	CA	6	California	91	900	850	-10	0	0
23	Los Angeles, CA	CA	6	California	91	900	857	-3	0	0

Figure 7-4. Flight delay of 75 minutes on departure

So in this case, the attribute DepDelay15 was a good indicator of whether a flight was actually also delayed on arrival. Now, how good would our prediction have been if we relied only on the DepDelay15 information? Head over to the third worksheet of the Excel file, Confusion_Table, to see the confusion table (Figure 7-5).

	A	B	C	D
1	**Classifier Evaluation**			
2				
3		**LABEL** ▾	**COUNT**	**PERC**
4	**BASELINE PREDICTION**	⊟ 0	34169	90,1%
5	ACTUAL	0	32991	97,1%
6	ACTUAL	1	1178	30,0%
7	**BASELINE PREDICTION**	⊟ 1	3737	9,9%
8	ACTUAL	0	988	2,9%
9	ACTUAL	1	2749	70,0%
10		Total	37906	100,0%
11				
12		ArrDel15	TRUE	10,4%
13			FALSE	89,6%

Figure 7-5. Evaluating the baseline classifier

Before we dive into the details, look at the last two rows, which read, ArrDel15 True = 10.4% and False = 89.6%. This summary tells us that we are dealing with an *imbalanced classification* problem as explained previously in Chapter 3. Only 10% of all flights are actually flagged with the ArrDelay15 attribute and are thus more than 15 minutes late on arrival.

Why should this imbalance be important to us? Because it affects our evaluation metric. Imagine that if we predicted that all flights will be on time with less than 15 minutes' delay, this would give us an astonishing accuracy score of 90%. Would this prediction be useful? No. That is why we have to come up with a smarter evaluation metric.

Look at the confusion table in Figure 7-5. This shows us how our baseline prediction (the DepDelay15 label) performed. If we used the Departure Delay heuristic in the past, we would have misclassified 2,166 observations: 1,178 flights were actually delayed, although we predicted they would be on time. And 988 flights were actually on time, even though we predicted there would be a delay.

As you learned in Chapter 3, *precision* is a measure that captures a classifier's exactness; higher precision indicates fewer false positives. If we manage to improve this metric, the 988 flights that have been predicted as delayed, but were actually on time, would be reduced. The precision is calculated by dividing the true-positive values (TP: 2,749) by the sum of the true positives and false positives (FP: 988).

Recall measures a classifier's completeness; higher recall indicates fewer false negatives (FN: 1,178 flights that were delayed, although predicted on time). Recall is calculated by dividing the true positives by the true positives plus the false negatives.

To compress both bits of information into a single metric that is easier to track, we will use the *F1-score*, which is the harmonic mean of precision and recall and is calculated as follows:

$$F1 = 2 \times (precision \times recall) / (precision + recall) = 2TP / (2TP + FP + FN)$$

As you can see in Figure 7-6, the F1-score for our baseline classifier is 0.72.

BASELINE		
True Positive	2.749	
False Positive	988	
True Negative	32.991	
False Negative	1.178	
Precision = TP / (TP + FP)		0,74
Recall = TP / (TP + FN)		0,70
F1-Score = 2TP / (2TP + FP + FN)		**0,72**

Figure 7-6. F1-score for the baseline classifier

Our goal is to come up with a new classifier that manages to beat this 0.72 F1-score baseline, so we can make even more accurate predictions about flight delays.

Solution Overview

To improve the prediction for a late arrival, we will use an AI classifier trained on historical data. Figure 7-7 shows a conceptual overview of the architecture for this use case. As you can see, this use case is getting slightly more advanced than the use cases from previous chapters. That is mainly because we are now looking beyond the capabilities of Power BI and adding more functionalities in the analysis layer.

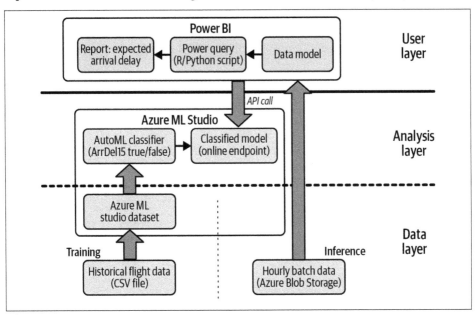

Figure 7-7. Automated classification use case architecture

We have two data sources in this architecture. On the bottom left of the figure is a set of historical flight data provided as a CSV file. And on the bottom right, we have the hourly batches of data being consumed by our BI system (in this case, Power BI).

In this example, we are using an AI service that will learn patterns from historical flight data and use this information to classify new data points (hourly flight batches), whether these flights will be likely delayed or not.

We could use many approaches to tackle these classification problems. Since we don't want to bring in rare and expensive AI/ML experts at this stage, we will use AutoML to train an ML model for us. I'm demonstrating the workflow on the example of Microsoft Azure Machine Learning Studio as the AutoML platform, but it could really be anything; they all work more or less the same. We will first build and evaluate the model on Azure ML Studio and then deploy it as an online HTTP endpoint—all without writing a single line of code!

The actual predictions will be made directly from the user layer within Power BI. Here, we will send a prediction request to an online API so we can fetch the new data and integrate it into our data model using Power Query. For this part, we will rely on a small R or Python script that handles the API request. Once we have the predictions in our BI, we will present the results in a Power BI report.

Native Integration of Azure and Power BI

It's possible to connect Power BI and ML models on Azure without any R or Python scripting. However, this native integration has the following disadvantages:

- This integration might require a Power BI Pro or Premium license.
- You're less flexible in terms of which data is sent to the model.
- This works only with Power BI and Azure.

The last point is especially important to me. I'm using Power BI and Azure here as examples. But as I pointed out before, my goal is for you to be able to build such systems even with other web services (such as AWS or GCP) or other BI platforms as well. That's what the R/Python scripts will allow you to do.

If you'd like to learn more about the native integration of Power BI and Azure ML models, I recommend "Tutorial: Consume Azure Machine Learning Models in Power BI" (*https://oreil.ly/eSHT0*) in the Microsoft documentation.

Model Training with Microsoft Azure Walk-Through

Visit Azure ML Studio (*https://ml.azure.com*), which you set up in Chapter 4. Since we want to train an AI model by using AutoML, select Start Now in the Automated ML pane and choose "New Automated ML job" to fill up the blank rows.

An *AutoML job* is the process that takes you all the way from providing a dataset up to getting a validated ML model as a result. We will go through this process step by step.

First, you need some data. On Azure, data is organized in datasets that are linked to your workspace. Datasets will ensure that your data is correctly formatted and can be consumed by ML jobs. As shown in Figure 7-8, select "Create."

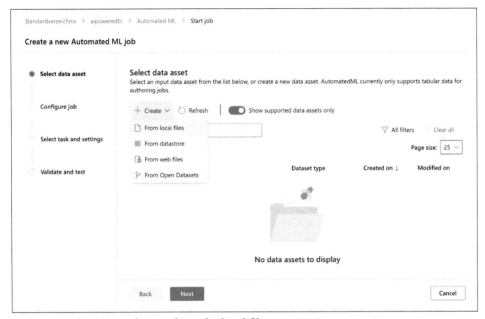

Figure 7-8. Creating a dataset from the local file

You can import data from various sources. In this case, we will upload a local file, so go ahead and select "From local files," as shown in Figure 7-8. In the "Basic info" form shown in Figure 7-9, give your dataset a telling name and add a description if you like. In this example, I named the dataset **aa_flights_ontime**. The version will default to 1, and the dataset type will be Tabular, as AutoML currently supports only tabular data.

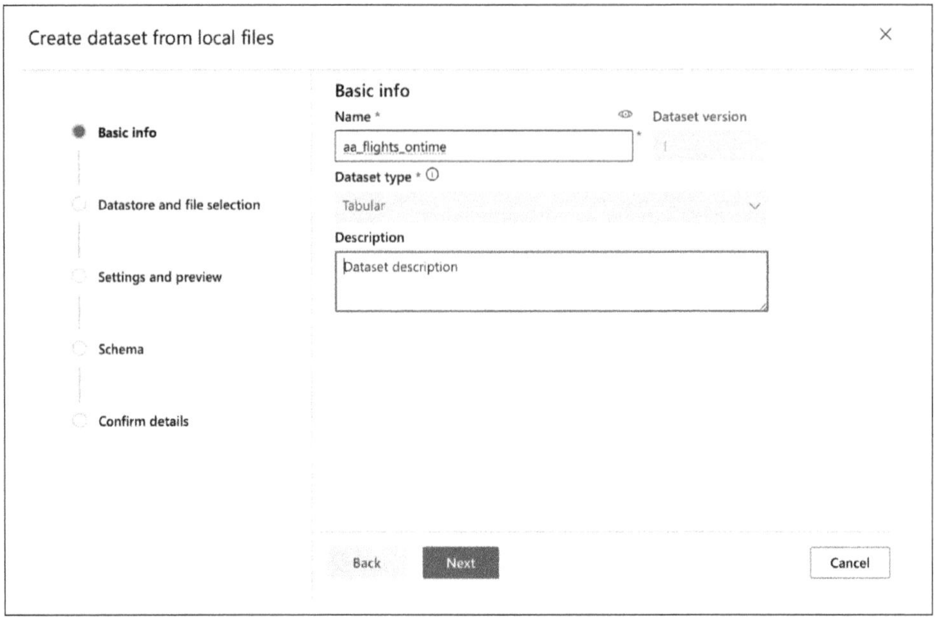

Figure 7-9. Adding basic info

Click Next to head over to the next section. You need to provide information as shown in Figure 7-10. You'll choose where the data should be stored and from where it should be uploaded. Select the default datastore that was automatically set up during your workspace creation (in this example, mine is called *workspaceblobstore*). This is where you'll physically upload your data file to make it available to your current workspace.

We can't upload the Excel file here. Azure ML Studio supports CSV, TSV, Parquet, and JSON files for tabular datasets. That's why we need to convert the Excel file to CSV first. For your convenience, I've done that already and created the file *AA_Flights_2021_01.csv*, which contains all flight data from January and is the first sheet of the Excel workbook *AA_Flights_2021.xlsx*. Click Next at the bottom of your screen to upload the file.

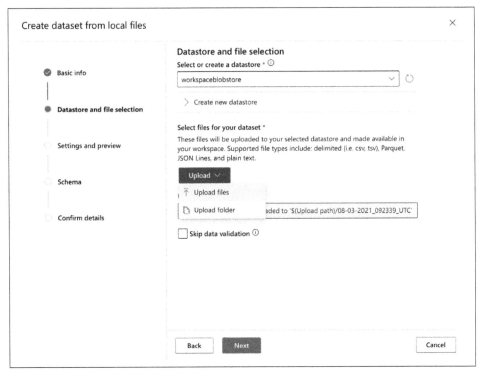

Figure 7-10. Selecting files to upload

After the file is successfully uploaded, you should see the "Settings and preview" form with some pre-populated information based on the uploaded file. Double-check that the settings are set as shown in Figure 7-11 and that the data preview at the bottom is displaying the first couple of rows correctly. If everything looks good, click Next.

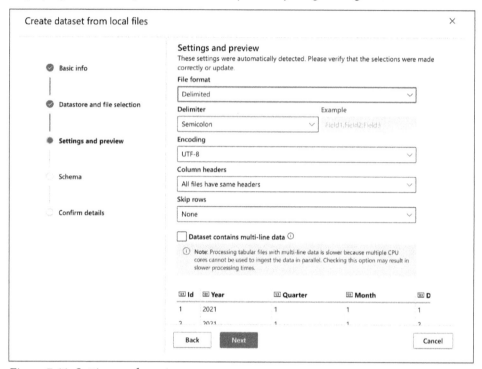

Figure 7-11. Settings and preview

The following form (Figure 7-12) will define the schema of your dataset. This schema is important for two reasons. First, the schema will allow you to define which columns in your dataset should be considered by the AutoML algorithm. And second, the schema will allow you to define the data type of the respective columns.

This step is important because both the columns you want to use and their respective data types are very hard for Azure ML Studio to guess automatically. For example, the column DayOfWeek looks numerical, but it's in fact categorical data: weekday 7 + 1 is not weekday 8, but weekday 1. Therefore, the column DayOfWeek should be interpreted as containing string values and not numeric ones.

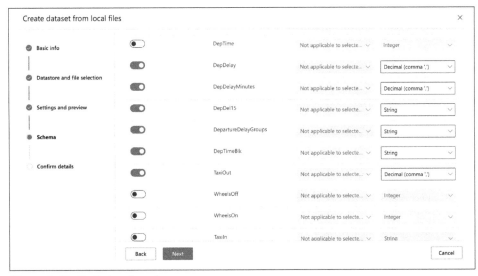

Figure 7-12. Defining the schema

Data types also define which AutoML tasks are possible for your data. For example, if we left the data type of the ArrDel15 variable to Decimal, we would not be able to select a Classification later. Similarly, if we want to predict a numeric value, we have to make sure it is correctly being set in the schema to enable a regression task. There is no way AutoML could reliably guess the data type on its own. That is something we have to define manually, and providing this information up front requires your expert knowledge.

In our example, we don't need all the data provided in the dataset. Some values don't provide any meaningful insight at all and would only increase the complexity of the project (such as Year, which has all the same values). And we don't want to include some other values in our prediction because it contains *target leakage* in the context of ML, which means that one feature includes the actual target in itself. For example, ArrivalDelay does tell us perfectly whether ArrDel15 is true or false.

Here's a list of all the columns we need for our use case. Make sure to include *only* these variables and that you set their data type correctly as shown in Figure 7-12:

- DayofWeek: String
- Origin: String
- Dest: String
- DepDelay: Dec/Comma
- DepDelayMinutes: Dec/Comma
- DepDel15: String

- DepartureDelayGroups: String

- DepTimeBlk: String

- TaxiOut: Dec/Comma

- ArrDel15: String

- ArrTimeBlk: String

- Distance: Dec/Comma

- DistanceGroup: String

Click Next. On the "Confirm details" page, double-check the information you provided and click Create to finish the creation of your dataset. You can select your dataset from the list that appears (click Refresh if necessary).

Process by clicking Next. You will see the "Configure job" screen, shown in Figure 7-13, which lets you specify how your AutoML job should work.

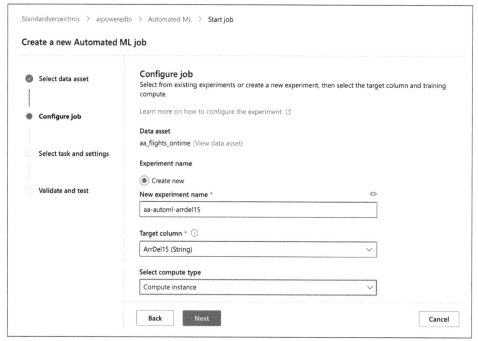

Figure 7-13. Creating a new AutoML job

What Is an AutoML Job?

Now that we have defined our dataset, we have to define which computation resources should be used for the AutoML training. In Azure, one AutoML training on a specific dataset is called an *AutoML job*. Jobs are organized in experiments. An *experiment* holds the information, such as the size of your compute environment, and specifies which column you want to predict.

Since we have not set up an experiment yet, select the "Create new" radio button. Enter a custom experiment name. In this case, I chose **aa-automl-arrdel15**. Specify ArrDel15 (String) as the target column. Finally, we have to specify which computing resources should be used for this training job. Select "Compute instance" as the compute type and then select the computing resource we initially created in Chapter 4. If the compute instance is stopped, you need to start it first. To do that, choose Compute from the Azure Machine Learning Studio main menu, select your instance from the list, and click Start. Tip: Open the compute instance menu in a new tab, so you don't interrupt the setup of your AutoML job.

 While there are no additional fees for using Azure Machine Learning, you will be charged for the underlying Azure services, such as Azure compute power or Azure Blob Storage. While greater compute power can improve AutoML speed (and thus lower the cost of the AutoML job), it is usually more cost-effective to choose cheaper compute resources and accept a slightly longer AutoML training time. Auto ML training in this use case should be more than covered by your free trial budget, even if you do it several times. To learn more about managing budgets, costs, and quotas for Azure Machine Learning, I recommend the Microsoft resource "Manage Budgets, Costs, and Quota for Azure Machine Learning at Organizational Scale" (*https://oreil.ly/LQo6K*).

Now it is time to specify what the AutoML task should do (Figure 7-14).

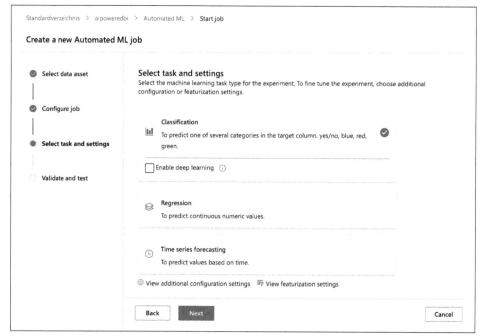

Figure 7-14. Select a machine learning task

We can choose from three task types here:

Classification
Predicting a categorical variable

Regression
Predicting a continuous numeric variable

Time-series forecasting
Regression for time-series data

Before you choose Next, click "View additional configuration settings." You will see the "Additional configurations" pane (Figure 7-15).

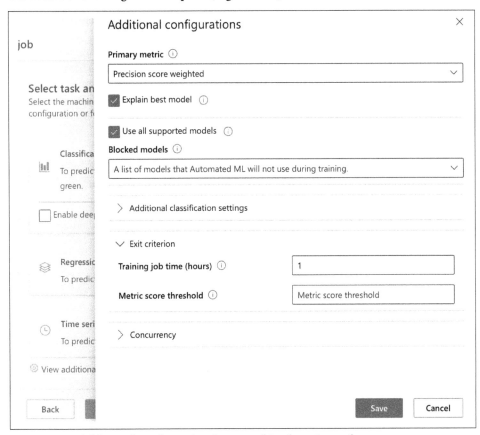

Figure 7-15. Additional configuration for a machine learning task

We want to customize some options here. First, we want to change the "Primary metric." Per default, this is set to Accuracy. As you have seen previously, accuracy isn't a good measure for imbalanced classification problems. We can't choose "F1-score" here. Instead, choose "Precision score weighted." This will also consider recall and therefore result in a better F1-score. Also, make sure that "Explain best model" is ticked.

Choosing the correct evaluation metric is a vital step in your AutoML process and can significantly affect the results. At the same time, it is hard for the AutoML service to guess which metric you need, since this depends on the problem at hand. For example, do you prioritize more false-positive over false-negative results, such as in clinical tests? Feel free to revisit Chapter 3 and become more familiar with various metrics as you need to. Experiment with them in multiple AutoML jobs. Visit "Evaluate Automated Machine Learning Experiment Results" (*https://oreil.ly/hNs4e*) in Azure ML Studio to compare your AutoML jobs according to different metrics.

Another setting we want to customize is the "Exit criterion." This will tell our AutoML algorithm when the model is "good enough." If a criteria is met, the training job is stopped. Typically, you can take two approaches here. You can end the training by time limit or by a minimum acceptance criteria for the metric. In this example, choose 1 hour as the maximum time limit. In fact, chances are that the training might even end before, if the algorithm can't get any more significant gains on training an even better model.

Confirm the additional settings with Save. Click Next and Finish to start your AutoML job. This will initialize your AutoML job and bring you to the "Run details" screen (Figure 7-16).

Figure 7-16. AutoML job details

This status updates as the experiment progresses. After a couple of minutes, the Status should change from "Not started" to "Running."

It will probably take 10 minutes or so before the first model is being trained. Some internal setups and checks occur on Azure first. One of these preparations is a service called *data guardrails*. Click the "Data guardrails" tab to find out more. After a few minutes, the screen should look like Figure 7-17. If this area is still empty, check back after a few minutes and refresh the page.

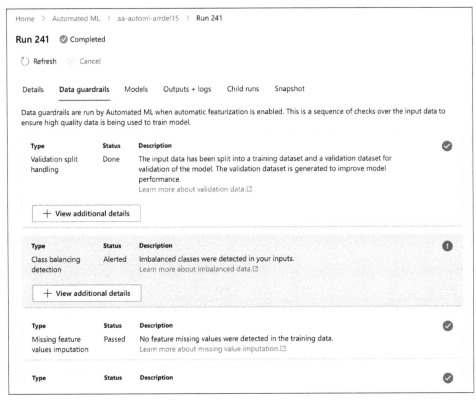

Figure 7-17. Data guardrails

Data guardrails on Azure AutoML are a series of automated checks over the training data to increase the chances of a high-quality training outcome. These checks include splitting the data into training and validation sets automatically, or checking for missing values in the training columns. Azure AutoML also checks for some assumptions related to the training task at hand—for example, it recognizes the imbalanced classes in the label and flags them as a potential problem area. If you click the "View additional details" button, you will see the underlying distribution of the class labels.

To find out how to tackle this problem, read the Azure documentation "Identify Models with Imbalanced Data" (*https://oreil.ly/dapAa*). Besides some built-in features that help tackle imbalanced classes, such as adding a weight column, one major point suggested is to pick an evaluation metric that is robust against class imbalances. It's a good thing that we chose precision over accuracy as our leading metric before.

While the overall training process is still running, head over to the Models tab. Here you will see a list of all the models and the preliminary evaluation metrics that the AutoML algorithm has come up with so far. After 15 to 20 minutes, you should already see a preliminary model with the respective evaluation metric. Consider that the model can only become better from here. If the AutoML algorithm finds an even better model, it will appear on top of this list. You can explore each model here and look further into the respective details. But the idea of AutoML is that we don't worry too much about what's going on during training. Let the algorithms do their job, grab a coffee, and check back in 30 minutes or so.

Has the training been finished? If so, you should see a screen like Figure 7-18, where the status indicates Completed.

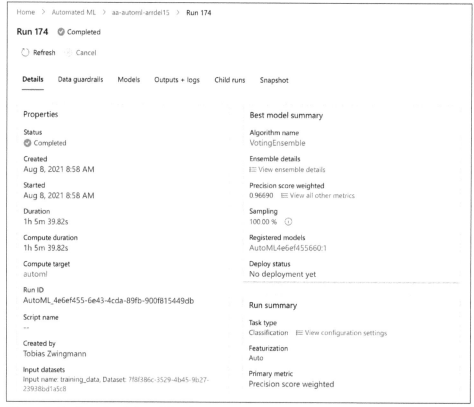

Figure 7-18. Completed AutoML job

Evaluating the AutoML Outputs

Now it's time to look at the best model the algorithm has found and explore it in a bit more detail. Head over to the models by clicking the Models tab. You should see a list similar to Figure 7-19. From this overview, we can see that the top five models are close together, with Precision scores ranging from 0.96340 to 0.96690 for the best model.

The best model in this case is a voting ensemble with a final Precision score of 0.96690. The actual results depend on the computing resources and the training time spent. They might look a little different if you chose different settings for the run configuration.

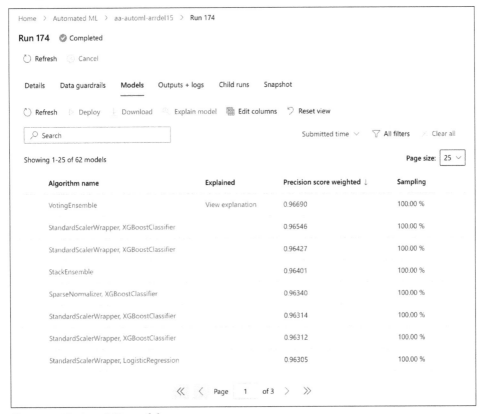

Figure 7-19. AutoML models

 The actual results for your AutoML job might slightly differ from the results in this book. While the AutoML process is deterministic, you might see different results due to stochastic procedures on the data preparation process (e.g., automated data sampling for training and testing). The big picture, however, should be similar.

Since we checked "Explain best model" in the advanced configurations before, the best model automatically shows the link "View explanation." We will come back to this in a bit. But first, click the algorithm name "VotingEnsemble" to see the model's detail page (Figure 7-20).

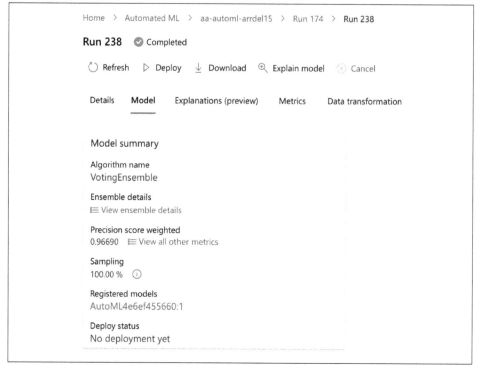

Figure 7-20. Details for best model

Most importantly, we want to find out how this model performs on our data. To find out more, click the Metrics tab. On this section, enable the following evaluation metrics and keep all other ones disabled for now:

- average_precision_score_macro
- average_precision_score_micro
- average_precision_score_weighted
- confusion_matrix
- f1_score_macro
- f1_score_micro
- f1_score_weighted

Your screen should look similar to the one in Figure 7-21.

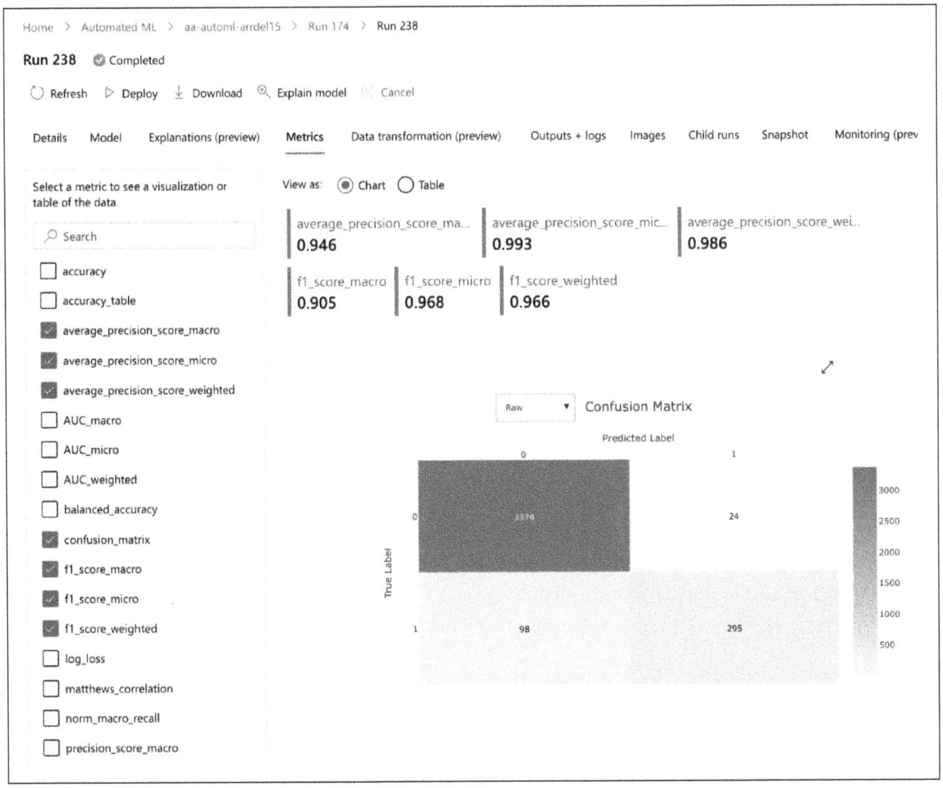

Figure 7-21. Model metrics

Before we worry too much about what micro, macro, and average metrics mean, let's take a look at the confusion matrix that the model evaluation has provided for us. This confusion table contains exactly the same information as our Excel table (Figure 7-5) in the problem statement—just the layout is a bit different.

The table contrasts the true data labels with the model's predicted labels. For example, for 3,374 observations, the actual label was 0 (no arrival delay > 15 minutes), and the model's predicted value was also 0. By contrast, 98 observations were predicted to be on time (predicted label = 0), but were in fact delayed by more than 15 minutes (actual label = 1). Note that this table does not contain all observations from the dataset, but only the sample data points from the validation set.

To make this screen more comparable to the Excel spreadsheet from our problem set, switch the drop-down menu at the top left from Raw to Normalized to show you the respective percentages (Figure 7-22). This makes it easier to compare the results to our Excel table from Figure 7-5.

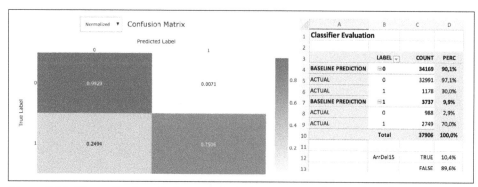

Figure 7-22. Normalized confusion matrix in Azure versus the Excel confusion matrix

Let's compare the model against our baseline model, which based its prediction solely on whether the plane was delayed more than 15 minutes upon departure. As you can see, our model makes significant gains compared to the baseline when it comes to flights predicted to be delayed (1) but were actually on time (0). The AI model misclassified only 0.71% of these observations incorrectly, whereas our baseline had an error of 2.9% in this category. Likewise, for flights that were predicted to be on time (0) but actually landed with more than a 15-minutes delay (1), we could reduce the error from the baseline from 30.0% to 24.94%.

Let's take a look at what this means for our acceptance criteria, the precision, recall, and F1-score. The metrics for the baseline model are as follows:

- Precision: 0.74
- Recall: 0.70
- F1-score: **0.72**

We can calculate the same metrics for our AI model by hand:

- Precision = TP / (TP + FP) = 295 / (295 + 24) = 0.92
- Recall = TP / (TP + FN) = 295 / (295 + 98) = 0.75
- F1-score: 2TP / (2TP + FP + FN) = 2 × 295 / (2 × 295 + 24 + 98) = **0.83**

As you can see, we could improve our baseline prediction by 11 percentage points, thanks to the approach of AutoML.

Let's come back to the Precision and F1-score metrics in the model Metrics tab. Why do we see much higher values here? That is because we are provided with the micro, macro, and weighted scores for our classification algorithm:

Micro

    Calculates metrics globally by counting the total true positives, false negatives, and false positives.

Macro

    Calculates metrics for each label and finds their unweighted mean. This does not take label imbalance into account.

Weighted

    Calculates metrics for each label and finds their average weighted by support (the number of true instances for each label).

For imbalanced classification problems, it is more informative to use a macro average with minority classes given equal weighting to majority classes.

In the case of a binary (two classes) classification problem, the macro F1-score is simply the average of the F1-score of the positive class and the negative class:

    *macro F1-score = (F1-score of positive class + F1-score of negative class) / 2 = (0.83 × 0.98) / 2 = **0.905***

As you see, that is exactly what the evaluation metric for the macro F1-score in Azure is showing us in Figure 7-23.

Figure 7-23. F1-score macro comparison

Be careful when you compare these aggregated evaluation metrics. Looking at things at a granular level (for example, in the confusion table) gives you a better picture of what is going on overall.

Sometimes the best model is not the best model for your purpose. Especially when the evaluation metrics are close together, you might want to check the first three models or so and explore the details—for example, in the confusion table as we did before. Depending on your preference, using the second- or third-best model may make sense if it better suits your problem at hand. Maybe you'll find a model that offers a better recall while sacrificing some precision?

Now that we have the confirmation that our model is working better than our non-AI baseline, let's understand why exactly this is the case. Head over to the Explanations tab of our best model. Select "raw" from the table in Figure 7-24 and shrink the list pane by clicking the double arrow.

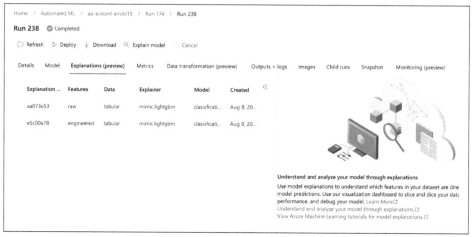

Figure 7-24. Model explanations

Next, click the "Aggregate feature importance" tab. This should result in a screen similar to Figure 7-25.

This visual briefly shows you the overall most important variables (features) that influence the outcome of a certain prediction. As we can see from the chart, the DepDelay (departure delay) attribute is unsurprisingly the most important influence factor by far.

But interestingly, three more variables are influencing the predictions by a good bit. The first is the TaxiOut attribute, which is nearly half as important as DepDelay. This should be no surprise since taxi-out is closely linked to the departure delay. But surprisingly, we also see that the variables Dest (destination) and Origin play a role when it comes to predicting arrival delays. Depending on the place a plane takes off and the airport it is scheduled to arrive at, the probability for an on-time arrival increases or decreases. These features are not as important as departure delay and taxi-out, but they do play a role in making better predictions.

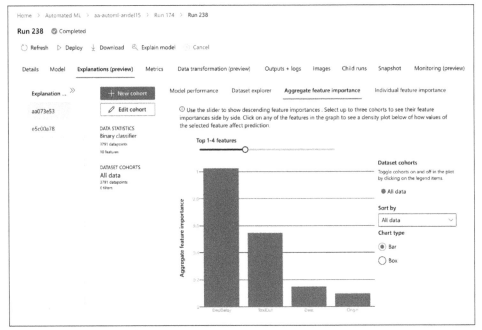

Figure 7-25. Aggregate feature importance

With more than four hundred unique combinations of departure and arrival airports in our dataset, this is an area where AutoML can play out its strengths, since it would be cumbersome for us to come up with handcrafted rules for these combinations, just to increase the overall quality of our predictions by a certain percent. Now that we have a rough idea of why the AutoML model works better than our baseline, let's move ahead and deploy our model for making predictions on new, unseen datasets.

Model Deployment with Microsoft Azure Walk-Through

Now that we've trained, validated, and understood our ML model, it is time to deploy it so we can use it to make predictions for new data. In Azure ML Studio, choose the model you want to make available and click "Deploy → Deploy to web service." The "Deploy a model" pane will pop up on the right side (Figure 7-26).

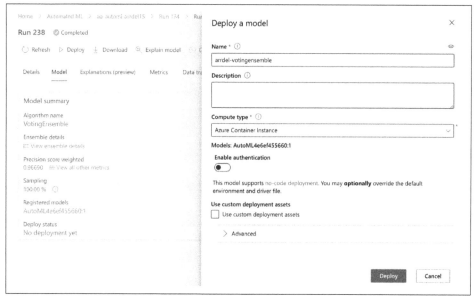

Figure 7-26. Deploying a model

Give your model deployment a name. I suggest using a combination of the model purpose (predicted variable) and the algorithm you are using. In our case, a good model name could be **arrdel-votingensemble**. Next, select the compute type. Here you can choose between Azure Kubernetes Services and Azure Container Instance. Both resources are typically used for real-time inference. The Kubernetes service is typically used for large-scale production deployments that require fast response time and autoscaling. This is exactly the opposite of our prototyping requirements. We're happy with the Azure Container Service, which is used for smaller CPU-based workloads that require less than 48 GB RAM. Make sure authentication is disabled for now and click Deploy.

After you click Deploy, you should see a notification telling you that the deployment is in progress (Figure 7-27).

Figure 7-27. Model deployment in progress

After a few minutes, you should see another notification that the deployment is complete. From the main menu on the left, click Endpoints and select your deployed model. You should see a screen similar to Figure 7-28. The deployment state of your model should be Healthy, and you should see a REST endpoint URL. That's one of the most important parameters from this whole page. We will use the REST endpoint later to make predictions (inference).

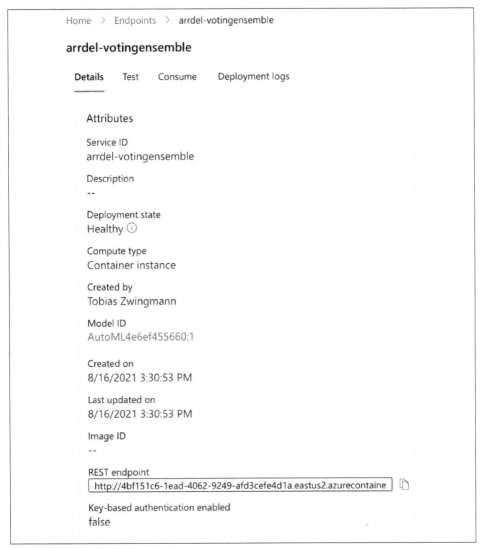

Figure 7-28. Deployed model endpoint

Congratulations, your first ML model is now ready for use! But before we integrate this model into our BI reports, let's quickly test it by using the built-in testing features in Azure ML Studio.

From the tab menu of the deployed model, choose Test. Here, you can quickly get online predictions for some sample data points. You can either input these values manually using the provided form, or you can toggle the small CSV icon to paste tabular data, as shown in Figure 7-29.

Figure 7-29. Testing the model using a real-time endpoint

Open the *AA_Hourly_Batches_2021-02-07_0800-0859.csv* file in a plain-text editor of your choice (not in Excel!). This file contains one batch of hourly flight data, which we want to use to make predictions about the expected arrival delay. In the text editor, select all, and then copy and paste the contents into the text area on the testing page. Click the Test button, and you should immediately see the results on the right (Figure 7-30).

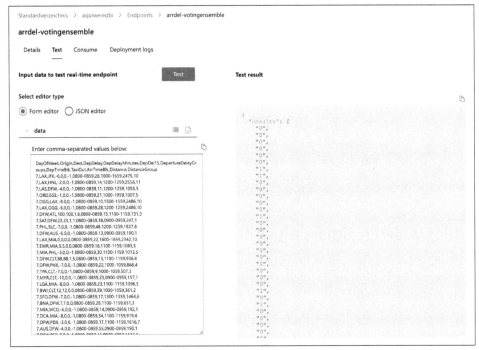

Figure 7-30. Testing model predictions

Now that our model is up and running, we are going to use R or Python to start getting inferences inside our BI dashboard. To call online predictions from our BI report, we need to run a small script that takes data from (in our case) Power BI, sends it to the HTTP API, retrieves the results, and feeds them back into the report.

Online Inference Versus Batch Inference

You can use your AI model in two ways, depending on how you want to make predictions. *Online* (or *real-time*) *inference* requires the model to make predictions anytime it is called upon and to respond immediately. This deployment type is often used with interactive application data. *Batch inference*, on the other hand, is an asynchronous process that makes its predictions based on a batch of observations. The prediction results are typically stored as files or written to a database, where they can be consumed by other applications.

While Azure ML Studio's AutoML service always returns an HTTP endpoint for online predictions, Azure ML Studio also provides ways to create batch predictions. You will see an example of batch predictions in Chapter 10.

 We are leaving Azure ML Studio for now and will come back to it only for the next use case. To avoid costs, I recommend you stop the compute resource you used for the Auto ML training by choosing Azure Machine Learning Studio → Compute → Stop.

Getting Model Predictions with Python or R

Depending on your preferred programming language, you can continue this section by using either Python or R. I demonstrate the examples with R, but the same steps apply to Python as well.

Visit Azure ML Studio. Select Endpoints and choose the model you want to use for requesting inference. On the following screen, select Consume and then choose R (or Python) from the tab menu. You will see two important things here, as shown in Figure 7-31: the public REST endpoint URL you need to use and a pre-written script to submit the request.

Figure 7-31. R script for model inference

The pre-written script is good enough if you want to process a single request for a single observation. If you want to process a whole table with multiple data points, you would need to rewrite the script in a way that multiple records are sent to the API, and not only one.

On the book's website (*https://oreil.ly/X9jmJ*), you can find two files, *azure-ml-inference-arrdel15.R* and *azure-ml-inference-arrdel15.py*. Both scripts share the same structure, sections, variable names, and code logic. I'll walk you through the code examples in R, but the same applies to the Python version as well.

Let's go through the script *azure-ml-inference-arrdel15.R* piece by piece. Section 0 of the script does some setup and housekeeping. First, the script loads all required packages. In the case of R, these are the following:

- *httr* (for making HTTP requests)
- *rjson* (for handling the API response)
- *dplyr* (for data preparation)

Make sure you have them installed for the R engine that Power BI is using, as described in Chapter 4.

Next, you need to customize two variables. For the variable API_URL, replace the dummy URL with the REST endpoint one from the Consume tab in your Azure portal.

The variable API_KEY is empty since we deployed our model without authentication. If you enable authentication, you would need to include your authentication key here:

```
# SECTION 0: Setup and Variables ----
# Make sure these packages are installed
library("httr")
library("rjson")
library("dplyr")

API_KEY = ""
API_URL = "http://xxxxxxxxxxxxxxxxxx.eastus2.azurecontainer.io/score"
```

 While we store our Azure credentials in plain text here within the code, please be aware that this is generally not good coding practice. We are doing this to keep things simple. If you want to learn best practices around handling authentication mechanisms, I recommend checking out the Microsoft resource "About Azure Key Vault" (*https://oreil.ly/cD2o6*).

Section 1 of the code contains the function for the actual API request, similar to the example script in Azure. The main difference is that you can pass a whole set of records to this function rather than just a single observation, which speeds up the overall process considerably.

As you can see from the code, the column names have a static reference. So if you have made changes to the dataset or chosen different columns for predictions, you will need to update them in the script as well:

```
# SECTION 1: API Request Function ----
inference_request <- function(DayOfWeek,
                              Origin,
                              Dest,
                              DepDelay,
                              DepDelayMinutes,
                              DepDel15,
                              DepartureDelayGroups,
                              DepTimeBlk,
                              TaxiOut,
                              ArrTimeBlk,
                              Distance,
                              DistanceGroup) {

  # Bind columns to dataframe
  request_df <- data.frame(DayOfWeek,
                           Origin,
                           Dest,
                           DepDelay,
                           DepDelayMinutes,
                           DepDel15,
                           DepartureDelayGroups,
                           DepTimeBlk,
                           TaxiOut,
                           ArrTimeBlk,
                           Distance,
                           DistanceGroup)

  req = list(
    Inputs = list(
      "data"=apply(request_df,1,as.list)
    ),
    GlobalParameters = list(
      'method' = "predict"
    )
  )
... (Truncated for brevity)
```

Section 2 contains the data processing part, which is simple in this case. This script is later embedded in a Power Query workflow, and Power Query passes the data from the previous step to the script as a table called `dataset`. As you can see from the script, we are assigning this source data to a new variable `df` to stay organized and keep the processed data separate from the original data:

```
# SECTION 2: Data preprocessing ----
# Fetch data from Power Query workflow
df <- dataset
```

Section 3 extracts the relevant columns for our prediction from the given dataset and actually calls the API, which is our hosted model:

```
# SECTION 3: Get Predictions ----
result <- inference_request(df$DayOfWeek,
                            df$Origin,
                            df$Dest,
                            df$DepDelay,
                            …)
                                            (Truncated for brevity)
```

Section 4 takes the result from the API and formats it in a way that it can be added to our original dataset as a new column called ArrDel15_Prediction:

```
# SECTION 4: Data postprocessing ----
result <- unlist(content(result))
df$ArrDel15_Prediction <- result
```

Finally, section 5 provides the output in a form that Power BI can take over from here again:

```
# SECTION 5: Format output for Power BI ----
output <- df
```

> Our dataset contains just a little more than 100 observations. If you need many more predictions than that (10,000+ rows), consider limiting the number of data points per API call or choosing a batch prediction instead of an online prediction. You will learn more about batch predictions in Chapter 10.

Model Inference with Power BI Walk-Through

Now that you know how to get predictions from your model programmatically, it is finally time to put your knowledge into action in Power BI. Note that although we are using Power BI here, you could use any BI tool that is able to process R or Python code.

Our goal is to enhance the arrival delay predictions for the dashboard we have seen in the problem statement (shown previously in Figure 7-2). To recap: the dashboard reads hourly batches of flight data and shows the expected proportion of delayed flights on arrival. We will now take this data, send it to our hosted model, get the predictions, and display the aggregated score for further use and improved decision making.

To follow along in Power BI, open the *Arrival_Delay.pbix* file. You should see the dashboard shown in Figure 7-32.

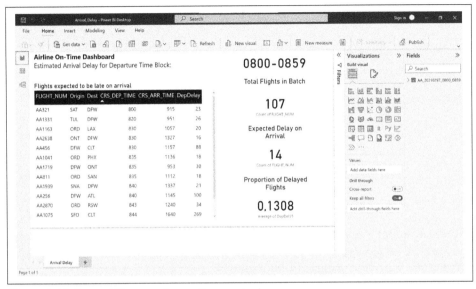

Figure 7-32. Power BI report for on-time arrivals

To add our AI predictions, we have to apply some data transformations. Click the Transform Data icon to launch Power Query from the toolbar, as shown in Figure 7-33.

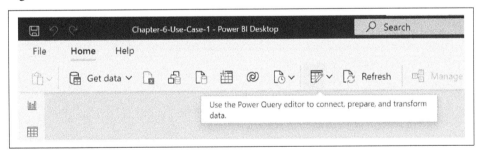

Figure 7-33. Transform Data icon

This opens the Power Query Editor. This tool allows you to manipulate your data, apply calculations, perform transformations, and execute Python and R scripts!

From the toolbar, click the Transform tab and then "Run R script" or "Run Python script," depending on which you prefer (see Figure 7-34). For this tutorial, I will continue with the example of R.

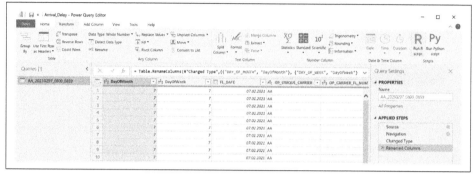

Figure 7-34. Power Query Editor

In the code editor, paste the code from the script file (*azure-ml-inference-arrdel15.R*), as shown in Figure 7-35. Double-check that you have replaced the endpoint URL with the one from your model in code section 0.

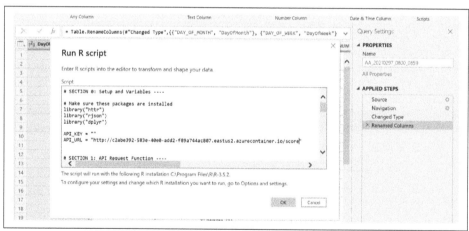

Figure 7-35. Running R/Python scripts inside Power Query

Click OK, and Power BI will evaluate the script. If you get a warning on data privacy, select "Ignore Privacy Levels checks for this file." The script should take a moment, depending on the number of rows you send to the API endpoint. Remember, we are still in the phase of prototyping here. In a production setting, you would apply these AI predictions on a database level and just consume them from your Power BI or reporting system. Check out Chapter 11 for more details.

Once the script is finished, you should see a prompt with two tables in Power Query. Select the "output" table. You will notice two things in the editor. First, another step is added under the Applied Steps pane on the right. And second, you will see a new column, ArrDel15_Prediction, if you scroll to the right (Figure 7-36). Double-check that the data type of this column is recognized as numeric. If it isn't, right-click the column and choose Change Type → Whole Number.

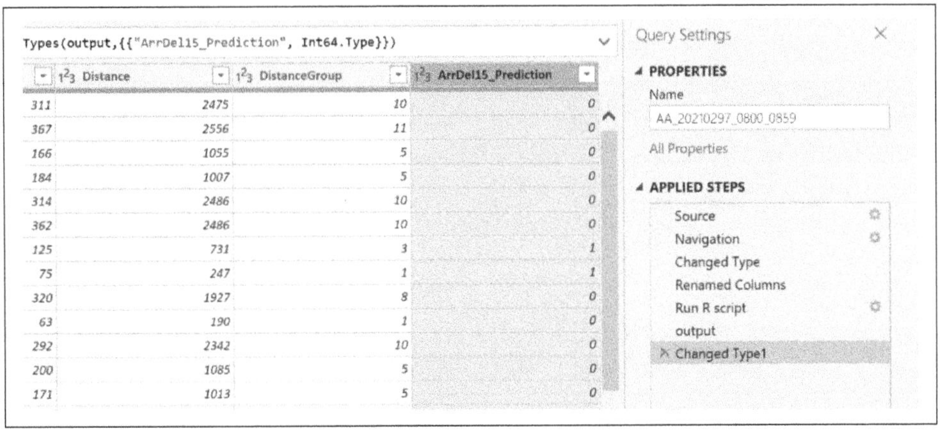

Figure 7-36. Prediction column in Power Query

In the Power Query Editor, select Home and then Close & Apply. Your data model is being updated and populated with the new additional information. You can see the new column in the updated model. Whenever you want to update the data or the predictions, you need to refresh the data model, as shown in Figure 7-37. This will reload the data from the file or an external source and rerun the steps in the Power Query Editor.

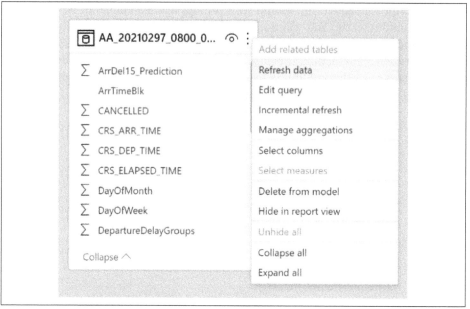

Figure 7-37. Refreshing data

Building the AI-Powered Dashboard in Power BI

We are now ready to populate our dashboard with the new information. Go back to Report and select the Card visual with the Proportion of Delayed Flights. Drag and drop the new dimension ArrDel15_Prediction from the Fields pane to the value field of the card visual, replacing the old metric DepDel15. Right-click the updated field and select Average. The Settings pane should now look like Figure 7-38, and the metric should update to 0.1495.

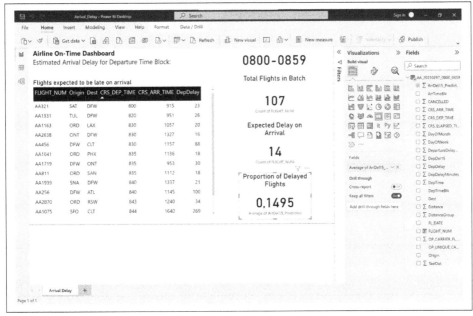

Figure 7-38. Updated dashboard with AI predictions

Go ahead and replace the DepDel15 field with the new ArrDel15_Predicted dimension for the rest of the visuals in the dashboard. This includes the filter value for the card visual Expected Delay on Arrival as well as the filter on the flights table.

Alternatively, you can open the file *Arrival_Delay_AI-Powered.pbix* and follow along from there. Your final dashboard should look like Figure 7-39.

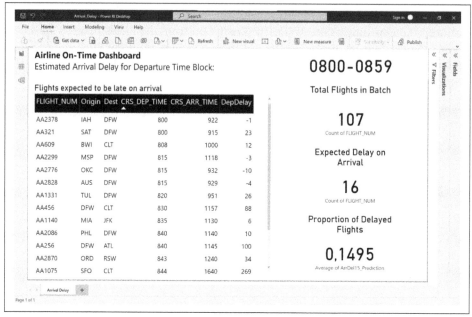

Figure 7-39. Final AI-powered dashboard with online predictions for flight delays

From the count of delayed flights alone, we might intuitively assume that the predictions from our baseline and the AI model are not that different. But don't fall for that trap! Just because the AI predicts one more flight in total to be delayed, the actual flights that are expected to be delayed are quite different. Have a look at the flights table. In the AI-powered dashboard, we can see flagged flights that did not have a departure delay of 15 minutes. Examples include flights AA2378 from IAH to DFW, flight AA2776 from OKC to DFW, and flight AA2828 from AUS to DFW that even started ahead of time.

As we know from the real dataset shown in Figure 7-40, we can confirm that flights AA2378 and flights AA2828 were in fact delayed by more than 15 minutes. Flight AA2776 did not have the ArrivalDelay15 flag, but the plane landed 12 minutes late, despite having a head start of 10 minutes. While technically the AI prediction here was wrong, it was definitely a good guess.

FL_DATE	OP_ UNI QUE _	OP_CAR RIER_FL _NUM	ORIGIN	DEST	CRS_ DEP_ TIME	DEP_ TIME	DEP_ DELAY	DEP_ DEL15	CRS_ARR _TIME	ARR_T IME	ARR_ DELAY	ARR_ DEL15
07.02.21	AA	2828	AUS	DFW	815	811	-4	0	929	954	25	1
07.02.21	AA	2378	IAH	DFW	800	759	-1	0	922	1003	41	1
07.02.21	AA	2776	OKC	DFW	815	805	-10	0	932	944	12	0

Figure 7-40. Actual delay of flights AA2378 and AA2776 on 7/2/21

I hope you enjoyed building this dashboard and found out how AI can help you to make better predictions for your dataset. Keep track of a baseline and see if and how well AI can possibly outperform this.

Spot the Error

When you look carefully at the flights table, you will find a small hitch in our approach that is also likely to happen in real life. See, for example, the last row in Figure 7-38, the flight from SFO to CLT. The flight is delayed by 269 minutes. This is what we call a *training-serving skew*. If this was real-world data, this information would actually be available only 4.5 hours later. So depending on which point in time we are looking at, the data might have information available or not. In training, we have all information available. In reality, though, we don't.

We could use various approaches to tackle this issue—for example, introducing a "minimum delay" that counts the delay "up to now" or by not serving a prediction for these flights. Or we could take off the DepDelay variable from our AI model and just keep the field Departure_Delay_15 as a proxy for the flight delay (in addition to all other attributes) and see how our AI model performs.

When you decide to put a prototype into production, these are the questions you want to ask: How often do we get the data? Is the frequency enough? To which extent will the business benefit from a better prediction, and is it worth the effort of scaling up the data pipeline? These are the questions you want to discuss and focus on. Thanks to your prototype, you don't need to discuss whether AI could beat the current baseline. You built the PoC yourself.

Use Case: Improving KPI Prediction

For this use case, we will continue with the previous scenario. We are on the BI team of American Airlines. Only this time, we don't want to improve our live reporting, but rather our planning even ahead of time.

For that purpose, we will need to deal with the Elapsed Time metric, which measures the difference between actual departure time and actual arrival time of a given flight. The elapsed time is planned well ahead and called the Computer Reservation System (CRS) Elapsed Time. In contrast to the preceding use case, this is not a categorical, but a continuous numerical variable.

Welcome to the world of regression problems! Let's find out more about the problem by introducing the problem statement as follows.

Problem Statement

We want to identify bottlenecks in the flight schedule for the next month and flag those flights that have a high chance of being delayed, meaning the actual elapsed time was higher than the planned elapsed time. The BI team has built a dashboard that analyzes historical data and shows a key performance indicator (KPI) that compares CRS (scheduled) Elapsed Time to Actual Elapsed Time. You can see this dashboard in Figure 7-41 or open it yourself in Power BI with the file *Elapsed_Time.pbix*.

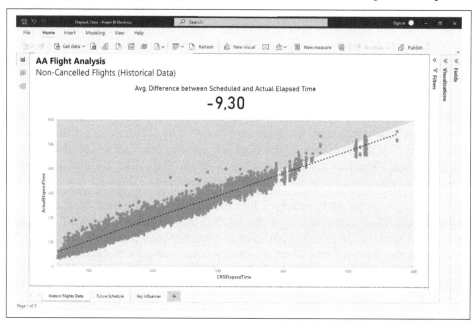

Figure 7-41. Flight analysis dashboard

From the dashboard, we find out that, on average, flights need 9.30 minutes less than actually planned. This intuitively makes sense, as we know that the schedule is optimized to minimize delays. At the same time, we can see from the scatterplot on the left that some flights exceed the planned elapsed time. The scatterplot shows CRS Elapsed Time versus Actual Elapsed Time. Each point is a flight. Points in the upper dark area of the plot needed more time than originally scheduled. The key question is, are we able to create a model that will flag these flights at times when the flight schedule is generated?

Based on the historical data, the analysts have built a simple regression model that is also shown as a trend line in the dashboard. The model takes the scheduled CRS Elapsed Time and calculates a prediction for the Actual Elapsed Time based on the historical data. The analysts have told us that the regression model has a Standard Error (RMSE) of 14.30, as shown in Figure 7-42. If you struggle with the interpretation of these metrics, revisit Chapter 3 briefly. While the model seems to be good on paper, it turns out to be quite useless for predicting the actual elapsed time.

SUMMARY OUTPUT

Regression Statistics	
Multiple R	0,98047362
R Square	0,96132851
Adjusted R Square	0,96132749
Standard Error	14,3004254
Observations	37906

	Coefficients	P-value	Lower 95%	Upper 95%
Intercept	9,2120	9,781E-121	9,9820	8,4420
X Variable 1	0,9498	0	0,9479	0,9517

Root Mean Square Error (RMSE)	14,3004254

Figure 7-42. Baseline regression model

Open the Future Schedule report in the file *Elapsed_Time.pbix* (Figure 7-43). As we can see from this report, applying the model to the flight schedule for February 2021 will flag 114 flight numbers for which the actual elapsed time will probably exceed the scheduled elapsed time by five minutes or more. However, by looking at the bar chart on the right, we can see that the biggest difference between the scheduled elapsed and actual predicted elapsed time is only marginal, with 6.50 minutes more than planned. That is the highest difference the regression model is able to predict. Look at the scatterplot on the left. It shows the average expected delay by flight number. You can see that all of these flights are close to the threshold of being exactly in line with the scheduled elapsed time. This makes it hard for us to identify those flights that are likely to encounter a long delay.

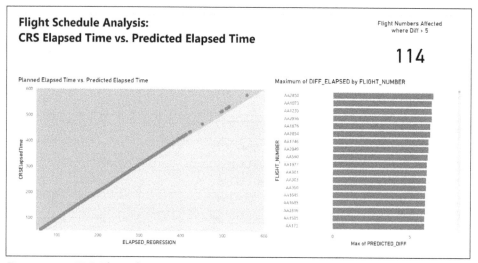

Figure 7-43. CRS Elapsed Time versus Predicted Elapsed Time baseline

The regression model that has been built is just not flexible enough to capture variations in the elapsed time that are caused by variables other than the scheduled CRS time. But what are these influencing variables, anyway? The BI team has further conducted an analysis and identified key drivers that cause the difference between the scheduled elapsed time and the actual elapsed time to increase. You can find a screenshot of this analysis in Figure 7-44 or in the "Key influencers" report page in the Power BI file *Elapsed_Time.pbix*.

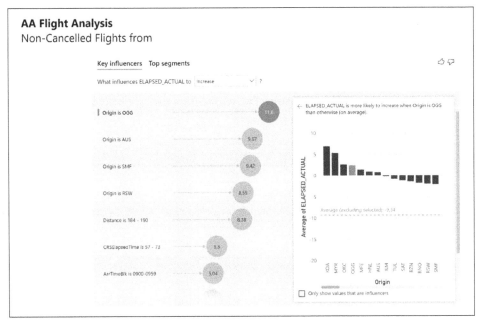

Figure 7-44. Key influencers analysis for predicted flight delays

From the analysis, we find out that a variety of factors drive the discrepancy between scheduled and elapsed time. Among them are the origin airport, flight distance, planned flight duration, and the arrival time block. So, you probably don't want to schedule a meeting shortly after arrival if you take a short-distance flight from Austin that is expected to land sometime between 9:00 a.m. and 9:59 a.m.

But how can we as an airline turn these insights into actionable information for our customers? How can we flag those critical bottlenecks in a flight schedule and surface them automatically without having to run through the key influencers analysis over and over again? Let's find out how by proceeding to the solution overview.

Solution Overview

To identify bottlenecks in the flight schedule, we will take all information available to us when the schedule is created and train an ML model on historical data to predict the actual elapsed time using this information. The information includes attributes such as origin airport, destination airport, arrival and departure time blocks, and more. All these attributes are known before the flight even happens, so we don't run into a training-serving skew and can react to the model outputs well ahead of time.

Figure 7-45 shows the high-level architecture of this use case. It's similar to what we did previously in "Use Case: Automating Classification Tasks" on page 138. We will train an ML model on historical data and deploy it using Azure ML Studio, so we can get predictions from an online endpoint from within Power BI. The only major difference is that this time we are not training a classification model, but a regression model. Again, we are using Power BI to make the request, but we could use other BI tools as well.

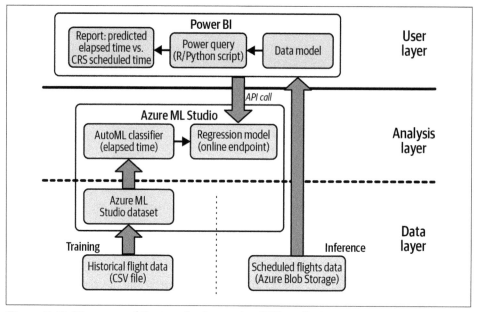

Figure 7-45. Use case architecture for improving KPI prediction

Model Training with Microsoft Azure Walk-Through

Head over to Azure ML Studio by navigating to *ml.azure.com*. From the home screen, choose Create new → Automated ML job, as shown in Figure 7-46.

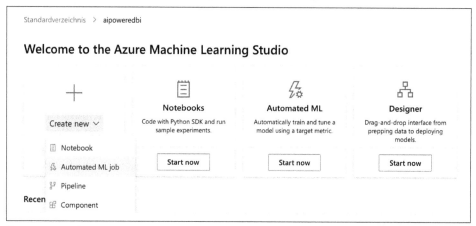

Figure 7-46. Creating a new automated ML job

Choose Create Dataset → From local file. You will see the form for providing basic information about your dataset (Figure 7-47). Give your dataset a name that you can relate to the AutoML training job. In this example, I chose **aa-flights-elapsedtime**. Proceed with Next.

Figure 7-47. Creating a dataset from local files

Click the Upload button and select the *AA_Flights_2021_01.csv* file. Once the upload is complete, the Next button should appear at the bottom of the screen.

Although we are technically using the same data source as in the previous use case, it is still a good idea to re-upload the file as a separate dataset in Microsoft Azure in order to keep organized. The training dataset we are using now has a different schema than the training dataset from the first use case. For example, this time we are predicting the Actual Elapsed Time attribute. You can also update the schema in Azure for a dataset by adding a new version, but this will be complicated to track if you want to retrain your ArrDel15 classifier from the use case before. A good rule of thumb: keep a separate dataset for each AutoML task, meaning that the target column should stay fixed. Use the schema update function and version control to add or remove features or tweak the data types of your input data, but don't touch the target column.

Continue to the "Settings and preview" form. Double-check that the file format is set to Delimited, the delimiter is set to Semicolon, and the encoding is set to UTF-8. You should see a properly formatted preview of the data, as shown in Figure 7-48.

Figure 7-48. Dataset settings and preview

Click Next to proceed to the schema settings. Include *only* the following attributes with their respective data types:

- DayOfWeek: String
- Origin: String
- Dest: String
- DepTimeBlk: String
- ArrTimeBlk: String
- CRSElapsedTime: Decimal (Comma)
- ActualElapsedTime: Decimal (Comma)
- Distance: Decimal (Comma)
- DistanceGroup: String

Click Next, confirm the details, and you should see the new dataset appear in the list of available datasets (Figure 7-49).

Figure 7-49. List of available datasets

Select the new dataset and click Next. On the following screen, I suggest creating a new experiment to keep the models and results from the classification and regression tasks separated. Choose an experiment name that will differentiate well from the previous experiment, such as **aa-automl-time**. Choose ActualElapsedTime (Decimal) as the target column. For the compute resource, you can use the same "automl" resource that we have used in the previous use case. Proceed with Next.

On the following screen, AutoML will guess that you are trying to solve a regression problem, as you specified a continuous numeric target variable. In our case, this is absolutely correct! Before we finish the setup process, open the advanced settings shown in Figure 7-50 by clicking "View additional configuration settings."

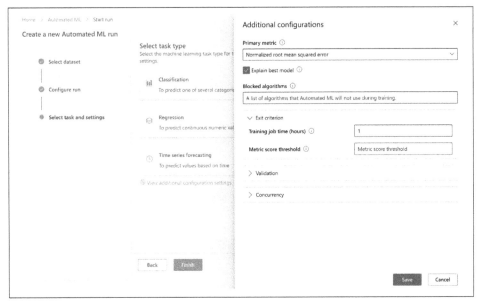

Figure 7-50. Additional configurations for AutoML

In the additional configurations, make sure that "Primary metric" is set to "Normalized root mean squared error." This way, we can compare the AutoML model pretty well with the existing baseline from the regression model we already have. Also double-check that the option "Explain best model" is checked. Under "Exit criterion," set the training job to a maximum of 1 hour. In fact, we probably don't even need that much time, and the algorithm should converge after roughly 30 minutes. Confirm the settings with Save, and submit the AutoML job by clicking Finish.

The run can take a while, so take a break and come back after a few minutes. You can check the status of your run by choosing Experiments → aa-automl-time (or whichever name you gave to it) and examining the status of your current run. Once the status changes to Completed, the run details should look similar to Figure 7-51.

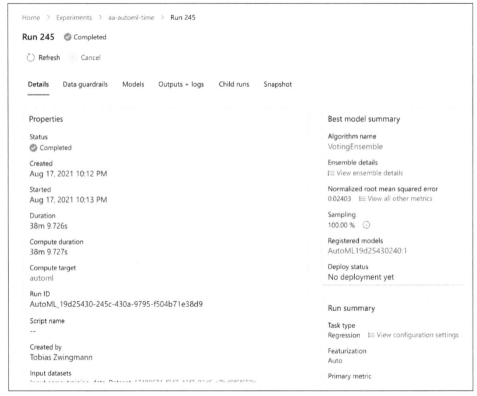

Figure 7-51. Completed job details for the lapsed time prediction

As you can see, in this case, the overall run took about 38 minutes and resulted in a model that uses VotingEnsemble as an algorithm—again! In fact, AutoML often comes up with a VotingEnsemble or Stacked Ensemble as the final model. Both techniques combine the results of numerous models that either "vote" for the final result or are "stacked" on top of each other to come up with the final decision (if you want to know more, revisit Chapter 3 for more details). It is common for AutoML algorithms to end up with ensemble models.

In our case, the model achieved a normalized RMSE of 0.2403. How can we compare that to the RMSE baseline of 14.30 from our simple regression model?

Click the VotingEnsemble link and choose Metrics. Uncheck all boxes except for r2-score, the residuals, and root_mean_squared_error, as shown in Figure 7-52.

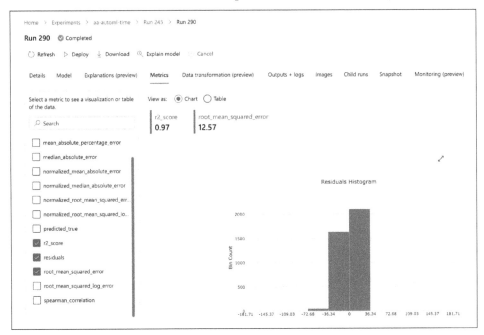

Figure 7-52. Regression evaluation metrics

From the metrics, you can see that the RMSE of our AutoML regression model is 12.57. That is less (and therefore better) than the simple regression model, but actually not that much, considering the amount of computing power we threw at this problem. But as you learned from the previous use case in this chapter, we should be skeptical about aggregated quality metrics and look at the results in a bit more detail.

Take a look back at the Residuals histogram in Figure 7-52. A *residual* is the error a regression model makes, the difference between the actual and the predicted outcome. For our simple regression model, the regression almost always predicted less than what was actually the real value. In our AutoML scenario here, we can see that the residuals are centered around the 0 value, with some predictions being a little bit on top of the actual metric and other predictions below that. This type of variance is a good sign, because we need this variation to identify flights that have a high probability of exceeding the scheduled elapsed time. So with some good faith in our AutoML model and the confirmation that at least on paper it is better than our regression baseline, head over to the Explanations tab to find out which factors are influencing our predictions.

In the Explanations tab, select the first list item with the raw features. Then select the "Aggregate feature importance" tab from the submenu. Select the Top 5 features and you should see a screen similar to Figure 7-53.

Figure 7-53. Aggregate feature importance for the regression model

In this case, the top five features are CRSElapsedTime (no surprise, by far) and Distance, Dest, Origin, and ArrTimeBlk. This selection makes sense from a logical standpoint. Bigger airports are busier than smaller ones, so there should be a higher probability that a delay happens. Also, ArrTimeBlk confirms what we have seen from the key influencers tool previously. At certain arrival times, especially in morning hours, airports are typically busier, and delays are more likely to happen.

The actual results in your case might look a little different, as some random elements are involved in the AutoML process (for example, the way the data is split into training, testing, and validation sets). Unfortunately, we can't set the seed for these random procedures fixed in Azure so we have 100% reproducible results. However, the overall big picture should be the same when you conduct the analysis on your own.

Let's take a minute to understand our model even a little better and see what is going on. Click the "Individual feature importance" tab, shown in Figure 7-54. You will find a scatterplot there. In the scatterplot, click the title of the y-axis and choose Predicted Y. Do the same for the x-axis and choose True Y. This will give an overview of all data points (flights) and their corresponding true and predicted values for the Elapsed Time attribute.

The great thing about this visualization is that we can individually select single data points and inspect the concrete feature importance that led to the individual predicted result. Choose three data points from this chart:

- One point with a predicted value that's higher than the actual value
- One point with a predicted value that almost matches the actual value
- One point with a predicted value that's much lower than the actual value

Figure 7-54 shows how this looks for my selection.

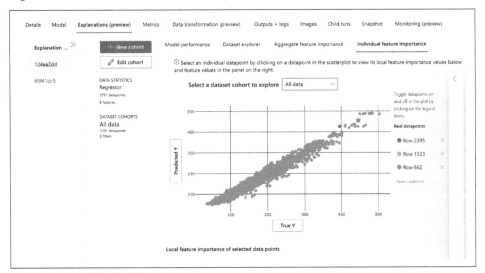

Figure 7-54. Individual feature importance

To provide a little more context, you can also open the menu pane on the right to reveal more details about the data points. For example, data point Row 662 is a flight from Honolulu Airport to Dallas Fort Worth, departing on a Saturday evening and landing in the morning, as you can see in Figure 7-55. The prediction for this point was pretty accurate, with a predicted elapsed time of 454.2 minutes and an actual time of 446 minutes.

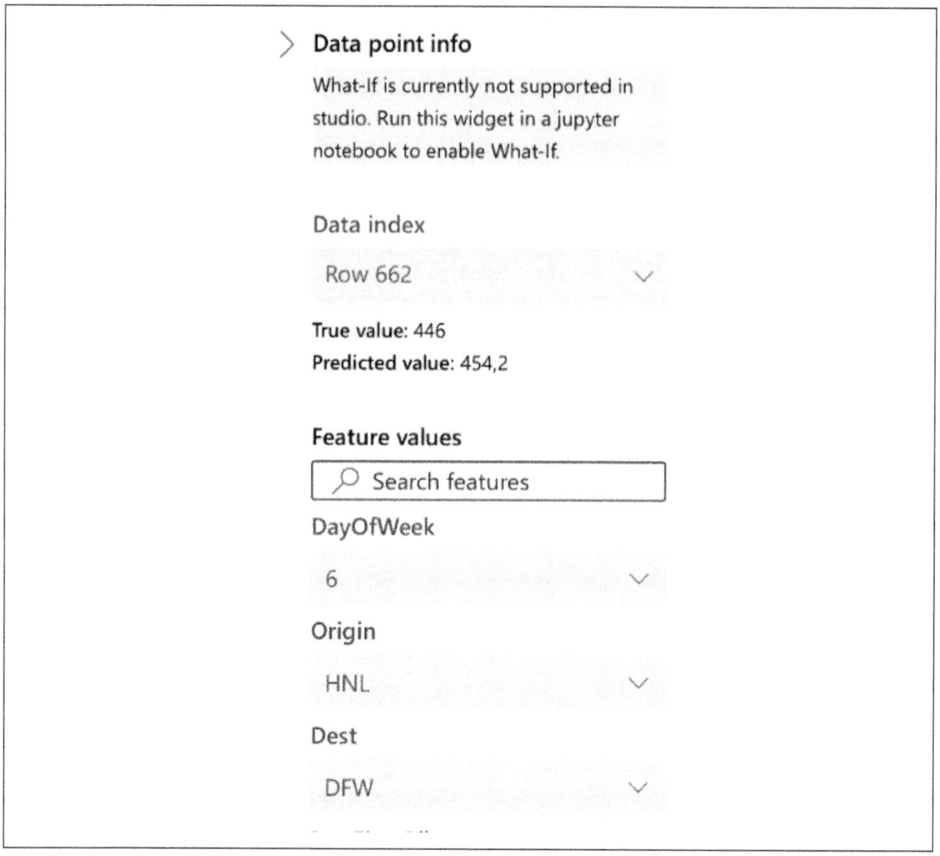

> **Data point info**
>
> What-If is currently not supported in
> studio. Run this widget in a jupyter
> notebook to enable What-If.
>
> Data index
>
> Row 662 ⌄
>
> **True value:** 446
> **Predicted value:** 454,2
>
> **Feature values**
>
> 🔍 Search features
>
> DayOfWeek
>
> 6 ⌄
>
> Origin
>
> HNL ⌄
>
> Dest
>
> DFW ⌄

Figure 7-55. Data point feature importance

Likewise, I chose a point with a prediction value that was much higher than actual
(426 minutes versus 395 minutes for Row 2395) and one point with a prediction
value that fell short (84 versus 140 minutes in the case of Row 1523).

Now, with three points selected, scroll down to see a graphic similar to the one in Figure 7-56.

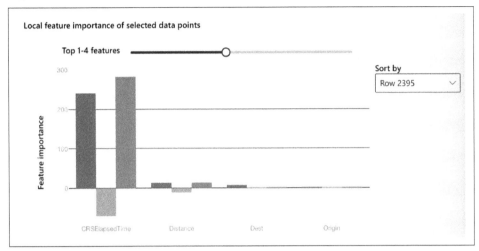

Figure 7-56. Local feature importance of selected data points

This graphic shows what led to the individual prediction for the selected data points. For example, we can see that for Row 1523 (the bar in the middle), at the point where the prediction was too low, the feature CRSElapsedTime was actually weighed down by the model. For some reason, the model decided that in this special case, the original scheduled time should not be considered as much. As it turns out, in this case, this was a bad decision. In contrast, for Row 662 (the bar on the right), where the prediction was almost exactly like the true outcome, the scheduled departure time had a high influence factor. The model did not consider any other factors here as important in potentially causing a delay.

Looking at single predictions and understanding which factors have an influence on them will help you feel more comfortable in applying as well as explaining your ML model, instead of just accepting it as a "closed box." This process is also a good tool for debugging. In this example, we can see that the model is working pretty much as expected.

Let's go deploy this model to production so we can get some inference from it.

Model Deployment with Microsoft Azure Walk-Through

The deployment steps will be identical to the previous use case, so I will keep it short here. Select the model you want to deploy and click "Deploy → Deploy to web service" from the menu bar as shown in Figure 7-57.

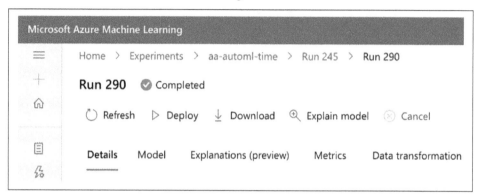

Figure 7-57. Deploying the model from Azure ML Studio

In this pane that pops up, give your model a name, such as **elapsedtime-votingensemble**. Choose Azure Container Instance as the Compute Type. Click Deploy.

The deployment is complete when your model is listed under Endpoints and has the status Healthy (Figure 7-58). Select the model to see the REST endpoint URL, which you will need in the further steps.

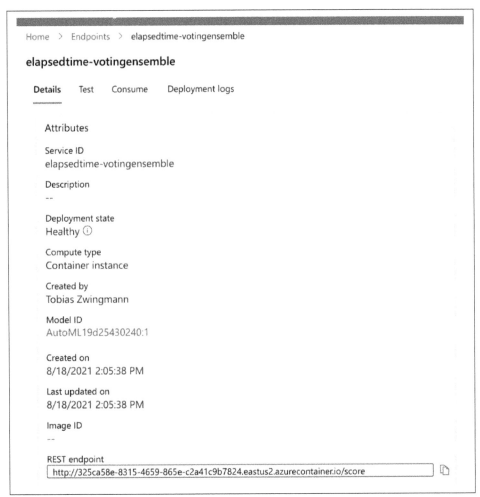

Figure 7-58. Deployed model details

Feel free to test your model online by choosing Test from the navigation menu. You can explore how to make requests against your model programmatically by using the Consume tab. Let's go ahead and get some predictions from our online endpoint.

Getting Model Predictions with Python or R

To send data to our hosted model endpoint and get predictions back, we'll use the same approach as in the previous use case ("Automating Classification Tasks"). This means that you can find two script files named *azure-ml-inference-elapsedtime.R* and *azure-ml-inference-elapsedtime.py* on the book's website (*https://oreil.ly/X9jmJ*).

You can continue in your preferred programming language. I will walk you through the example using R code, but all sections, variable names, and the overall code logic will be the same in the Python file. The script contains six sections that serve different purposes.

Section 0 again contains the setup, where you can review the required packages and update your API parameters. Make sure you replace the API_URL with your custom endpoint from the previous deployment:

```
# SECTION 0: Setup and Variables ----

# Make sure these packages are installed
library("httr")
library("rjson")
library("dplyr")

API_KEY = ""
API_URL = "http://xxxxxxxxxxxxxxxxxxxxxx.eastus2.azurecontainer.io/score"
```

Section 1 again contains the API request function. The main difference compared to the previous example is that we are now passing different columns to the function, because this endpoint expects different data. Also, GlobalParameters must be set to 0.0 as specified by the Azure endpoint example. Otherwise, the function works just the same:

```
# SECTION 1: API Request Function ----

inference_request <- function(DayOfWeek,
                              Origin,
                              Dest,
                              DepTimeBlk,
                              ArrTimeBlk,
                              CRSElapsedTime,
                              Distance,
                              DistanceGroup) {

  # Bind columns to dataframe
  request_df <- data.frame(DayOfWeek,
                           Origin,
                           Dest,
                           DepTimeBlk,
                           ArrTimeBlk,
                           CRSElapsedTime,
```

```
                                    Distance,
                                    DistanceGroup)
    … (Truncated for brevity)
```

Section 2 contains the preprocessing steps with a new detail. While in the previous use case we were looking at only a one-hour batch of data (about 100 rows), in this case we are dealing with an entire month of data—more than 32,000 rows in total for February 2021! While this would likely work given the size of the query, we are pushing the limits of online inference here; the processing time for this request would be nearly a minute.

Also, this data contains a lot of redundant information for the inference API. Keep in mind that we trained on weekdays. Some flights in the schedule occur daily, which means that each day of the week is in the dataset four or more times. It would be inefficient not only computationally but also financially to send a data point with the same information to the API multiple times. Therefore, the code includes a `distinct` statement that deletes redundant rows based on the columns we use for AI predictions:

```
# SECTION 2: Data preprocessing ----
# Fetch data from Power Query workflow
df <- dataset

# Create subset of dataframe that holds distinct flight information for predic-
tion
df_inference <- df %>% select(DayOfWeek,
                              Origin,
                              Dest,
                              DepTimeBlk,
                              ArrTimeBlk,
                              CRSElapsedTime,
                              Distance,
                              DistanceGroup) %>%
    distinct()
```

The `distinct` operation will shrink our dataframe from 32,048 rows to only 13,826 rows that contain unique information for inference. That is a reduction of our data workload by more than 50%!

Section 3 finally makes the actual call to the API by using the reduced dataset:

```
# SECTION 3: Get Predictions ----
result <- inference_request(df_inference$DayOfWeek,
                            df_inference$Origin,
                            df_inference$Dest,
                            df_inference$DepTimeBlk,
                            df_inference$ArrTimeBlk,
                            df_inference$CRSElapsedTime,
                            df_inference$Distance,
                            df_inference$DistanceGroup)
```

Eventually, however, we want to report on all flights, not only the distinct combination that we sent to our model. We are solving that in section 4:

```
# SECTION 4: Data postprocessing ----
result <- unlist(content(result))
df_inference$ELAPSED_TIME_PREDICTED <- result

# Bring results back to original dataframe
df <- df %>%
  left_join(df_inference, by = c("DayOfWeek",
                                 "Origin",
                                 "Dest",
                                 "DepTimeBlk",
                                 "ArrTimeBlk",
                                 "CRSElapsedTime",
                                 "Distance",
                                 "DistanceGroup"))
```

In section 4, we will join the prediction results back to the original dataframe so that we get a prediction for each row in the original dataset. As a result, the dataframe df contains all of the 32,048 original observations with their respective prediction results, but we send only 13,826 rows from that to our model. Isn't that beautiful?

Section 5 cleans up the environment and provides the output for further downstream processing in Power BI (or any other BI tool):

```
# SECTION 5: Format output for Power BI ----
rm(df_inference)
output <- df
```

Now it's time to put our script to work and see our model in action within our BI tool!

Model Inference with Power BI Walk-Through

Open *Elapsed_Time.pbix* in Power BI Desktop. Select the Model icon on the left navigation pane to open the Modeling view. You will see two data sources here (Figure 7-59).

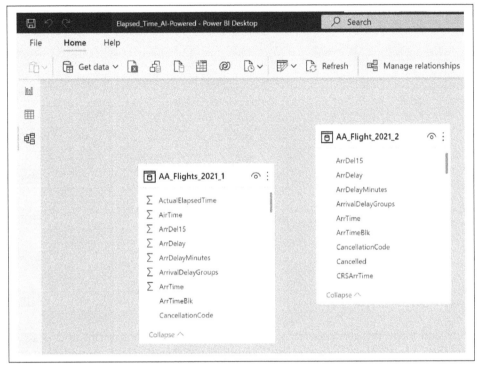

Figure 7-59. Data model in Power BI

The data source *AA_Flights_2021_1* contains all the historical flights from January 2021. This is the data we used to train our model on. We don't need to modify this data. The second source, *AA_Flight_Schedule_2021_2*, contains the flight schedule data we are interested in. For this data model, we want to run predictions for the Elapsed Time attribute.

We will do this by applying the R or Python script we have written before to create a new column in the model. Open the Power Query Editor and make sure you choose the AA_Flight_Schedule_2021_2 table on the left, as shown in Figure 7-60. In the menu pane, select the Transform tab and then choose "Run Python script" or "Run R script," depending on your preference.

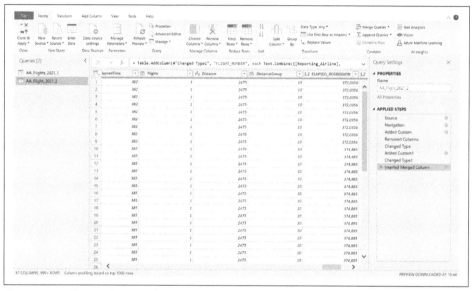

Figure 7-60. Power Query Editor

Copy and paste the contents from the file of the R or Python script and paste it into the code window in Power BI. Double-check that the URL provided in the script is the one of your healthy REST endpoints. Also make sure that you have all the required packages (*httr, rjson*, and *dplyr* for R, or *requests, json*, and *pandas* for Python) installed in the code environment used by Power BI, as explained in Chapter 4.

Click OK, and Power BI will run your script. Select "Ignore Privacy Levels checks for this file" if Power BI gives you a warning message. Depending on your machine, the inference process might take some time. Remember that we are doing calculations here for more than 32,000 rows of data. And while we reduced the data amount sent to the API, that's still over 13,000 rows. If you want to see what your computer is doing, feel free to open the Windows Task Manager, click the Performance tab, and see your computer at work.

After the process has been completed, you should see a prompt for showing you the two result tables from the script, called "df" and "output." Select the "output" table and you should see that one step was added on the right under Applied Steps and that your dataset now contains an additional column called ELAPSED_TIME_PRE-DICTED, as shown in Figure 7-61.

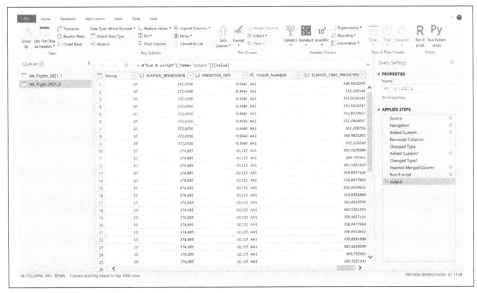

Figure 7-61. ELAPSED_TIME_PREDICTED column in Power BI

Before we close the Power Query Editor, let's quickly create a new column that creates the difference between the AI predictions and the CRS scheduled time, so we can later filter for flights that are likely to be delayed.

To insert a new column in Power Query, choose Add Column → Custom Column and enter the custom column formula shown in Figure 7-62. Confirm with OK.

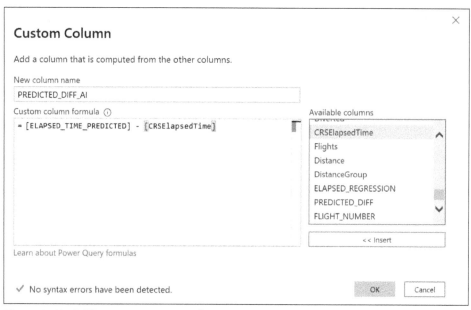

Figure 7-62. Adding a new custom column in Power Query

To double-check that this new column is formatted correctly as a numeric value, right-click the column PREDICTED_DIFF_AI and choose Change Type → Decimal. Now choose File → Close & Apply to exit the Power Query Editor and apply your transformations. Power BI will update the data model accordingly, which again can take a couple of minutes. The waiting time in this case should not bother us too much, since this process will be done only once for each monthly flight schedule.

Building the AI-Powered Dashboard in Power BI

After the data model has been successfully updated, head over to Reports in Power BI. We want to put our new predictions to work. Select the report Future Schedule, where you can see the baseline regression predictions. Time to tune them up.

Select the scatterplot on the left. Replace the value for the y-axis. Instead of ELAPSED_REGRESSION, put the new measure ELAPSED_TIME_PREDICTED here. Update the other two visuals on the page accordingly. In addition, replace the filter on the KPI visual at the top right by deleting PREDICTED_DIFF and adding "PREDICTED_DIFF_AI is greater than 5" to consider your AI predictions instead. Figure 7-63 shows the updated dashboard.

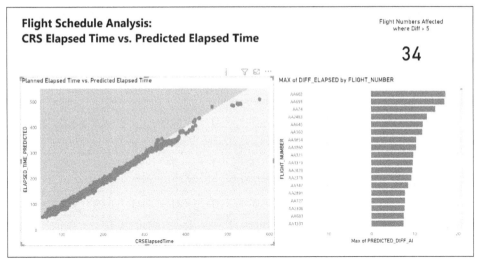

Figure 7-63. Updated dashboard with AI-powered predictions

What have we achieved so far?

First, by applying our AI model, we have reduced the number of flights that are predicted to need at least five minutes longer than scheduled, from 114 to 34 observations.

Second, if we look at the scatterplot on the left, we can see more variation; the points do not form a single straight line as in the simple regression model.

And third, if we look at the bar chart on the right, we can see that we have identified two flights that are predicted to take 15 minutes longer than planned. If we compare that to the previous regression model, where the highest difference was only about 6.5 minutes, this is a significantly bigger amount.

Let's see if we can tweak this report even a little bit more to make it more interactive and actionable. Right-click on the Future Schedule tab and click Duplicate Page to create a copy of the current report. Rename the copy from Duplicate of Future Schedule to **Interactive Schedule**.

In the Interactive Schedule report, select the bar chart on the right and add the field DistanceGroup to the legend, as shown in Figure 7-64.

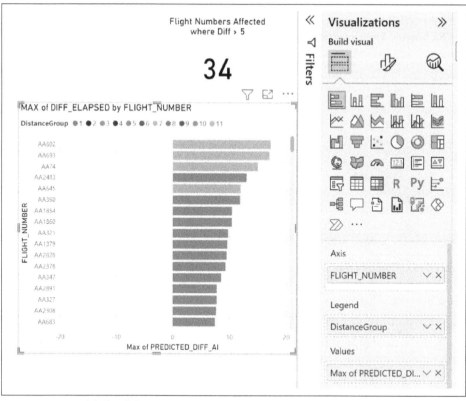

Figure 7-64. Highlighted distance groups in the bar chart

From this additional information, we can see that the flights that have the highest discrepancy between predicted and scheduled elapsed time are long-distance flights (distance group 11). The majority of flights on the chart, however, are short-distance flights.

Also, let's get rid of the scatterplot. It has provided a good overview of how the model is working, but it is not so interactive. Select the scatterplot and replace it with a treemap visual. Adjust the settings for the treemap as follows (see Figure 7-65):

- Add the fields Origin and Dest to Group.
- Put the field PREDICTED_DIFF_AI into Values.
- Aggregate PREDICTED_DIFF_AI by Average.
- Filter this visual to "PREDICTED_DIFF_AI is greater than 0."
- Delete any field from Details.

Figure 7-65. Treemap visual and settings

As a result, you should see an updated visual, as shown in Figure 7-66. Enable the drill-down function at the top.

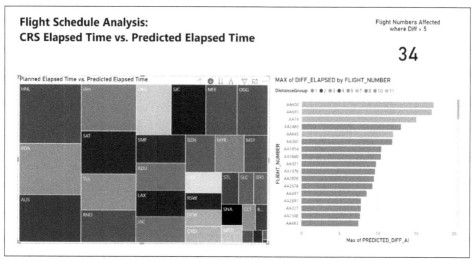

Figure 7-66. Treemap visual with drill-down function

The treemap shows origin airports for which the field size is the average of the difference between the predicted and scheduled elapsed time for flights from this airport. Every time we interact with this tree, the bar chart on the right will change and we can drill down. For example, click the origin airport Honolulu. You will see that the treemap updates, and the bar chart as well, as shown in Figure 7-67.

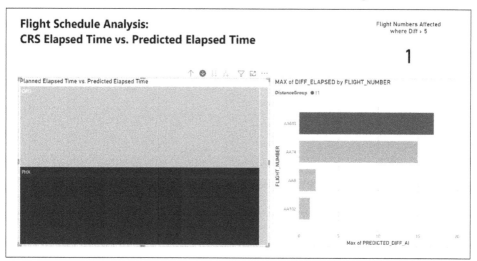

Figure 7-67. Drilling down for Honolulu (Flight AA693 selected)

From this drill-down, we can see that there are four flight numbers, two of which have more than five minutes' predicted delay.

This provides us with a great interactive resource to locate the bottlenecks in our flight planning. We can clearly see that flights scheduled to depart from Honolulu are on a tough schedule and that the connection from Honolulu to Phoenix, Arizona has the highest chance of exceeding the scheduled time, at least according to the best knowledge we have so far.

Similarly, we can search vice versa and select a bar from the bar chart to show us which airports are associated with the probably delayed flight numbers, as shown in Figure 7-68.

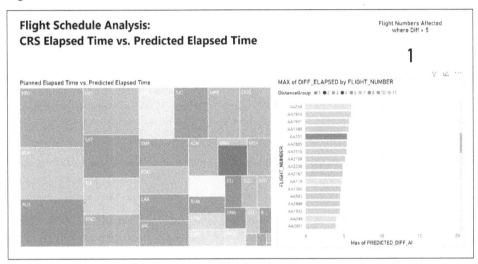

Figure 7-68. Drilling down by flight number (Flight AA301 selected)

While the model is not perfect, we have improved our baseline, and who knows—maybe we can think of even more criteria that can make the model more accurate. At least now we have a good showcase to demonstrate how a better AI model could be beneficial for improving our schedule ahead of time.

You can download the final Power BI file (*Elapsed_Time_AI-Powered.pbix*) from the book's website (*https://oreil.ly/X9jmJ*).

Use Case: Automating Anomaly Detection

In the previous use cases, you learned how to leverage AI to predict categorical and numeric variables and how to use that skill to create business value. In the following use case, we are not so interested in whether a value is categorical or numeric, but we want to know if a certain value is abnormal. To identify whether a value is an anomaly, the algorithm will consider the points to be a series of events in time, also known as a *time series*. Let's head over to the problem statement of our use case.

Problem Statement

We are analysts working with the operations team of American Airlines, and our job is to maintain a service level. This includes observing what is happening at the airports where American Airlines takes off, especially the ones used most frequently. The most important airports that counted more than 1,000 flight departures in January 2021 were Dallas Fort Worth (DFW), Charlotte Douglas Airport (CLT), Phoenix Sky Harbor (PHX), Miami International Airport (MIA), Chicago O'Hare (ORD), Philadelphia International (PHL), and Los Angeles International Airport (LAX). Among other metrics, we have to closely monitor the taxi-out time that is occurring at these airports.

Taxi-out time is defined as the time between the plane leaving the gates and actually taking off. A high taxi-out time is a proxy for busy or overcrowded airports and can lead to unexpected flight delays (as you have seen in the previous use case).

While a natural fluctuation of the taxi-out time is normal and considered by the flight schedule, too many peaks in long taxi-out times can lead to recurring delays. A stable taxi-out time is an important precondition for guaranteeing a smooth departure process at an airport. Also, long taxi-out times increase congestion and excessive emission of greenhouse gases.

Monitoring the taxi-out status and flagging unwanted spikes to airport operators are effective approaches to eliminating delays and improving the utilization of resources. The way this process is currently handled is through a BI dashboard, which shows an overview of the daily average taxi-out time for the high-traffic airports previously mentioned. The dashboard is shown in Figure 7-69.

Our primary goal, as analysts looking at this dashboard, is to identify those peaks that are abnormal for an airport in order to raise these issues for further investigation to the operations team. The main problem is, what is an abnormal point?

The line chart in the graphs shows the average daily taxi-out time for the month of January for the seven airports mentioned. The dashed horizontal line displays the average taxi-out time for each of these airports in January. As we can see from the dashboard, the value of these averages varies depending on the airport. The average taxi-out range is between 15.3 minutes for LAX and almost 20 minutes for DFW. That is why it is hard to judge abnormal taxi-out time generally, but instead they must be considered by the airport.

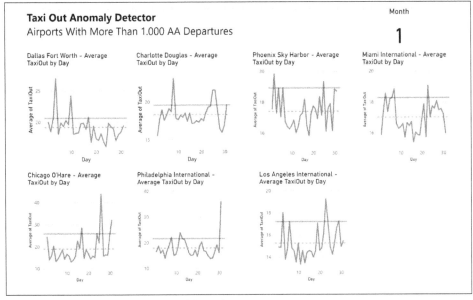

Figure 7-69. Taxi-out baseline dashboard

Flagging all above-average taxi-out times, however, is not practical because the time has too many fluctuations. Instead, the team has decided to set a 90-percentile threshold for each airport, which is indicated by the solid horizontal line in the graphs. This threshold covers 90% of all taxi-out averages for a specific airport. All daily taxi-out averages that exceed this threshold will be flagged and considered anomalies. For example, the average taxi-out values for DFW on January 4 and January 10 have been flagged.

However, this approach does have limits:

- The 90-percentile mark is static and does not consider any trends that are happening in the data.
- It is sensitive to extreme values, meaning one day of high average taxi-out values can raise the bar to unnecessary heights.
- It is tedious and time-consuming to look at these charts manually and flag problematic events on a case-by-case basis.

The team is looking for an overall improved approach of identifying peak values for taxi-out times for these airports.

Solution Overview

Our goal is to make the prediction of abnormal data points more dynamic and more responsive to the overall development of the timeline. Figure 7-70 shows the overall architecture for this use case from a high level.

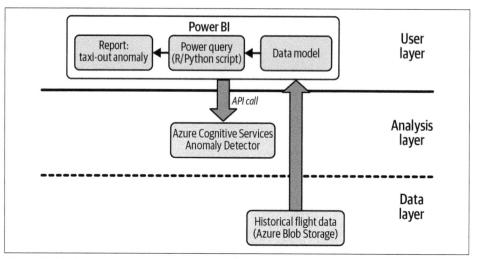

Figure 7-70. Anomaly detection use case architecture

This time, we are not going to train our own AI model. Instead, we will use an off-the-shelf AI service for the first time in this book. This means we will consume an AI model that has been pretrained before on the task that we want to achieve. That's why we don't need any training process here, but we can directly skip to inference.

The approach we take for this is an AI-powered anomaly detection that analyzes a series of events (value) over a certain period of time (timestamp). The anomaly detection will calculate dynamic upper and lower margins for the expected value and flag all values that exceed these boundaries as positive (above upper boundary) or negative (below lower boundary) anomalies.

In this example, we are using the Anomaly Detector by Azure Cognitive Services. To do this, we will enable the endpoint through our Azure portal, learn how to prepare our data, get predictions from this endpoint by using Python or R, and finally apply these predictions in Power BI to build an enhanced version of the taxi-out anomaly detection report.

Note that the anomaly detection service can be used for both batch and real-time prediction. *Real-time prediction* in this case means that we send any points we observe directly to the API and will get the prediction back of whether this point is an anomaly based on the points we sent previously. For our use case, however, we are taking the *batch* approach, meaning we upload all available data at once to the API.

Without further ado, let's head over to the Azure portal.

 Anomaly detection can be considered a tool for both predictive and diagnostic analytics, depending on how and for what purpose it is used. If the focus is more on analyzing historical data, anomaly detection can be considered a tool for diagnostic analytics. However, as soon as we analyze new data points in real time, it has more of the characteristics of a tool for predictive analysis.

Enabling AI Service on Microsoft Azure Walk-Through

Our first task is to enable the Cognitive Services Anomaly Detector API in Azure by creating a resource for it. To do that, you can either visit the Create Anomaly Detector (*https://oreil.ly/D38ul*) page or navigate there manually: visit *portal.azure.com*, search for **Cognitive Services**, and in the Decision section you will find the card "Anomaly detector," where you can click Create (Figure 7-71).

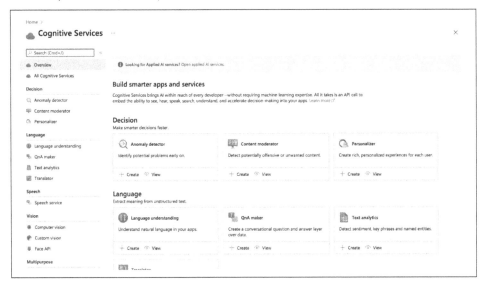

Figure 7-71. Cognitive Services overview

The Create Anomaly Detector form requires you to specify more details. Choose your Azure subscription and select the same resource group you have created for the previous use cases. In addition, you need to specify the geographic region where the service should be running. Choose your preferred region and give your service a descriptive name. Note that this name is globally unique; think of it as a subdomain for the final endpoint.

Finally, you will need to choose the pricing tier. Different pricing tiers affect the performance and pricing model of the AI service. For our purposes, the Free tier should be enough; it allows 10 calls per second and 20,000 transactions per month. See Figure 7-72 for an example of the filled-out form. Proceed by selecting "Review + create." Review your settings on the subsequent page and confirm by clicking Create.

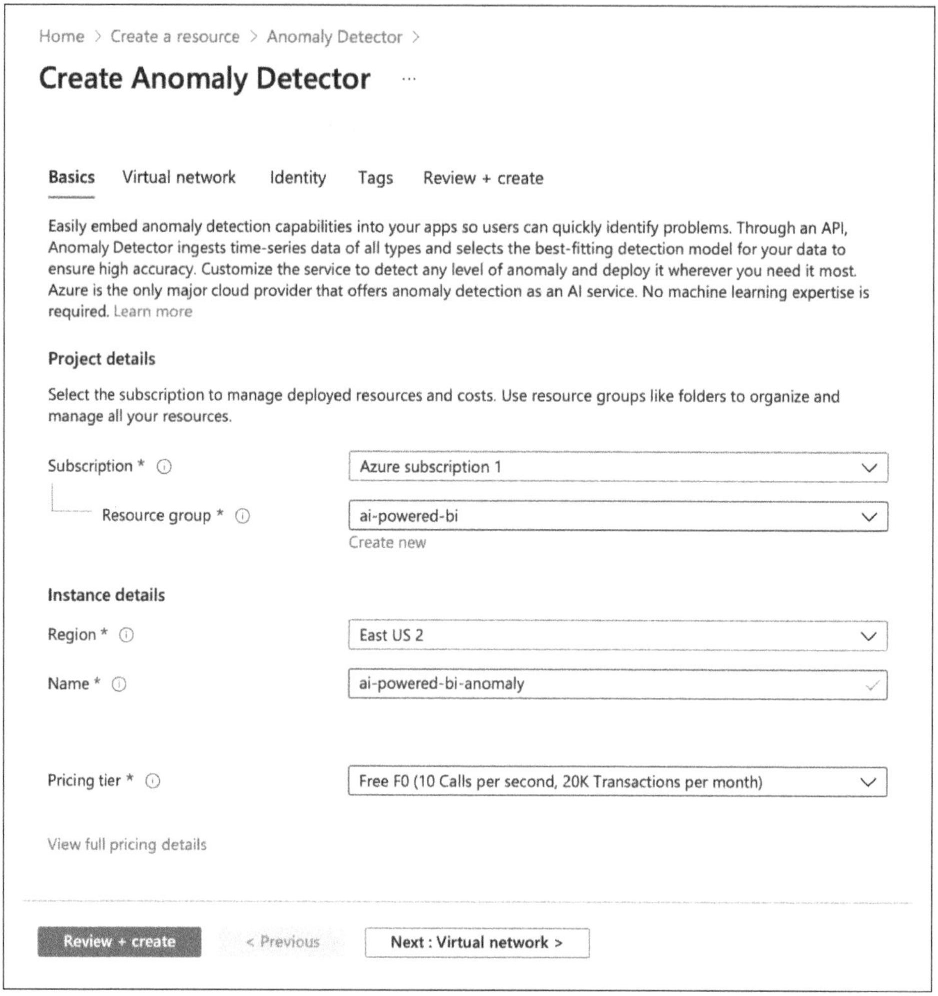

Figure 7-72. Creating the anomaly detector in Azure

The deployment of the service might take a few minutes. After it is completed, you should see a notification in Azure and a success message (Figure 7-73).

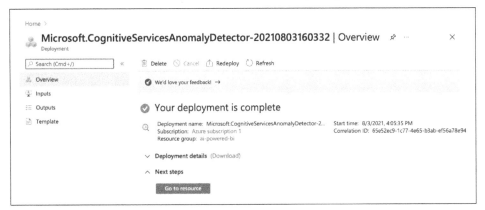

Figure 7-73. Cognitive Services deployment complete

Navigate to the newly created resource by clicking "Go to resource." Alternatively, you could navigate from the Azure portal home page to Cognitive Services, choose "Anomaly detector" from the menu on the left, and click the name of the endpoint from the list, as shown in Figure 7-74.

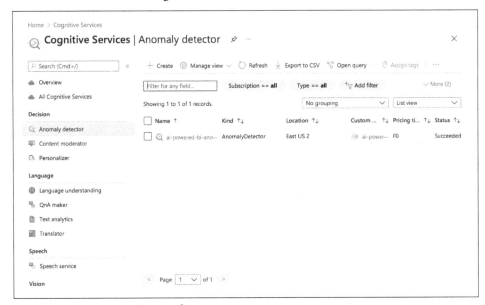

Figure 7-74. Cognitive Services list view

When you have selected the anomaly detector resource, you will be prompted with the quick start guide. This is a good place to come back to if you want to integrate the endpoint into further applications. The most important page we will need is Keys and Endpoint, which you can find in the menu on the left (Figure 7-75).

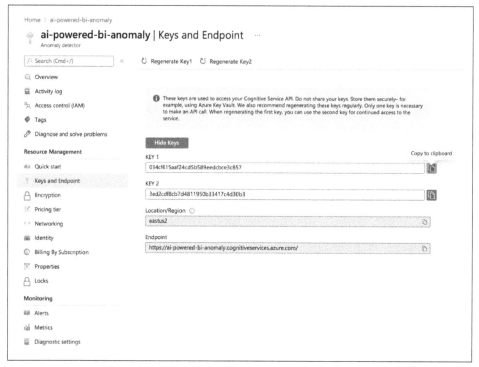

Figure 7-75. Access keys for Cognitive Services

On this page, you will find three essential components. The first two are your secret credentials, which you will need to access the AI service. Think of them as something like a password that authorizes you to make requests against the service. As it goes for passwords, you should not save these keys somewhere in plain text and you should not share them publicly anywhere. If you did, either accidentally or on purpose (like printing them in a book), click the Regenerate Key 1 or Regenerate Key 2 button to generate a new pair of keys. This will void the previous key and create a new one for you.

Why do we need two keys, you might ask? Think about it as having a guest key for your home. You have a second key that you can share and distribute to colleagues for quick prototyping purposes, so there is no harm when the key is regenerated often. The first key should be safely integrated in your running applications, and you don't want to replace this key that much (most likely, never).

And finally, the third component on this page is the API endpoint. Be careful, however: this is not the complete endpoint you can use to make inference requests, as we did in our previous examples. Instead, you need to add the path to the actual service, the service version, and the service settings to it. To find out how to construct the final REST endpoint, you can refer to the API documentation (*https://oreil.ly/ iWMNi*) or the quick start you visited before.

For example, the final REST endpoint for the anomaly batch inference looks like the following (replace *ai-powered-bi-anomaly* with your own service name):

```
https://ai-powered-bi-anomaly.cognitiveservices.azure.com/anomalydetector/v1.0/
timeseries/entire/detect
```

That's it. Now we're all set to start making prediction requests from our newly set-up AI service. Let's find out how to do it in either Python or R, depending on your preference.

Getting Model Predictions with Python or R

On the book's website (*https://oreil.ly/X9jmJ*), you will find the files *azure-anomaly-detection-flights.r* and *azure-anomaly-detection-flights.py*. You can use either to follow along in your preferred code language. I'll demonstrate the example in R, but all code sections, variable names, and intermediate steps will also appear in the equivalent Python version.

The structure of the code is similar to what you have seen previously in the AutoML example. The script has a total of six sections, and each section handles a different part. Let's go through them piece by piece.

Section 0 is again the place where the script loads all required packages such as *httr*, *rjson*, and *dplyr* in the case of R. Furthermore, you need to specify your custom `API_Key` and `API_URL` for the Azure Cognitive Service from the Azure portal, as described previously. Make sure to replace the *xxxxxxxx* values with your custom parameters. Also, double-check that the `REGION` is set accordingly, as shown under the access keys:

```
# SECTION 0: Setup and Variables ----
library("httr")
library("rjson")
library("dplyr")

API_KEY = "xxxxxxxxxxxxxx"
API_URL = "https:// (https://xxxxxxxxxxxxxxxxxx.cognitiveservi
ces.azure.com/)xxxxxxxxxxxxxxxxxx (https://xxxxxxxxxxxxxxxxxx.cognitiveservi
ces.azure.com/).cognitiveservices.azure.com/
anomalydetector/v1.0/timeseries/entire/detect"
REGION = 'eastus2'
… (Truncated for brevity)
```

In section 0, we are also defining the `MIN_FLIGHTS` threshold for the airport selection. Remember that we don't want to check for anomalies for all airports, but just for the busiest ones, defined as airports with a minimum of 1,000 departing flights.

Section 1 contains the `inference_request` function. It is similar to the request function we used before but contains some variations. The biggest change is that the request body has been structured differently to fit the requirements of the Azure Anomaly Detector API. The API expects a JSON object that contains information about the time-series granularity first (in our case, that is daily), and secondly the actual time series with the corresponding timestamps and values. The function takes two vectors (R) or lists (Python) as inputs (timestamps and values). Within the function, these two lists will be brought into a format that can be consumed by the API

```
# SECTION 1: API Request Function ----

# Expects a list of columns and gets predictions for each row
inference_request <- function(timestamp, value, granularity) {

  # Build request dataframe based on timestamp and value
  request_df <- data.frame("timestamp" = timestamp, "value" = value)
  … (Truncated for brevity)
```

Section 2 is handling the data preprocessing steps needed before we actually send data to the API. First, we are reassigning the variable `dataset`, which is the default placeholder for data flowing in from the Power Query workflow. Assigning a different variable name will make it clear to us which variable refers to the original source data (`dataset`) and which one to the preprocessed data (`df`):

```
# SECTION 2: Data preprocessing ----

# Fetch dataset variable from Power BI and convert Timestamp to string
df <- dataset
```

Second, we are applying our threshold value to filter for airports that cater to at least 1,000 American Airlines flights:

```
# Get airports where threshold is met
airports <- df %>%
  group_by(Origin) %>%
  count() %>%
  filter(n >= MIN_FLIGHTS) %>%
  arrange(desc(n))
  … (Truncated for brevity)
```

Section 3 handles the code that applies the function `inference_request` to the daily average taxi-out times for the airports individually. We do that by running a preprocessing script inside a `for` loop that iterates through the list of the airports selected by the threshold criteria. All results will be collected in a dataframe called df_inference_all:

```
# SECTION 3: Get Predictions ----
# Loop through all airports in list and calculate average taxi-out time
for (airport in airports$Origin) {

  # Create aggregated dataframe for average TaxiOut per Airport
  df_inference <- df %>%
    select(FlightDate, Origin, TaxiOut) %>%
    filter(Origin == airport) %>%
    group_by(FlightDate, Origin) %>%
    summarize(AvgTaxiOut = mean(TaxiOut)) %>%
    mutate(Timestamp = paste0(FlightDate, "T00:00:00Z"),
           AvgTaxiOut = round(AvgTaxiOut,2))

  # Submit request to get anomaly predictions
  result <- inference_request(df_inference$Timestamp, df_inference$AvgTaxiOut,
"daily")
  result <- (content(result))

  # Convert result object to dataframe
  results_df <- data.frame(lapply(result, function(x) Reduce(c, x)))

  # Add inference results to inference_df (collects results for all airports)
  df_inference <- bind_cols(df_inference, results_df) %>%
    select(-Timestamp)

  df_inference_all <- bind_rows(df_inference_all, df_inference)

}
```

Finally, in section 4, we join the information back to the original dataframe so we can make use of the new columns in our BI tool, just as we did previously. This process is handled by the following code:

```
# SECTION 4: Data postprocessing ----
# Add inference information to original dataframe
df <- df %>%
  left_join(df_inference_all, by = c("FlightDate", "Origin")) %>%
  mutate(upperMargins = expectedValues + upperMargins,
         lowerMargins = expectedValues - lowerMargins)
```

And last but not least, section 5 returns the output, so Power Query can use our transformed dataset for further processing:

```
# SECTION 5: Format output for Power BI ----
rm(df_inference, df_inference_all, airports, results_df)
output <- as.data.frame(df)
```

Don't worry if the code looks too overwhelming or too complicated at first glance. You can always go back and revisit it step by step if you need to. Otherwise, feel free to copy and paste everything while replacing your custom variables in section 0.

Model Inference with Power BI Walk-Through

Our goal is to utilize the anomaly detector to create a better report and more actionable insights. We want to make the overall report more accurate and interactive, and to free it up from manual efforts.

First, let's plug the AI into our data model. Open *Anomaly_Detection.pbix* in Power BI Desktop and navigate to the data model. Open Power Query Editor, as shown in Figure 7-76.

Figure 7-76. Power Query Editor

Before we can plug in our R or Python script, we need to include a small preprocessing step. Our script expects the flight date in a specific format (YYYY-MM-DD). However, Power BI converted the FlightDate column from String to a proprietary Datetime format, which is difficult for us to process in Python or R. But we don't want to delete this type conversion, because it will allow a better reporting experience. Therefore, we will generate the YYYY-MM-DD string manually and use a simple Power Query formula to store the string in a separate column. From the ribbon menu, choose Add Column → Custom Column. Enter the new column name **Flight DateTxt** (pay attention to the correct spelling and letter case!) and include the custom formula shown in Figure 7-77.

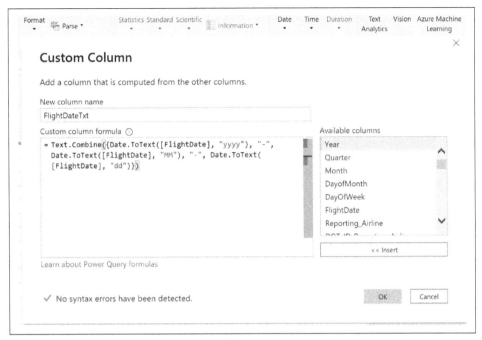

Figure 7-77. Power Query new custom column

As a result, you should see a new column called FlightDateTxt in the preview. Finally, convert the original column to text by right-clicking the column name and choosing FlightDate → Change Type → Text. We are now ready to integrate our R or Python script.

From the ribbon menu, select Transform and then choose either "Run R script" or "Run Python script" as per your preference. I'll continue the example with R, but the same steps apply to Python as well.

When the script editor opens, paste the code from either *azure-anomaly-detection-flights.r* or *azure-anomaly-detection-flights.py* and replace the *xxxxxxxxx* values with your personal API key and URL from the Keys and Endpoint page of your Azure portal (Figure 7-78).

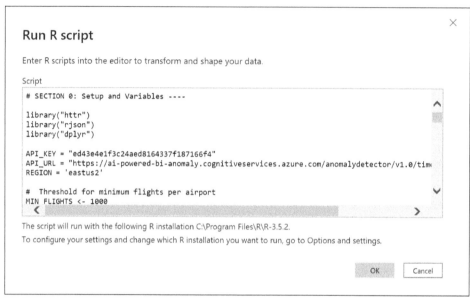

Figure 7-78. Power BI code editor (R example)

Click OK and wait for the script to be executed. Select "Ignore Privacy Levels checks for this file" when prompted. The script could take a few minutes, depending on the performance of your computer. If the script is completed, select the "output" table that appears as a result.

You should eventually see the new columns expectedValues, isAnomaly, isPositiveAnomaly, and upperMargins in your preview table. It is OK if the first rows show null values, since we did not do inference for the whole dataset but for just some airports. If you scroll down, you should see results popping up from line 32 onward.

Before we close Power Query, transform the column FlightDate back to the original format (right-click and choose FlightDate → Change Type → Date). Your final preview and Power Query steps should look like Figure 7-79.

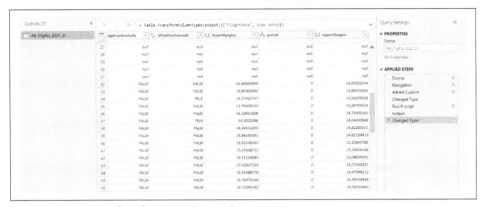

Figure 7-79. Anomaly columns in Power Query

Choose File → Close & Apply to exit the Power Query Editor. Back in the data model menu, you should see the new list of columns in your model.

The heavy lifting is done. Now, we can proceed to the dashboard and make our predictions visible for report users.

Building the AI-Powered Dashboard in Power BI

In the Report section, add another report page by clicking the plus icon next to the first report page. We don't want to update the existing visuals, but come up with an approach that better fits the information we have.

Our goal is to build a line chart showing not only the actual average taxi-out time, but also the predicted upper boundaries for the time series. Also, we want to highlight those data points that exceeded the upper boundaries and therefore mark them as anomalies. And finally, we want to provide the user an interactive way to switch airports easily.

Before we add any visuals, open the Filters pane and add a page filter to this report page, as shown in Figure 7-80. Remember that we want to analyze only a selected group of airports so it is convenient to filter them out for all charts. Add the data field **Origin** to the "Filters on this page" area and select the following airports: CLT, DFW, LAX, MIA, ORD, PHL, and PHX.

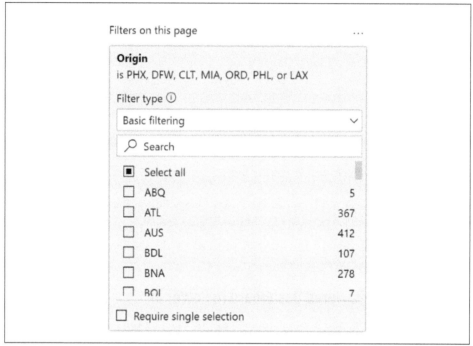

Figure 7-80. Page filter options

Let's continue by adding the line chart visual. Double-click the line chart icon from the Visualizations pane. Drag the line chart so that it covers roughly half of the report page. Add the following fields to the axis and value areas, as shown in Figure 7-81: FlightDate (Axis), TaxiOut, upperMargins (Values).

Figure 7-81. Field settings for line chart

Below FlightDate, delete the Year, Quarter, and Month hierarchy by clicking the small x icon so that only Day is left (Figure 7-82). Also, right-click TaxiOut and upperMargins and choose Average as the aggregation function instead of Sum. The field labels should now read "Average of TaxiOut" and "Average of upperMargins."

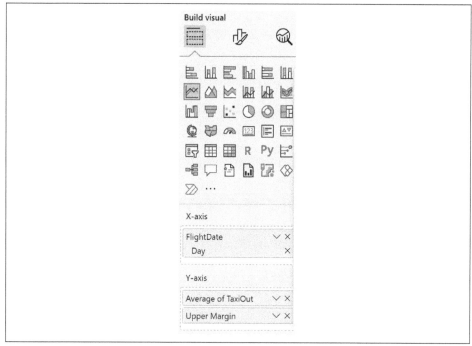

Figure 7-82. Field settings with aggregation method

You should see two lines (Figure 7-83).

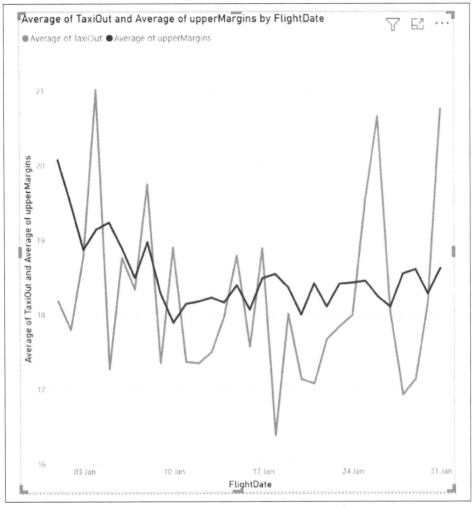

Figure 7-83. Line chart with Average of TaxiOut and Average of upperMargins

The chart shows the average taxi-out and the average upper margins for the airports we specified on the page filter. But we want to analyze the airports individually. Therefore, open the Filters pane once again and set a filter just for this visual, which is "Origin" is "DFW," as shown in Figure 7-84. We will add the interactivity later so that users can choose the airport they want to analyze.

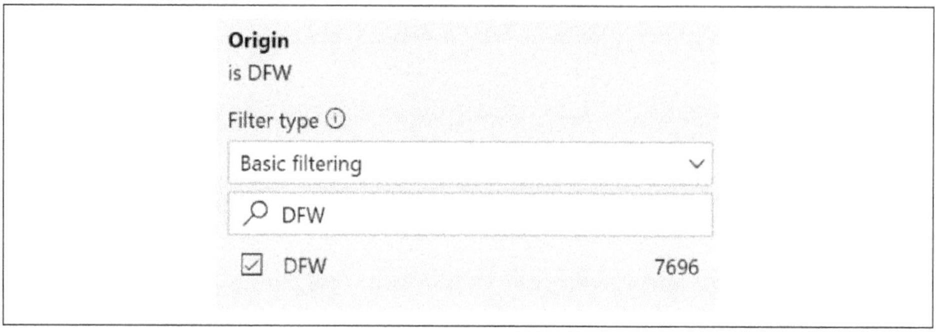

Origin
is DFW

Filter type ⓘ

Basic filtering	⌄
🔍 DFW	
☑ DFW	7696

Figure 7-84. Airport filter on line visual

You've set two filters now: one filter on the page for seven airports, and one filter on the visual for DFW airport. Also, we have two lines already on the chart: one line showing the daily average taxi-out and one line showing the predicted upper boundary. What's missing is the highlight of outliers. We're getting there!

Add the field isPositiveAnomaly to the values as the third line. Right-click and choose New Quick Measure. In the window that pops up, set the settings as shown in Figure 7-85: select the Calculation option to "Filtered value," set "Base value" to Average of TaxiOut, and set Filter to isPositiveAnomaly equals True. Confirm the settings by clicking OK. Delete Count of isPositiveAnomaly from the values area if it still appears here. You should see three values now: Average of TaxiOut, Average of upperMargins, and Average of TaxiOut for True. Right-click Average of TaxiOut for True and choose "Rename for this visual." Rename this field to **Anomaly**. Likewise, change the name of "Average of upperMargins" to **Upper Margin** for this visual.

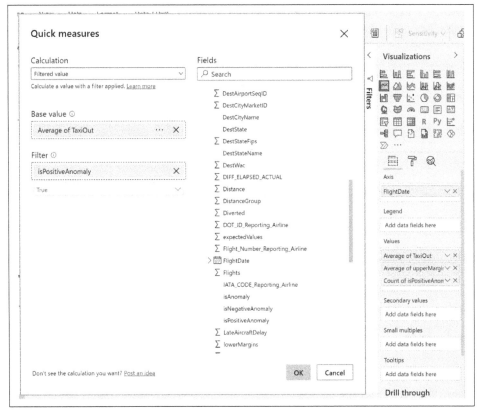

Figure 7-85. Adding a quick measure

With these three values, we have all the information we need on the plot. The rest is "just" formatting. So head over to the Format settings (Figure 7-86).

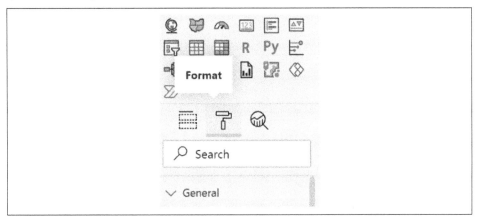

Figure 7-86. Formatting pane

Choose "X axis" and change the type from Continuous to Categorical, as shown in Figure 7-87.

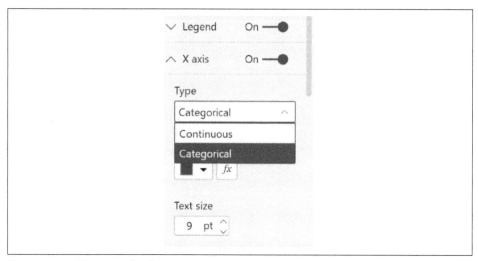

Figure 7-87. Changing the formatting type

Head over to "Data colors" and change the color for both Upper Margin and Anomaly to Red.

Next, select Shape and set the stroke width to 6. From the drop-down menu shown in Figure 7-88, select Upper Margin.

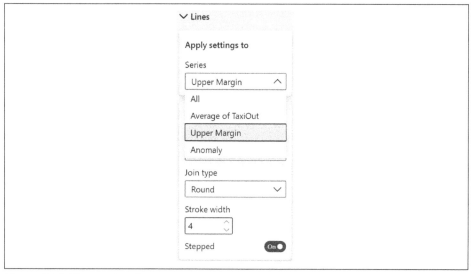

Figure 7-88. Formatting shapes

We want to give this upper band a different style to make clear that this is a boundary, not an actual data value. So set the line style to Dotted and then toggle Stepped to On. Next, select Anomaly from the drop-down menu in Shape and set the stroke width to 0. Then scroll down to Markers and switch them to "on." Select Anomaly from the drop-down menu. Switch the marker shape from circle to square, and increase the marker size to 10, as shown in Figure 7-89. Switch off markers for the other two series.

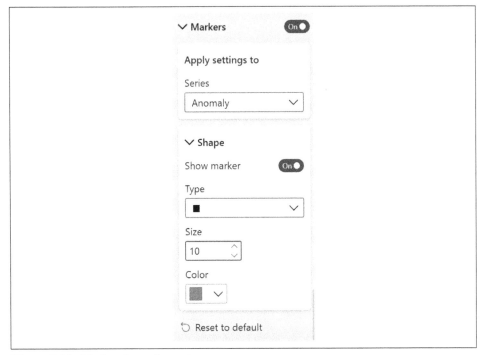

Figure 7-89. Marker shape format

Your line chart should look like Figure 7-90, and we are almost ready! The only thing missing now is for users to be able to choose the airport they want to examine. We will use the cross-filter feature in Power BI to make this process more convenient for the user.

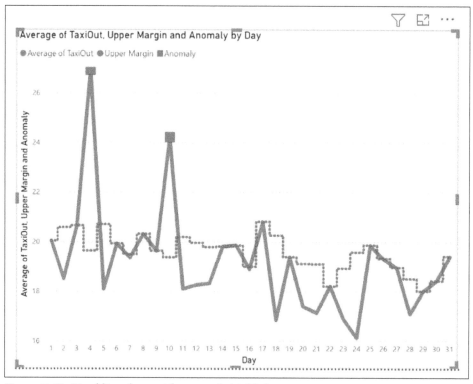

Figure 7-90. Final line chart with anomaly highlights

Add a stacked bar chart from the Visualizations pane to the report page with a double-click. Make sure that your line chart is not selected; otherwise, it will replace this visual. The bar chart should automatically fill the empty space right next to the line chart. Add Origin to the axis and TaxiOut to the values. Right-click TaxiOut and choose Average as the aggregation measure. Under Format, choose "Y axis" and increase the inner padding to 50%.

The cross-filter functionality in Power BI will have the effect that once a user selects a bar from the bar chart, the other visuals on the same page will be filtered accordingly. To allow the dynamic filtering for our line chart, select the line chart, open the Filters pane, and remove the visual filter "Origin is DFW" that we set for the purpose of designing the chart. Leave the page filter untouched.

Now, whenever we select a bar on the right side, the left side will show the daily average taxi-out time with the anomaly values highlighted; see Figure 7-91.

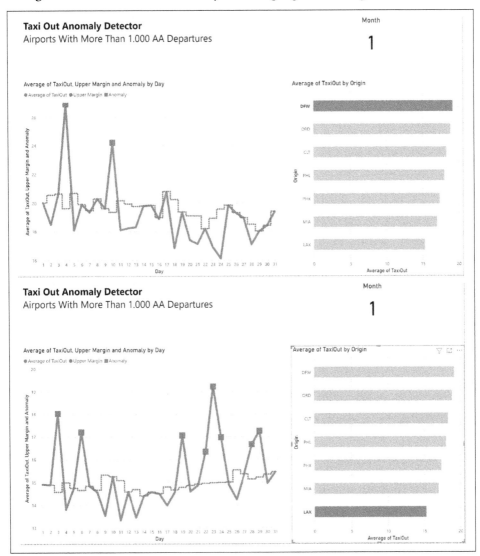

Figure 7-91. Report interactivity

To finish off our report, let's add a headline and the current month to the top by copying those elements from the first report page. Figure 7-92 shows our final dashboard in action. You can find the final state in the *Anomaly-Detection_AI-Powered.pbix* file on the book's website (*https://oreil.ly/X9jmJ*).

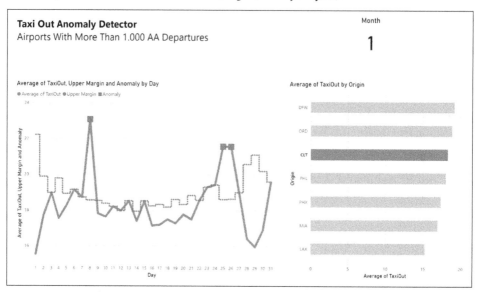

Figure 7-92. Final AI-powered dashboard

Since we now have the attribute isAnomaly in our dataset, we can easily run further analysis or automated reports for this metric. To find out more about how the anomaly detection is working in detail, how to run inference results in real time, and general best practices around this API, I recommend "Best Practices for Using the Anomaly Detector Univariate API" (*https://oreil.ly/9RHAY*) by Microsoft.

With our AI-powered approach, we have helped the operations team identify anomalies quicker and without adhering to a fixed rule set. Thanks to the AI prediction, the data label isAnomaly is now also available in the data model, which allows further analysis or automated reporting of this metric, thus supporting the data teams by removing a lot of manual workload.

Cleaning Up Resources

Consider stopping or deleting the following resources we have used in this chapter to avoid any ongoing charges:

- Stop the compute instance.
- Delete model endpoints for regression and classification.
- Delete the Azure Cognitive Services Anomaly detector resource.

We will still use some of these resources for the other chapters. If you don't plan to do the use cases in the following chapters, you can delete all resources at once. Select "Resource groups" in your Azure portal, select the resource group that you created, and choose "Delete resource group." Confirm the resource group name. Then click Delete.

Summary

Congratulations! Give yourself a pat on the back because what you just did was nothing less than applying state-of-the-art AI tools to real-world data and building actionable BI dashboards for predictive analytics. You have not only learned how to use historical information in a dataset to predict future categorical or numeric variables, but also touched on AI services that provide automated estimations (in this case, for anomaly detection).

It does not matter whether you are a Power BI or Tableau user, or whether you prefer AWS, Azure, or GCP. The fundamental building blocks that you learned and applied in this chapter will help you to get up to speed quickly on any of those platforms. Try out what you've learned on your own dataset to get more hands-on experience. In the next chapter, we will touch on the realms of prescriptive analytics, making intelligent recommendations for decisions on a microlevel.

## CHAPTER 8

AI-Powered Prescriptive Analytics

Now that you have learned how to leverage AI to analyze data from the past and make predictions about the future, it's time to discuss recommended actions! In this chapter, you will learn how to support data-driven decision making by letting an algorithm suggest the best option out of a range of possible actions. Let's go!

Use Case: Next Best Action Recommendation

For this use case, we are building on the suggestions of a predictive model and selecting the best option for a specific customer.

Problem Statement

We are working on the BI team of a large telco provider. The company sells various products, such as monthly or yearly cable and cell phone subscriptions, and has millions of active customers each year. The company is facing an increasing problem of churning customers.

The data scientists on the team have successfully built a customer churn model that predicts the likelihood of single customers to churn by the end of the current quarter. The churn predictions have been calculated as a churn score: 100 means highest churn probability, and 0 means lowest churn probability. While the churn predictor has proven quite accurate and useful in identifying those customers who are likely to cancel their subscription with the company, the business still struggles with the right measures to counter churn. The BI team has incorporated a churn prevention dashboard, shown in Figure 8-1.

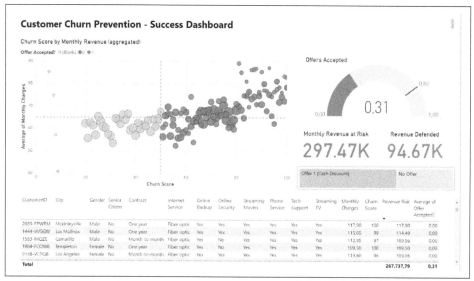

Customer Churn Prevention - Success Dashboard

Churn Score by Monthly Revenue (aggregated)

Offer Accepted? ☐ (Blank) ● 0 ● 1

CustomerID	City	Gender	Senior Citizen	Contract	Internet Service	Online Backup	Online Security	Streaming Movies	Phone Service	Tech Support	Streaming TV	Monthly Charges	Churn Score	Revenue Risk	Average of Offer Accepted?
2889-FPWRM	Mckinleyville	Male	No	One year	Fiber optic	Yes	Yes	Yes	Yes	Yes	Yes	117.80	100	117.80	0.00
1444-VVSQW	Los Molinos	Male	No	One year	Fiber optic	Yes	Yes	Yes	Yes	Yes	Yes	115.65	99	114.49	0.00
1583-IHOZE	Camarillo	Male	No	Month-to-month	Fiber optic	Yes	No	Yes	Yes	Yes	Yes	112.95	97	109.56	0.00
1984-FCOWB	Templeton	Female	No	One year	Fiber optic	Yes	No	Yes	Yes	Yes	Yes	109.50	100	109.50	0.00
9158-VCTQB	Los Angeles	Female	No	Month-to-month	Fiber optic	Yes	Yes	Yes	Yes	Yes	Yes	113.60	96	109.06	0.00
Total														267.737,79	0.31

Offers Accepted: 0.31

Monthly Revenue at Risk: 297.47K   Revenue Defended: 94.67K

Figure 8-1. Baseline churn prevention dashboard

The dashboard shows a scatterplot at the top left, comparing churn score against monthly revenues. In the upper-right quadrant are customers who are on an expensive monthly plan and at the same time have a high churn likelihood, which makes them a particularly relevant target group for churn prevention measures.

Currently, all customers that are labeled as Churn get the same retention offer. On average, this offer is accepted by 31% of the customers, depicted by the respective dots in the scatterplot. These 31% accepted offers translated to a defended revenue of $94,670. Sales staff members have indicated that they could provide other offers but were unsure of which offer to show customers. Simple A/B testing has proven to be ineffective because of the large variety of customer segments and offer types.

The head of the analytics department suggests following a data-driven approach to find out which retention offer should be shown to the various customer segments. Our goal is to come up with an approach that at least beats the existing baseline and supports the ability to experiment with new offer types in real time.

Solution Overview

Figure 8-2 shows our use case architecture for tackling this problem.

As you can see, the heavy lifting will be done in the data layer. That's because we are relying on an out-of-the-box AI service in the analysis layer to predict the best offers for us.

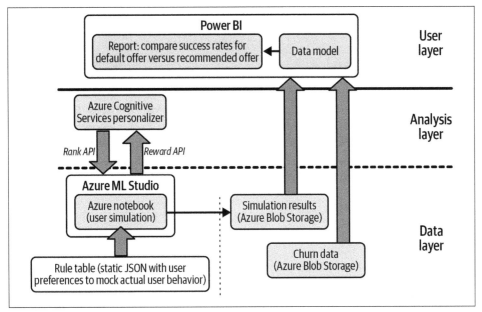

Figure 8-2. Next Best Offer use case architecture

The AI service is using an approach called *reinforcement learning*. By experimenting with different offers for different customer groups, the reinforcement model will finally figure out which offer to show to which customer group. The model will learn based on a reward system. If a customer accepts the offer, the model will get a reward; if not, the model will be penalized. We will use a Microsoft AI service called *Azure Personalizer* to run and maintain the model.

However, in order for this service to work, we need to provide user interaction data. And since we don't want to send out offers to clients in this example, we are going to simulate user behavior based on a rule table that contains the user preferences. In a real-world setting, we naturally don't know these user preferences and have to find them out through experimentation, but for the sake of our simulation, we will keep the ground truth stored in a plain JSON file. Of course, the model will not have access to this file and needs to find the patterns alone.

A small script running inside an Azure notebook will mimic offer proposals to users with the help of the Personalizer service and generate rewards based on the users' (hidden) preferences. The results of our simulation will be logged using a CSV file and stored in Azure Blob Storage so we can access them later through Power BI for further analysis.

Finally, we will use Power BI to monitor our model performance and get an overview of which offers are going to be recommended for which user cohorts. With this approach, we should be able to see how much better our personalized recommendation is compared to the baseline recommendation.

Setting Up the AI Service

Navigate to your Azure dashboard by visiting *portal.azure.com*. Type **Personalizer** in the search bar at the top and choose Personalizers under Services. Click Create, which brings you to the Create Personalizer form (Figure 8-3). Choose the resource group you created in Chapter 4 and give your recommendation service a name such as **offer-engine**. Choose the Free F0 pricing tier. Click "Review + create." After the final validation passes, confirm with Create. The deployment might take a few minutes to complete.

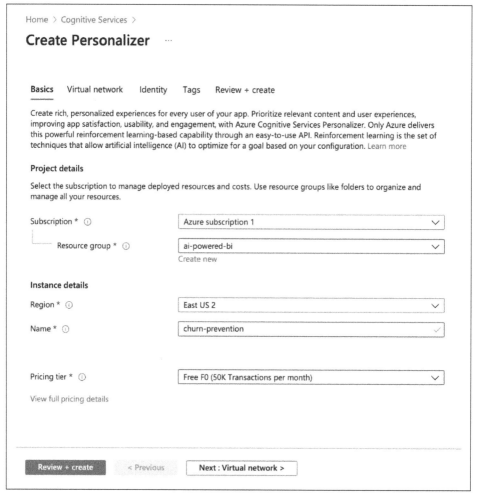

Figure 8-3. Creating a Personalizer form

Once the deployment of your Personalizer service is finished, navigate to the service by clicking "Go to resource." Let's head over there to see what's going on. On the service home page, you should be greeted with a quick start that looks like Figure 8-4.

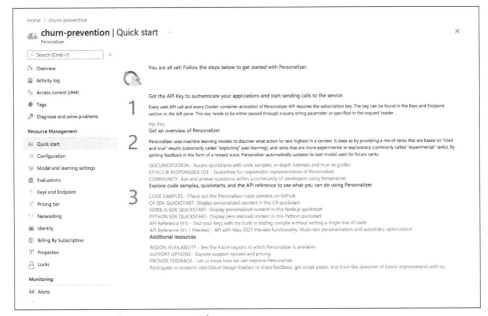

Figure 8-4. Personalizer service quick start

This interface can be a bit overwhelming at first, but we don't need to do very much here. First, click Configuration in the left menu pane to review your model settings. This is the place where you can tweak the learning behavior of your model. Which time to choose here depends on the data you work with. It is usually OK to start with the standard settings and see how quickly the model picks up any patterns. But for our use case, because we are going to simulate user interactions, we want to keep the wait and model update cycles short. Set the "Reward wait time" to 10 minutes and the "Model update frequency" to 1 minute, as shown in Figure 8-5. Also, we can lower the exploration percentage to 15%, because we know that the user preferences are not changing during our experiments.

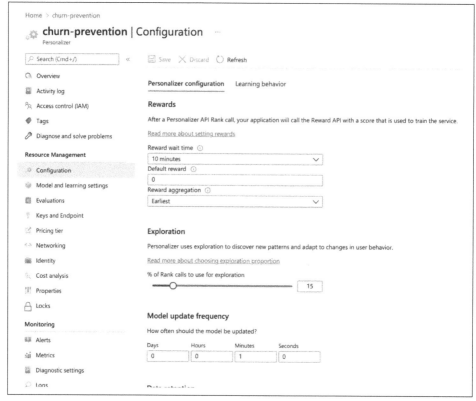

Figure 8-5. Personalizer learning configuration

Don't forget to save your changes by clicking the small disk icon at the top and verify that the settings have been applied by refreshing the page.

Next, check out the "Learning behavior" tab. This is a practical feature for real-world settings. Here you can adjust whether the service should immediately deliver the predicted result or should run in *apprentice mode*, which means serving a baseline prediction and collecting data until this baseline can be topped. You can find more information about the learning behavior of the Personalizer service by looking at the Microsoft document "Configure the Personalizer Learner Behavior" (*https://oreil.ly/ ndze1*). For our setting, we will leave everything as it is and stay with "Return the best action, learn online."

To access the model and send requests to it, we need both the unique model URL and the corresponding access keys. You can find both by clicking the "Keys and Endpoint" menu in the navigation pane on the left to access the screen shown in Figure 8-6.

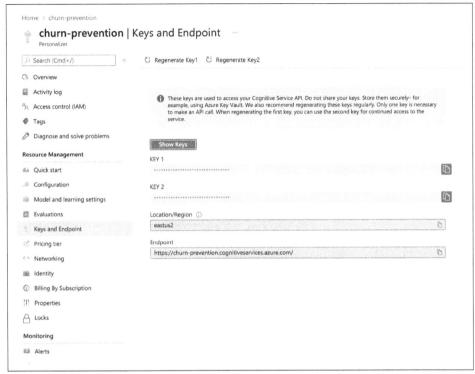

Figure 8-6. Access keys and URL to Personalizer service

This screen is showing you two essential pieces of information. First, it gives you two access keys that you need to authenticate against the API so you are allowed to make rank and reward requests. And second, you will find the URL that you will need to access the model. Leave this page open for later, because we will need this information when we interact with the model.

How Reinforcement Learning Works with the Personalizer Service

Now that we have set up our model and have the credentials to use it, it is a good time to review how the process of learning actually happens and how the model works. Figure 8-7 shows this conceptually.

A typical request to the model incorporates both a rank and a reward call. Together, this is referred to as a *learning loop*: the rank function suggests something to the user and decides whether the model should *exploit* (show the best action based on past data) or *explore* (select a different action to see if the overall recommendation result can be still improved).

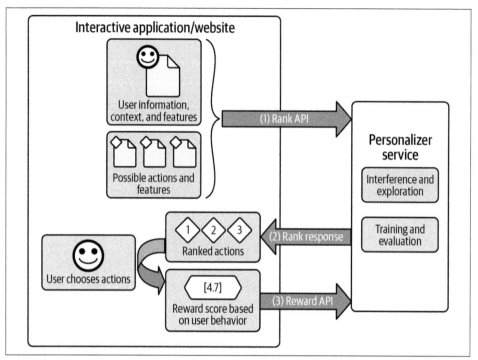

Figure 8-7. Conceptual flow of Personalizer service interacting with an application

After the service has suggested an action to the user, the model expects a reward. This can be anything from a simple flag such as 0 for "not successful" or 1 for "successful" (in our case, indicating whether an offer was accepted), or it can be a continuous value that can represent anything from the scroll depth of news articles to profit won from a stock trade. Reinforcement learning is a pretty universal concept that can be applied in any scenario where the system follows a defined set of rules.

In the case of Azure Personalizer, the service works as follows, as you can see in Figure 8-7:

1. Information about the user (context features) and about the available actions to choose from is sent to the Personalizer service over the Rank API.

2. The service will do its magic and send a rank response back. The rank response returns a ranked list of actions by their highest chance of receiving a reward (if running in exploit mode).

3. Depending on which action the user takes, a result score is calculated by the application and sent back to the service using the Reward API. The model will take this feedback and update itself according to the learning policies that were defined up front.

Equipped with this new knowledge about reinforcement learning, let's move on to get some hands-on experience about how a learning loop looks in practice and how we can utilize this in our BI.

Setting Up Azure Notebooks

To simulate user interactions with our offers, we need to run some code outside of Power BI. To run the code, we will use Azure Notebooks. This service offers a quick way to execute Python or R code without having to install any software on your machine.

To set up Azure Notebooks, navigate to *ml.azure.com*, choose your preferred workspace, and navigate to Notebooks, as shown in Figure 8-8.

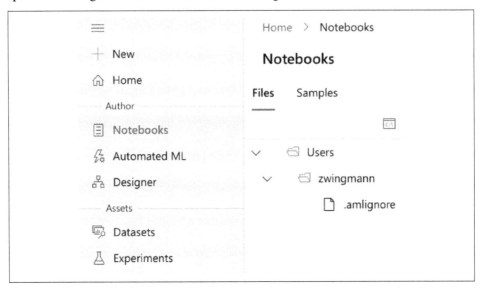

Figure 8-8. Azure Notebooks

Choose Upload → Upload files, as shown in Figure 8-9. Select the following files:

- *user-simulations.ipynb*
- *customer-information.csv*
- *preferences.json*
- *offers.json*

You can find all the files on the book's website (*https://oreil.ly/aLTWS*). Check the "I trust the contents of this file" option and click Upload.

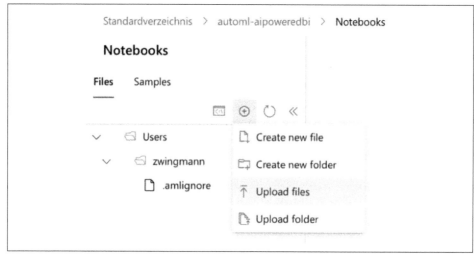

Figure 8-9. Creating a new Azure notebook

Click the *user-simulations.ipynb* file. You should see the notebook on the right side of the screen and all files on the left, as shown in Figure 8-10.

Figure 8-10. Azure Notebooks interface

Before we can run our code, we need to provision a compute resource where the code is actually being executed. If you have not created a compute resource yet, refer to "Create an Azure Compute Resource" on page 83. If the resource is stopped, start the resource for this exercise. Otherwise, select the compute resource from the drop-down menu and click "Start compute," as highlighted in Figure 8-10.

Once the compute resource has started and connected to this notebook for the first time, you should see a notification prompting you to authenticate your Azure compute resource. Click the authentication button, and as a result, you should see a green badge (Figure 8-11). This authentication process makes it much easier to access Azure resources from within Azure Notebooks.

Figure 8-11. Authentication in Azure Notebooks

From the top right, you can now choose which programming language you would like to use. To follow along with the code example, choose "Python 3.6 - Azure ML" (or newer), as shown in Figure 8-12.

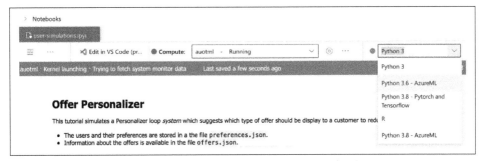

Figure 8-12. Switching programming languages in Azure Notebooks

 We will use some Azure packages needed in this code for authentication and blob storage that are currently not supported in R. While it is still possible to execute this workflow in R, it would be very heavy. So in this case, I provide only the Python version. All R users, please follow along here.

Simulating User Interactions

Let's finally simulate some user interactions with offers. For this, we will make two assumptions. First, we define a finite set of offer possibilities with a rather simple complexity. And second, we assume that we know which user segment accepts which offer. With this information, we can let our model start to randomly suggest offers to various customer segments, and it should pick up the underlying patterns through exploration.

We also keep the complexity of the user segments relatively low because we don't want to exceed the 50,000 API calls of our free tier. Remember, we need one call each for each rank and reward function, and a typical reinforcement model needs a couple thousand iterations to start learning meaningful patterns. Therefore, we'll keep the complexity low at the beginning so we can get good learning results with fewer learning loops (and you stay within the free credits). However, we will adhere to one principle: the model does not know which customer segment prefers which offer type, and it has to find this out on its own.

Don't be limited by this example. You can freely add more context features about customer segments or action features or new offers if you'd like to shoot for higher goals.

For our simulation, we need four components:

- Information about the available offer types and offer attributes
- Information about customers (context features)
- Information about customers' true preferences (ground truth) to calculate the reward offline
- A place where we can store the interaction data so we can analyze it later through Power BI

The first component is contained in the *offers.json* file, which lists the available offers and the corresponding features. Three offers are available to prevent churn: Free Month, Free Upgrade, and Cash Discount. To be fair, we assume that all of these offers have the same value, so there isn't any offer that is a bigger bargain than the others. It's purely a question of preference.

The second part is the information about customers (context features). This information is contained in the *customer-information.csv* file. As mentioned before, we keep the complexity low by considering only the variables "Senior citizen" and "Contract," but of course the Personalizer service can handle a lot more features. In fact, the more features we provide about the offer context, the better—given we have enough time and credits to learn.

The third component is in *preferences.json*. It includes the information about which customer segment prefers which offer type. Table 8-1 shows this information in tabular form. These are the patterns that are unknown to our model, and that we want the model to pick up automatically.

Table 8-1. Rule table with customer preferences

Senior citizen	Contract	Preferred offer
Yes	Month to month	Cash Discount (offer 1)
Yes	One year	Free Month (offer 2)
Yes	Two years	Free Month (offer 2)
No	Month to month	Performance (offer 3)
No	One year	Performance (offer 2)
No	Two years	Cash Discount (offer 1)

And finally, we will need a place to store the results of our simulation. To keep this example simple (and maintain accessibility via Power BI), we will save the results as a plain CSV file. To provide a bit more real-world experience, we will write the outputs to Azure Blob Storage (created in Chapter 4) and load it from there into Power BI.

Running the Simulation with Python

In Azure Notebooks, take a look at the code in front of you. My goal is for you to understand what this code is doing, even if you are not familiar with Python, so let's walk through it.

The code consists of five sections. The first is called User Inputs, and you'll need to customize some options:

OFFERS_FILE_PATH
> The filepath where the *offers.json* file is located.

PREFERENCES_FILE_PATH
> The filepath where the *preferences.json* file is located.

USER_TABLE_FILE_PATH
> The filepath where the *user-information.csv* file is located.

PERSONALIZATION_BASE_URL
> The endpoint shown on the Keys and Endpoint screen in the Azure portal.

KEY
> One of the access keys from the same page in the Azure portal (it does not matter which key). Make sure you replace this key if you decide to regenerate it.

AZURE_CONNECTION_STRING
> The Azure connection string to authorize for the blob storage, which will be ignored if empty.

```
AZURE_CONTAINER_NAME
```
The name of the Azure blob container, which will be ignored if empty.

If you uploaded the files to Azure Notebooks as shown previously, you can leave the filepaths as they are.

Replace the *xxxxxxxx* values in this section with your custom variables for the Personalizer URL, the Personalizer key, and the Azure connection string from your Azure Blob Storage account. Also, double-check that you created a storage container called *simulation*, as explained in Chapter 4.

That's all you have to customize for this script. The rest is just reading and understanding before we run the whole script at once.

The second code section, called Dependencies, loads all required packages for this script. All these packages should be preinstalled with the "Python 3.6 - Azure ML" kernel we just selected.

The third section, called Functions, contains four main functions:

```
add_event_id
```
This function generates a unique ID for each rank call. The ID is used to identify the rank and reward call information. This value could come from a business process such as a web view ID or transaction ID.

```
add_action_features
```
This function adds the entire list of offers to the JSON object to send to the rank request.

```
get_reward_from_preferences
```
This function is called after the Rank API is called, for each iteration. It compares the user's preference for an offer, based on their seniority and contract type, with the Personalizer's suggestion for the user for those filters. If the recommendation is correct, a reward of 1 is returned; otherwise, the reward is 0.

```
loop_through_user_table
```
This function contains the main work of the script. It will iterate through each line of the provided user table, request a personalized offer from the API, compare to the actual user preferences, and calculate a reward score that is then sent back to the Personalizer service. All results will be collected in a list called `results`, and this will be returned by the function upon completion.

The fourth section, called Execution, will invoke these functions and run the actual workflow.

The fifth section, Export, will persist the results by saving locally to a flat file called *results.csv*. If Azure storage credentials were provided, the results file will also be uploaded to Azure Blob Storage.

Verify again that you have customized all the inputs in the first code section. Now, run the code by selecting "Restart kernel and run all cells," as shown in Figure 8-13.

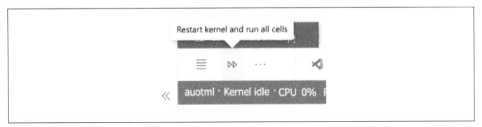

Figure 8-13. Running the entire Azure notebook

An iteration over the whole customer table should take roughly 10 minutes. When the process is completed, you should see the new file *results.csv* being created on the file tree on the left. This is basically the artifact of our experiment (and would be the log files of a real-world scenario). If you specified an Azure connection string and a valid container name in the inputs, this file will automatically be uploaded to your Azure container. If something fails with the upload, make sure that you don't run the whole script again, but only the last code cell of the script that handles the file upload.

Evaluate Model Performance in Azure Portal

To quickly get a glimpse of how the model is working, we can check the model performance in the Azure portal. Navigate to your Personalizer resource and select Evaluations from the menu on the left side. Scroll down and you should see the average reward score, as shown in Figure 8-14.

In this example, you can interpret this number as a percentage of how often the model chose the correct offer for a customer. At this time, the reward score should still be relatively low.

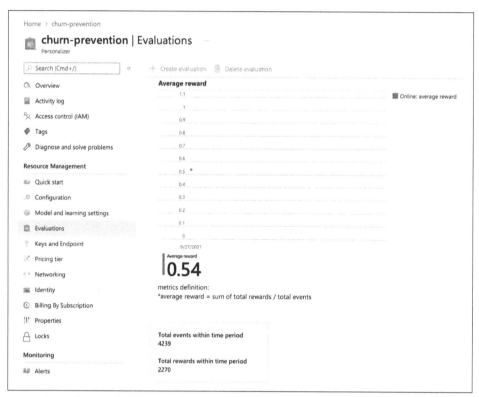

Figure 8-14. Personalizer evaluation

Remember that we started with a naive model making random guesses and figuring out potential patterns only after a couple thousand experiments. Personalization services typically require tens of thousands of examples to really perform well in real-world scenarios. If you run the preceding simulation code two or three more times, you should consequently see this number increasing. If this is not the case, it's a clear sign that something is going wrong with the learning behavior of the model. You can check the Microsoft FAQ (*https://oreil.ly/dojWy*) to troubleshoot errors in model learning.

We can still do one thing to improve the performance without having to run through the whole dataset again: *offline evaluation*. This technique allows you to use existing data and retrain your model with various learning policies to find out which one works best for your data. Let's try this out to see if we can get an even better model than the one we trained so far. From the top menu, choose "Offline evaluations," as shown in Figure 8-15.

Figure 8-15. Creating an offline evaluation

Double-check that the date range matches the day that you ran the simulation experiment and leave all other settings as they are. Click OK to start the offline evaluation, as shown in Figure 8-16.

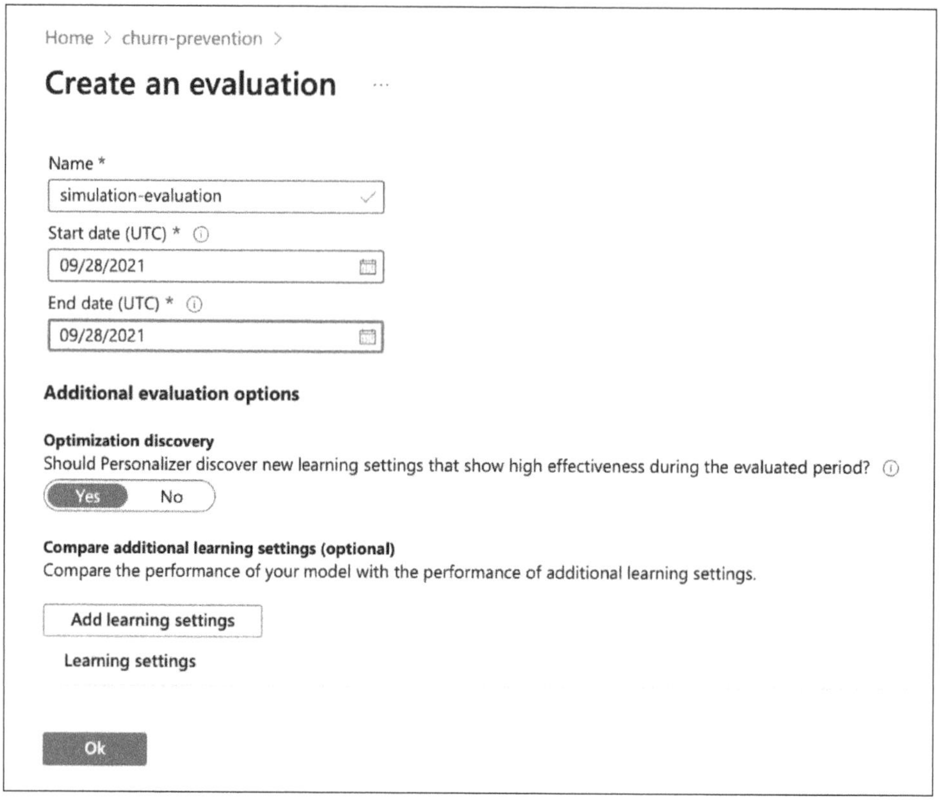

Figure 8-16. Offline evaluation form

The evaluation process takes a couple of minutes. Once it is completed, select the evaluation from the list to see further details. Click the link "Compare the score of your application with other potential learning settings" to see the evaluation metrics, shown in Figure 8-17.

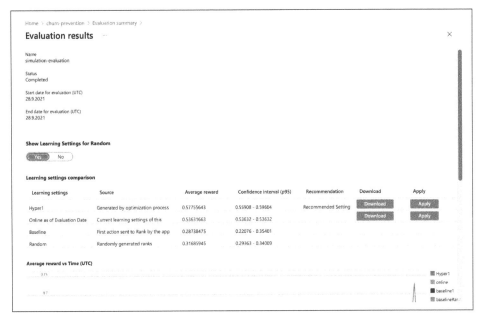

Evaluation results ···

Name
simulation-evaluation

Status
Completed

Start date for evaluation (UTC)
28.9.2021

End date for evaluation (UTC)
28.9.2021

Show Learning Settings for Random

Yes   No

Learning settings comparison

Learning settings	Source	Average reward	Confidence interval (p95)	Recommendation	Download	Apply
Hyper1	Generated by optimization process	0.57755643	0.55908 - 0.59604	Recommended Setting	Download	Apply
Online as of Evaluation Date	Current learning settings of this	0.53631663	0.53632 - 0.53632		Download	Apply
Baseline	First action sent to Rank by the app	0.28738475	0.22076 - 0.35401			
Random	Randomly generated ranks	0.31685945	0.29363 - 0.34009			

Average reward vs Time (UTC)

0.75

0.7

■ Hyper1
■ online
■ baseline1
■ baselineRan

Figure 8-17. Offline evaluation results

As you can see, from the offline evaluation we learned that we can improve our model from a 0.5363 average reward (Online as of Evaluation) to a 0.5775 average reward if we apply the learning setting Hyper1. This is closer to the ideal scenario of 0.85, considering that we leave 15% out for exploration. Choose a new learning setting by clicking the Apply button next to it. This will retrain your model and deploy it with the new learning setting.

You could now go back to your code and run the simulation again to see how the model improves. But first we want to incorporate our AI recommendations into our BI dashboard. Let's explore this in the last step of this use case.

Model Inference with Power BI Walk-Through

As you might remember, our use case scenario already provides a BI dashboard that shows the current customer churn prediction as well as the overall acceptance rate of the standard offer, indicating the success of our customer retention strategy. What we want to do now is blend this information with insights on how our Personalization service is performing and see if our initiative leads to more customers accepting offers.

To start, open the Power BI workbook *Offer_Recommendation.pbix* from the book's website (*https://oreil.ly/aLTWS*) and head over to the data model. You should see the existing table structure here for the churn predictions. Let's add the results from our model by importing the result CSV file that we created during the simulation. If you decided earlier to save the CSV file locally, choose Get data → Import Text/CSV and find the CSV file on your local computer.

If you decide to save the file in Azure Blob Storage, choose Get data → Azure → Azure Blob Storage. Provide the name of your storage account that you provided earlier. In the next step, paste your access key that you got from the Azure portal. After you confirm these options, you should see a list with all containers and files on your blob storage, as shown in Figure 8-18.

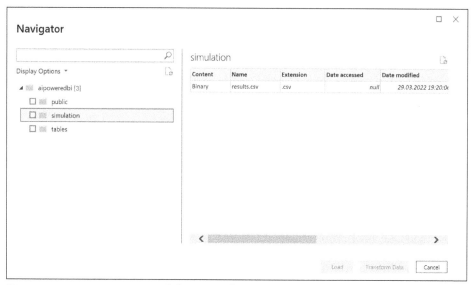

Figure 8-18. Accessing Azure Blob Storage from Power BI

Choose the container with your simulation data. But don't load the file yet! Instead, click the Transform Data button. This will allow you to use Power Query to extract the actual contents of the CSV file. Otherwise, you would see only the CSV metadata such as its filename, creation date, and size.

In the Power Query Editor, click the Binary data link, as shown in Figure 8-19.

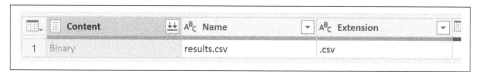

Figure 8-19. Accessing blob files with Power Query Editor

This will bring you to the contents of the CSV file; the conversion from binary to tabular data is shown as a processing step in the Applied Steps pane on the right (Figure 8-20).

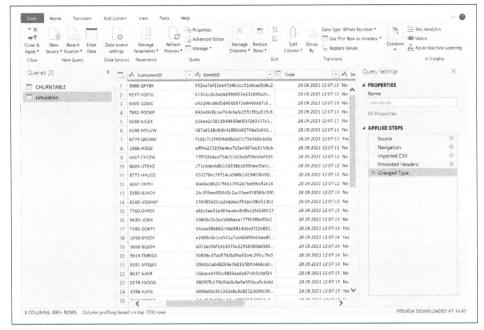

Figure 8-20. Importing table data from blob storage

Confirm the transformation by selecting Close & Apply from the top menu. The contents of the new CSV file will be added to your data model. Power BI will automatically generate the relationship between the Churntable and the simulation data models based the field CustomerID, as shown in Figure 8-21.

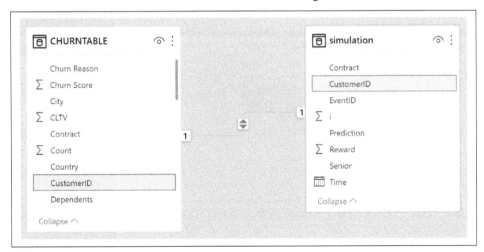

Figure 8-21. Data relationship in Power BI

Building the AI-Powered Dashboard in Power BI

Head over to the BI report page and let's do some modifications to include our new AI-based recommendations. Make the following changes to the report:

1. Update the scatterplot visual:

   - Legend field: replace "Offer accepted?" with "Reward" from the simulation data model.

   - Change the color scheme under formatting and data colors: set Blank to gray, 0 to red, and 1 to blue.

2. Update the gauge visual:

   - Replace "Average Offer accepted" with "Reward" from the "simulation" table. Apply the calculation "Average" to "Reward."

3. Update the metric visual for the defended revenue:

   - Add Reward = 1 to the visual filter.

   - Delete "Offer Accepted" from the visual filter.

4. Update the treemap visual:

   - Replace "Displayed offer" with "Prediction" in the group field. Adjust data colors in the formatting pane so that Blank matches gray, and all offers match shades of blue.

The final dashboard should now look similar to Figure 8-22.

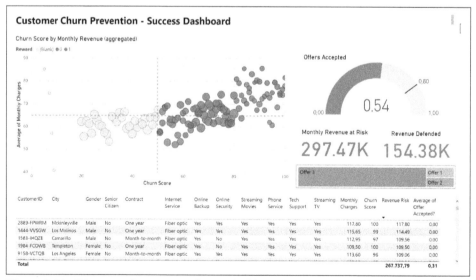

Figure 8-22. AI-powered recommendation dashboard

Let's briefly compare this dashboard to the original one from the beginning of this chapter (Figure 8-1). You will notice two major changes.

First, the gauge has increased from 0.31 to 0.54, an increase of 23 percentage points in accuracy compared to our existing baseline. This means that by using the AI-based approach, we could convince more customers to accept our retention offers. The defended monthly revenue consequently increased as well, to 154.38K, which is a plus of almost $60,000.

Second, we can see that the proportions of offers increased. The former most popular Offer 1 (Cash offer) is now only rarely happening. Most customers accepted Offer 3—the higher performance.

Can we improve these KPIs even more? Remember that we tweaked our model through an offline evaluation previously. But we haven't applied the new model yet.

Go back to the simulation code and rerun it once again without making any changes. After another 10 minutes, the code will have gone through the dataset once so the Personalizer service could use the updated learning settings. The *results.csv* file in your Azure Blob Storage should have been automatically updated. Therefore, all we need to do in Power BI is go to the data model and hit "Refresh data" for the "simulation" table, as shown in Figure 8-23.

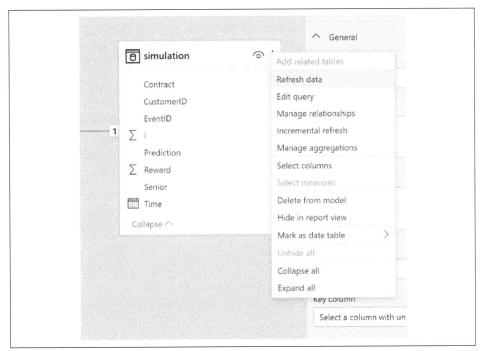

Figure 8-23. Refreshing the data

After a few seconds, Power BI has fetched the updated data. If we go back to the report, we can see the updated recommendations in action (Figure 8-24).

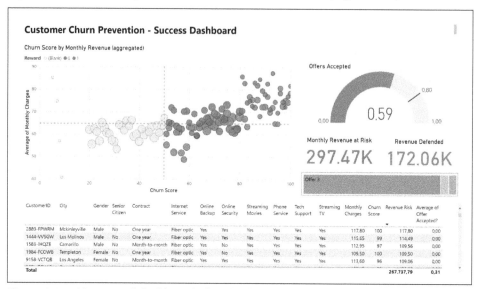

Customer Churn Prevention - Success Dashboard

Churn Score by Monthly Revenue (aggregated)

Reward ☐ (Blank) ●0 ●1

Offers Accepted

0.59 (0.00 — 0.80 — 1.00)

Monthly Revenue at Risk **297.47K**   Revenue Defended **172.06K**

Offer 3

CustomerID	City	Gender	Senior Citizen	Contract	Internet Service	Online Backup	Online Security	Streaming Movies	Phone Service	Tech Support	Streaming TV	Monthly Charges	Churn Score	Revenue Risk	Average of Offer Accepted?
2889-FPWRM	Mckinleyville	Male	No	One year	Fiber optic	Yes	Yes	Yes	Yes	Yes	Yes	117.80	100	117.80	0.00
1444-VVSGW	Los Molinos	Male	No	One year	Fiber optic	Yes	Yes	Yes	Yes	Yes	Yes	115.65	99	114.49	0.00
1583-IHQZE	Camarillo	Male	No	Month-to-month	Fiber optic	Yes	No	Yes	Yes	Yes	Yes	112.95	97	109.56	0.00
1984-FCOWB	Templeton	Female	No	One year	Fiber optic	Yes	No	Yes	Yes	Yes	Yes	109.50	100	109.50	0.00
9158-VCTQB	Los Angeles	Female	No	Month-to-month	Fiber optic	Yes	Yes	Yes	Yes	Yes	Yes	113.60	96	109.06	0.00
Total														267.737,79	0.31

Figure 8-24. AI-powered dashboard after the data refresh

Iterating through the dataset once more with the updated learning settings has improved our recommendations by another 5 percentage points, hitting an accuracy of 59% now. The defended revenue has increased by another $17,680.

For a real-world scenario, imagine that you are not iterating over the same dataset over and over again but over new customer data for each quarter, month, or day, depending on your business. This way, you can monitor how your recommendation model is performing and you can decide whether it is good enough to be released into production. At least the dashboard will give you a solid guideline to assess business value of the AI-backed recommendation service, in contrast to your existing baseline.

You can download the final Power BI file *Offer_Recommendation_AI-Powered.pbix* from the book's website (*https://oreil.ly/aLTWS*).

Cleaning Up Resources

Consider stopping or deleting the following resources we have used in this chapter to avoid any ongoing charges:

- Stop the compute instance.
- Delete the Azure Personalizer Service resource.
- Delete the CSV files in Azure Blob Storage.

We will still use some of these resources for the other chapters. If you don't plan to do the use cases in the following chapters, you can delete all resources at once. Select "Resource groups" in your Azure portal, select the resource group that you created, and choose "Delete resource group." Confirm the resource group name. Then click Delete.

Summary

I hope you can see from this use case how we can utilize AI to turn predictions into actions and how to find out which actions fit in a given context. While Azure Personalizer is only one of many services, the ideas and principles behind these reinforcement learning–based recommendation engines are similar, and you should find it easy to pick up other services as well if needed. Also, with Azure Blob Storage, you learned a way to monitor model updates in real time and bring them into your BI without too much friction.

In the next chapter, we will tackle unstructured data and see how to leverage AI on images, documents, and audio files to analyze their content in our regular BI workflow and blend it with existing information from the business.

## CHAPTER 9

Leveraging Unstructured Data with AI

In the previous chapters, we used AI quite a lot with structured data, or as most people call it, tables. However, a lot of data in businesses is not actually stored in clean tables, but comes in a plethora of formats such as PDFs, images, raw text, websites, and emails. When you consider these formats, the majority of data available within organizations is unstructured. With AI, we can unlock these treasure troves and get insights from data that has hardly been touched before by analysts or data that otherwise needs a lot of manual effort before anyone can get insights from it. In this chapter, we'll explore how AI can help us analyze texts, documents, and image files.

Use Case: Getting Insights from Text Data

Written language is one of the biggest and most diverse data sources humanity has collected. And businesses are no exception. The biggest creators of data are people, either within or outside organizations. Customers become content producers and share their opinions about products or services across the web and on various channels.

In this use case, we are going to deploy an AI service that will help us make sense of this data. In the concrete problem at hand, we are going to analyze user reviews at scale and communicate key insights through a BI dashboard. Let's go!

Problem Statement

Small rooms, unfriendly staff, and horrible breakfast—or not? The management of a large hotel is strained by the variety of customer feedback. Are there really problems that management needs to address, or are there just sporadic complaints that they have to accept, as someone running an accommodation business? The head of operations has hired you as an external analyst to find out what customers think about the hotel and how this trend has developed over time.

As a data source, the company provides a sample of text files of customer feedback that they have collected over time through the hotel's website and gathered from booking portals. Since the new season is just about to start, management wants the results today rather than tomorrow, so speed is clearly prioritized over accuracy. The management staff wants to know whether something is fundamentally wrong and to have the capability to dive in deeper if necessary.

Solution Overview

Take a look at the high-level use case architecture in Figure 9-1.

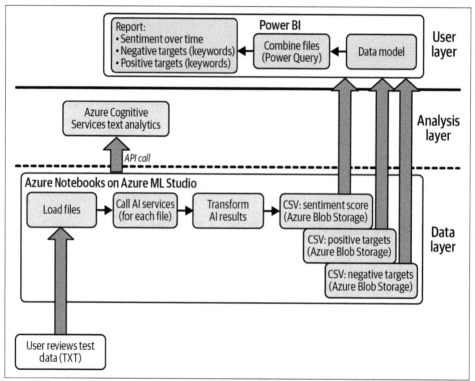

Figure 9-1. Use case architecture for getting insights from text data

From a first glance at this architecture, you should immediately recognize that the analysis layer seems to be pretty simple. The reason is that, in order to analyze many text files automatically, we will use an NLP AI service. As you have seen previously, this AI service doesn't need any training; instead, we can send data to the service and get a response right away.

In this case, our goal is to extract information about whether opinions in customer reviews stored as text files are negative or positive, which is also called *sentiment analysis*. Furthermore, we want to extract keywords so we can relate back to word phrases that carry a positive or negative emotion. The presentation should be in the form of a BI dashboard, in our case Power BI (user layer).

The most challenging part of this use case is in the data layer. We need to get the data into the right shape, send it to the AI service, and retrieve the results in a structured, tabular way so our BI system can handle them. We will achieve that by building a small data processing pipeline using a script in Azure Notebooks on Azure ML Studio that loads the files, calls the AI service, transforms the results, and exports flat CSV files that can be then consumed by our BI system (Power BI).

Setting Up the AI Service

First of all, we need to activate the Cognitive Services Text Analytics in our Azure subscription. This step is straightforward and similar to what we've done previously in other chapters. To activate Cognitive Services Text Analytics, go to your Azure portal (*https://portal.azure.com*) and search for **cognitive services** in the search bar, as shown in Figure 9-2.

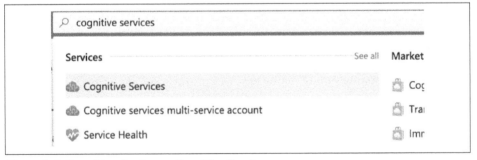

Figure 9-2. Searching for Azure Cognitive Services

Select Cognitive Services from the suggestions list and head over to the corresponding resource page. At this page, you can enable Cognitive Services for all kinds of data and use cases. Scroll down until you see the Language section, shown in Figure 9-3.

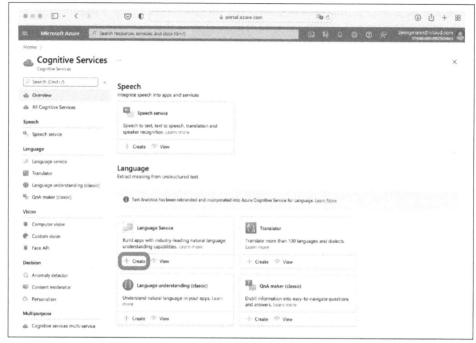

Figure 9-3. Cognitive Services for Language

From here, you can deploy a new Language Service resource by clicking the "+ Create" button. In the following form, which you should be quite used to by now, select your Azure subscription and the resource group, and give your Language Service a name. Also, make sure that you choose the Free Tier (F0), which allows 5,000 transactions per 30 days. One transaction is a text record that corresponds to the number of 1,000-character units within a document that is provided as input to a Language Service API—that's more than enough for our use case here. You can see an example of the filled-in form in Figure 9-4.

Click "Review + create" and then Create after the automatic review process has passed. The deployment will take a few minutes, but after that you should see a notification prompting that the new resource is ready.

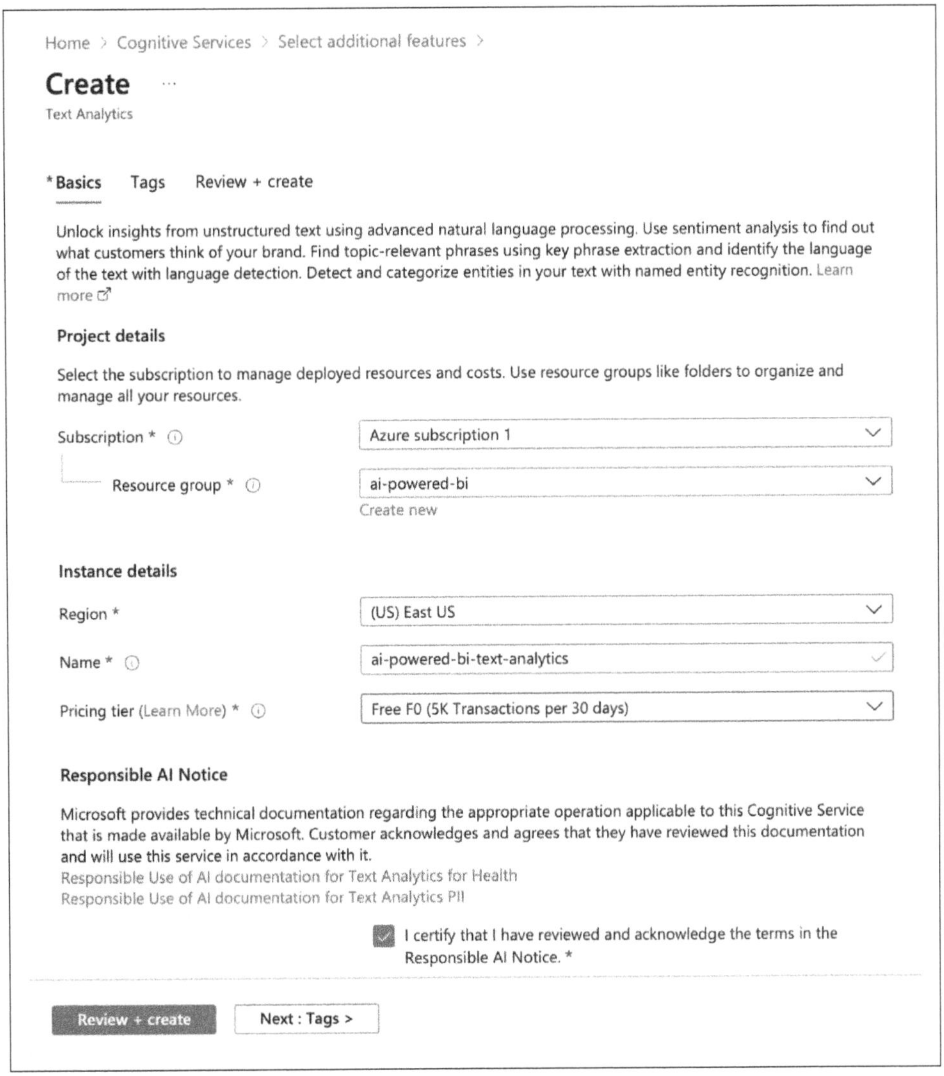

Home > Cognitive Services > Select additional features >

Create ...

Text Analytics

* Basics   Tags   Review + create

Unlock insights from unstructured text using advanced natural language processing. Use sentiment analysis to find out what customers think of your brand. Find topic-relevant phrases using key phrase extraction and identify the language of the text with language detection. Detect and categorize entities in your text with named entity recognition. Learn more ☐

Project details

Select the subscription to manage deployed resources and costs. Use resource groups like folders to organize and manage all your resources.

Subscription * ⓘ

      Azure subscription 1

      Resource group * ⓘ

      ai-powered-bi
      Create new

Instance details

Region *

      (US) East US

Name * ⓘ

      ai-powered-bi-text-analytics

Pricing tier (Learn More) * ⓘ

      Free F0 (5K Transactions per 30 days)

Responsible AI Notice

Microsoft provides technical documentation regarding the appropriate operation applicable to this Cognitive Service that is made available by Microsoft. Customer acknowledges and agrees that they have reviewed this documentation and will use this service in accordance with it.
Responsible Use of AI documentation for Text Analytics for Health
Responsible Use of AI documentation for Text Analytics PII

      ☑ I certify that I have reviewed and acknowledge the terms in the Responsible AI Notice. *

Review + create   Next : Tags >

Figure 9-4. Creating a text analytics service form

After the deployment is finished, navigate to the new resource either by clicking the notification, or—if you left the page—simply by searching for the resource name you provided in the form in the Azure search bar. In both cases, you should be greeted with the resource's overview page (Figure 9-5).

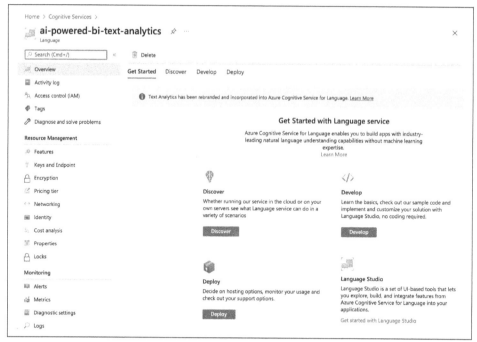

Figure 9-5. Text analytics overview page

We can do many things here, but for now we just want to focus on two. First, how do we authenticate against the API? Second, where do we find out how the API works (which code we need to write—or better, copy and paste)?

To answer the first question, you can click the Keys and Endpoint option in the left menu pane. Here you will find two keys, just as you did in the Azure Personalizer example in Chapter 8. You will need only one of these to call the API. Leave this window open in a new tab since we will soon need these resource keys.

To find out how the API works, you can explore the resources under "Develop" on the overview page. This will bring you to a site that explains various scenarios where you could use the Text Analytics API and the code you would use. This might seem like a lot for now, but don't get intimidated. You won't need all of this information. For now, it is enough to acknowledge that the majority of the code we are writing later in the data preparation step can be taken from this documentation page and adapted to your own needs.

Looking through the documentation for text classification, we can discover some more useful information regarding our new AI service. Navigate to Concepts → Data limits (*https://oreil.ly/9j6lt*), and you should find a table (Figure 9-6).

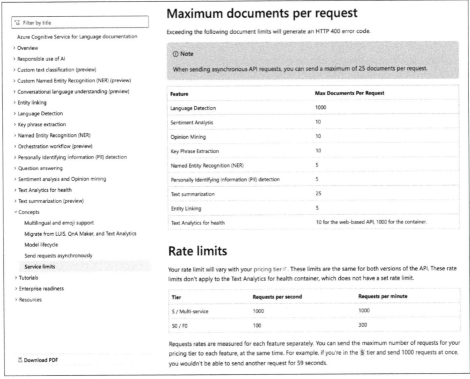

Filter by title
Azure Cognitive Service for Language documentation
Overview
Responsible use of AI
Custom text classification (preview)
Custom Named Entity Recognition (NER) (preview)
Conversational language understanding (preview)
Entity linking
Language Detection
Key phrase extraction
Named Entity Recognition (NER)
Orchestration workflow (preview)
Personally Identifying Information (PII) detection
Question answering
Sentiment analysis and Opinion mining
Text Analytics for health
Text summarization (preview)
Concepts
Multilingual and emoji support
Migrate from LUIS, QnA Maker, and Text Analytics
Model lifecycle
Send requests asynchronously
Service limits
Tutorials
Enterprise readiness
Resources
Download PDF
Maximum documents per request
Exceeding the following document limits will generate an HTTP 400 error code.
Note
When sending asynchronous API requests, you can send a maximum of 25 documents per request.
Feature | Max Documents Per Request
Language Detection | 1000
Sentiment Analysis | 10
Opinion Mining | 10
Key Phrase Extraction | 10
Named Entity Recognition (NER) | 5
Personally Identifying Information (PII) detection | 5
Text summarization | 25
Entity Linking | 5
Text Analytics for health | 10 for the web-based API, 1000 for the container.
Rate limits
Your rate limit will vary with your pricing tier. These limits are the same for both versions of the API. These rate limits don't apply to the Text Analytics for health container, which does not have a set rate limit.
Tier | Requests per second | Requests per minute
S / Multi-service | 1000 | 1000
S0 / F0 | 100 | 300
Requests rates are measured for each feature separately. You can send the maximum number of requests for your pricing tier to each feature, at the same time. For example, if you're in the S tier and send 1000 requests at once, you wouldn't be able to send another request for 59 seconds.

Figure 9-6. Text analytics request limits

If we look at this table and locate the row Sentiment Analysis, we can see that the API accepts 10 documents per request. We can send up to 10 text files at once to the API, which will greatly speed up our inference process, compared to sending the text files to the API one by one. We will come back to this during the data processing.

Now, everything has been set up for the AI service. Let's head over to build our mini data pipeline and run some inference on the customer feedback data.

Setting Up the Data Pipeline

To get from raw text files to a beautifully designed BI dashboard, we have to solve some intermediate steps. In a production environment, this would be called our *extract, transform, load* (*ETL*) process. For our prototype, we won't go as far as naming this a fully fledged ETL process, but in essence we are doing just that. Let's call it our mini ETL job.

We will write a short script to handle the essential parts of an ETL process:

1. Read plain-text files from a file.

2. Send the file contents to the AI service API.

3. Collect the results, transform them, and store them in a structured data object.

4. Export the files as flat tables so they can be easily consumed by our BI software.

For step 1, we need to get the text files and store them someplace where our script can access them. We will use Azure Blob Storage for this. Navigate to the book's website (*https://oreil.ly/0uHwu*) and download the *reviews.zip* file. In your Azure portal, navigate to storage, select the storage account you have set up previously, and create a new container named **texts**, as shown in Figure 9-7. This container will hold the raw input text files. The container "tables" should already be there from Chapter 4 and will receive the tabular output of our mini ETL process.

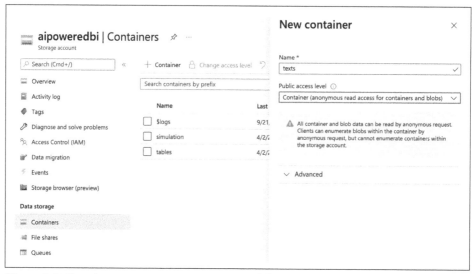

Figure 9-7. Creating a new container in Azure Blob Storage

After creating the "texts" container, upload all the individual text files here. Don't upload the ZIP file, but its contents. Your container should now look like Figure 9-8.

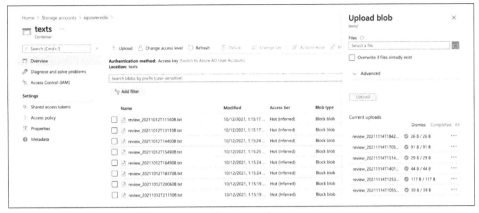

Figure 9-8. Azure storage container with review data

Our input data is now ready to be consumed by a script. You can leave the other container "tables" empty for now. We will populate it through our script, which we will take a look at next.

Download the *ETL_For_Text_Analytics.ipynb* file from the book's website (*https://oreil.ly/0uHwu*). This notebook contains all the code you will need to execute the mini ETL process. If you have a local IDE such as Jupyter Notebooks installed on your computer, you can go ahead and use this. If not, I suggest using Azure Notebooks as a hosted IDE as it comes as part of your Azure subscription.

I will walk you through the example using Azure Notebooks, but the same steps apply when you use your local IDE instead.

We will use some Azure packages needed in this code for authentication and blob storage that are currently not supported in R. While it is still possible to execute this workflow in R, it would be very heavy. So in this case, I provide only the Python version. All R users, please follow along here.

Let's start by creating a new Azure notebook:

1. Navigate to Microsoft Azure Machine Learning Studio (*https://ml.azure.com*) and select the workspace you have been using throughout the book.

2. Choose Notebooks from the menu on the left.

3. Click the plus icon and choose "Upload files," as shown in Figure 9-9.

4. Locate *ETL_For_Text_Analytics.ipynb* on your computer, check the "I trust the contents of this file" option, and click Upload.

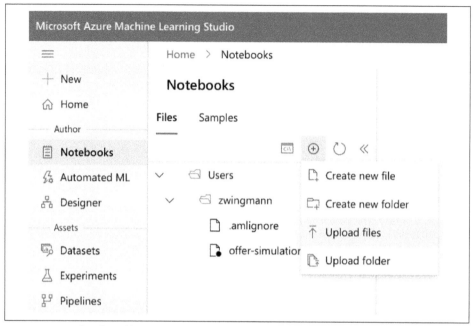

Figure 9-9. Uploading files to the notebook environment

You should see the notebook, as shown in Figure 9-10.

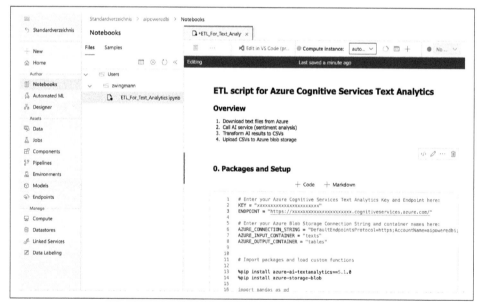

Figure 9-10. ETL notebook

The notebook will be displayed on the right side. While this file contains quite a lot of code, don't get intimidated by it. In fact, the only things you need to modify are the custom parameters for your access credentials and AI service endpoint in lines 2, 3, and 6 in section 0, Packages and Setup—just as you did in Chapter 8.

As an intermediate solution between letting you run the whole notebook at once, trusting that it will somehow work out, and discussing the code line by line, I will give you a high-level overview of what this code is doing by explaining the code sections. I recommend following along and executing the code cells.

This code has four main parts that roughly align to the four steps I mentioned previously during the ETL process:

1. Download text files from Azure: we will download the raw text files from Azure to the local machine that is running the notebook.

2. Call AI service (sentiment analysis): we will send the text files to the AI services and save the results.

3. Transform AI results to CSVs: we will transform the AI results from JSON outputs to flat CSV files so they can be consumed easily by our BI.

4. Upload CSVs to Azure Blob Storage: we will upload the files back to Azure Blob Storage that is connected to our BI.

Before we start, make sure that the notebook is connected to a compute resource that is running. If you have not created a compute resource yet, refer to "Create an Azure Compute Resource" on page 83.

If you are asked to authenticate again after the compute resource has started, just click the button that shows up to authenticate. You should then see a success prompt (Figure 9-11).

Figure 9-11. Authentication prompt

Now, head over to section 0 of the code. This is the place where we will make sure that all packages that we need are installed and loaded and, more importantly, your personal Azure credentials are provided. This is the only place in the whole notebook where you need to change something. Replace the dummy strings for the key, endpoint, and the Azure connection with your custom values from the Azure portal of the Text Analytics Cognitive Service and the Storage account, respectively.

Once you've updated your personal credentials, run the first code cell by placing the cursor inside it and pressing Shift+Enter. The output of this code should be relatively simple. All packages should have been installed on the Azure compute resource already, and you should simply see the Requirement already satisfied notifications, as shown in Figure 9-12.

While we store our Azure credentials in some plain text here within the code, please be aware that this is generally not good coding practice. We are doing this to keep the example simple and because the notebook is still hosted in a protected Azure environment. If you want to learn best practices around handling authentication mechanisms, I recommend checking out the Microsoft resource "About Azure Key Vault" (*https://oreil.ly/9U6Z7*).

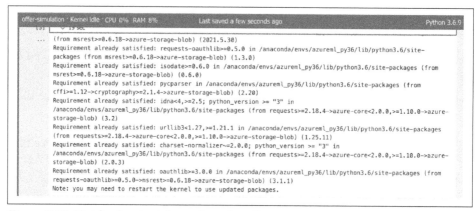

Figure 9-12. Notebook output for package installs

Let's move on to the first part of our mini ETL process: the file download. This first code cell of step 1 calls a class object that we defined in the preceding setup section. This code is essentially establishing a connection to your Azure storage account by using your connection string and downloading all files from the AZURE_INPUT_ CONTAINER that you provided. Run this cell, and it should be finished after a minute, printing output as shown in Figure 9-13.

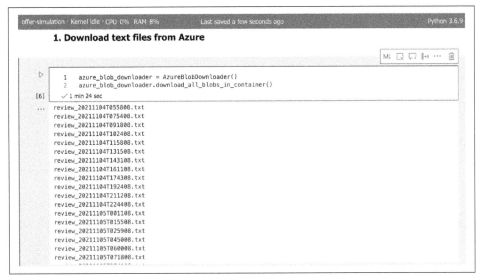

offer-simulation · Kernel Idle · CPU 0% RAM 8%   Last saved a few seconds ago   Python 3.6.9

1. Download text files from Azure

```
1   azure_blob_downloader = AzureBlobDownloader()
2   azure_blob_downloader.download_all_blobs_in_container()
```

[6]   ✓ 1 min 24 sec

```
review_20211104T055808.txt
review_20211104T075408.txt
review_20211104T091808.txt
review_20211104T102408.txt
review_20211104T115808.txt
review_20211104T131508.txt
review_20211104T143108.txt
review_20211104T161108.txt
review_20211104T174308.txt
review_20211104T192408.txt
review_20211104T211208.txt
review_20211104T224408.txt
review_20211105T001108.txt
review_20211105T015508.txt
review_20211105T025908.txt
review_20211105T045008.txt
review_20211105T060008.txt
review_20211105T071808.txt
```

Figure 9-13. Notebook output for blob download

If you wonder why this download takes so long, rest assured that there are methods to speed up the downloading process—for example, running multiple downloads at once. In fact, you could also pass over the file URLs of the AI services directly without downloading them at all. For our prototype, the slow download method is still OK. But if you move to production, you would consider faster alternatives.

Next, let's move on to section 2 of our code, calling the AI service. In this section, we will send the texts to the AI service for analysis. As mentioned previously, we are sending batches of 10 text files (documents) at once to the API so that we get the results faster. Run the code cell. Once it is finished, you should see the first result containing the first 10 results of the sentiment analysis, as shown in Figure 9-14.

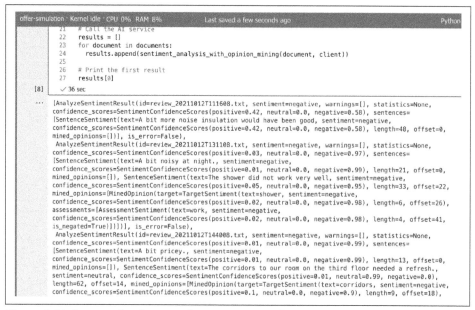

```
offer-simulation · Kernel idle · CPU 0%  RAM 8%               Last saved a few seconds ago                    Python
21    # Call the AI service
22    results = []
23    for document in documents:
24        results.append(sentiment_analysis_with_opinion_mining(document, client))
25
26    # Print the first result
27    results[0]
[8]    ✓ 36 sec

...   [AnalyzeSentimentResult(id=review_20211012T111608.txt, sentiment=negative, warnings=[],
      statistics=None,
      confidence_scores=SentimentConfidenceScores(positive=0.42, neutral=0.0, negative=0.58), sentences=
      [SentenceSentiment(text=A bit more noise insulation would have been good, sentiment=negative,
      confidence_scores=SentimentConfidenceScores(positive=0.42, neutral=0.0, negative=0.58), length=48, offset=0,
      mined_opinions=[])], is_error=False),
       AnalyzeSentimentResult(id=review_20211012T131108.txt, sentiment=negative, warnings=[], statistics=None,
      confidence_scores=SentimentConfidenceScores(positive=0.03, neutral=0.0, negative=0.97), sentences=
      [SentenceSentiment(text=A bit noisy at night., sentiment=negative,
      confidence_scores=SentimentConfidenceScores(positive=0.01, neutral=0.0, negative=0.99), length=21, offset=0,
      mined_opinions=[]), SentenceSentiment(text=The shower did not work very well, sentiment=negative,
      confidence_scores=SentimentConfidenceScores(positive=0.05, neutral=0.0, negative=0.95), length=33, offset=22,
      mined_opinions=[MinedOpinion(target=TargetSentiment(text=shower, sentiment=negative,
      confidence_scores=SentimentConfidenceScores(positive=0.02, neutral=0.0, negative=0.98), length=6, offset=26),
      assessments=[AssessmentSentiment(text=work, sentiment=negative,
      confidence_scores=SentimentConfidenceScores(positive=0.02, neutral=0.0, negative=0.98), length=4, offset=41,
      is_negated=True)])])], is_error=False),
       AnalyzeSentimentResult(id=review_20211012T144008.txt, sentiment=negative, warnings=[], statistics=None,
      confidence_scores=SentimentConfidenceScores(positive=0.01, neutral=0.0, negative=0.99), sentences=
      [SentenceSentiment(text=A bit pricey., sentiment=negative,
      confidence_scores=SentimentConfidenceScores(positive=0.01, neutral=0.0, negative=0.99), length=13, offset=0,
      mined_opinions=[]), SentenceSentiment(text=The corridors to our room on the third floor needed a refresh.,
      sentiment=neutral, confidence_scores=SentimentConfidenceScores(positive=0.01, neutral=0.99, negative=0.0),
      length=62, offset=14, mined_opinions=[MinedOpinion(target=TargetSentiment(text=corridors, sentiment=negative,
      confidence_scores=SentimentConfidenceScores(positive=0.1, neutral=0.0, negative=0.9), length=9, offset=18),
```

Figure 9-14. Raw notebook output for sentiment analysis

As you might notice from this preview output, the structure of the results is nested. The AI service provides not only the sentiment score for each text, but also a detailed breakdown for opinions on a word level for each text that was analyzed. This will be useful for the interpretation of the data, but on the downside it creates some hassle for us to untangle the whole object and convert it back into some nice flat tables. This is what section 3 of this code is all about. Let's move on!

Section 3 of the data preparation code is the most exhaustive. While the main AI workload has been done, a bit of postprocessing remains, to extract the sentiment scores for each text and the corresponding opinions discovered in each item.

Now, if you ask yourself, "How on earth should I ever come up with this code?" I have good news for you. Most of this code was borrowed from the AI services' documentation page. Do you remember the quick-start reference back in the Azure console? This is the place where most of this code is coming from. Once you understand the general behavior, making the adjustments you need is pretty straightforward.

In this example, I made three adjustments. First, I extracted only the high-level sentiment scores per text item and saved them as a flat table for better CSV compatibility. This table, or dataframe, also contains the original filename, the original text, and a datetime column extracted from the texts' filenames. This will result in a nice flat CSV output that we can later display in our BI. And second and third, I created a flat CSV each for all positive and negative terms or opinions found in the text documents, again stored with the reference to the original filename and the extracted datetime column so these terms can be linked back to their original context and also possibly filtered by time. If you feel lucky, go through the code line by line and see what's happening. If not, that's also fine. We're not wanting to become software engineers. In any case, click the Run button for this cell to see the output shown in Figure 9-15.

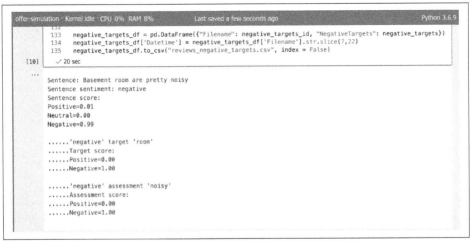

Figure 9-15. Formatted notebook output for sentiment analysis

For convenience reasons, the output printed the sentiment and opinions for each text document in an easy-to-read format. For example, you can see from Figure 9-15 that the sentence Basement room are pretty noisy (despite the grammar mistake) was recognized by the AI as a negative sentiment and that the AI service was able to identify the words room and noisy as the main drivers behind this negative opinion. Isn't that pretty?

At the end, this code also created the CSV files we wanted. If you take a look at the file explorer on the left and click Refresh, you should see three new CSV files, as shown in Figure 9-16.

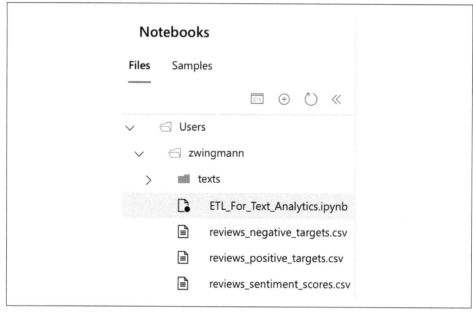

Figure 9-16. CSV outputs in notebook environment

To make these CSV files accessible to our BI, let's head over to code section 4, which is all about uploading these files to Azure Blob Storage. Compared to section 3, this will be a breeze.

Execute the last code cell. Within a blink of a second, you should see the output shown in Figure 9-17 confirming that the files have been uploaded successfully.

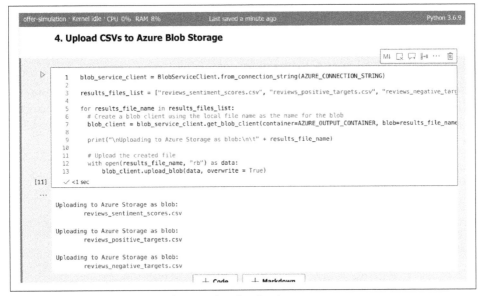

Figure 9-17. Notebook output for completed upload

Congratulations! You've completed the hardest part and survived the mini ETL challenge. Now, as with every ETL process, this process is reproducible. Whenever you update the text files in the blob input container and the files keep the same structure, you can simply rerun this whole workflow (at once), and the CSV files in the output container will be replaced and overwritten with the new results.

But let's leave the realms of ETL for now and move on to the fun part: visualizing and synthesizing our results in our BI.

 Don't forget to stop your compute resource after this exercise to avoid any ongoing charges!

Model Inference with Power BI Walk-Through

To display our results, we will once more come back to Power BI. Create a new report in Power BI and select Azure Blob Storage as the data source. Connect with your storage account and select the checkbox next to the folder *Tables*. Click Transform. In the Power Query Editor, you will find a list of all CSV tables found in the folder. We need to go through all three of them one by one.

Choose the first one and click the Binary link to see a preview of your data, as shown in Figure 9-18. Double-check that the Datetime column has been converted correctly to a datetime format. Click Close & Apply and redo these steps for the other two CSV files.

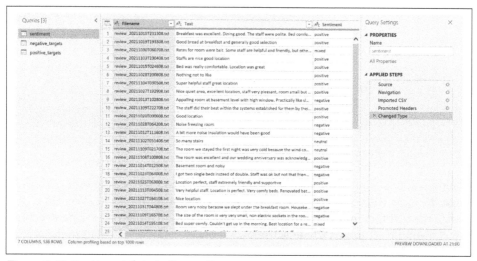

Figure 9-18. Sentiment data in Power Query

Your data model should now list three separate tables. We know, however, that these tables are related to one another and we want Power BI to know this as well. Right-click any table and choose "Edit relationship." In the editor that pops up, create a relationship between the table, "positive_targets," and "sentiment" based on the column Filename. The cardinality should be many to one, as shown in Figure 9-19. Click OK and redo this setup for the table "negative_targets."

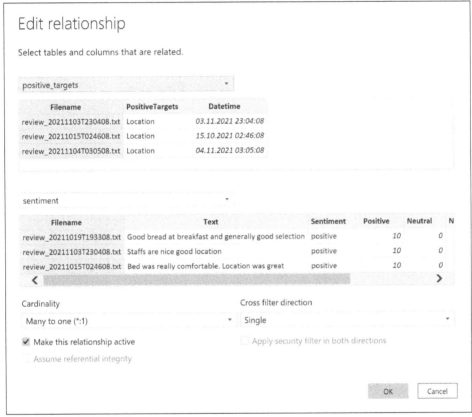

Figure 9-19. Data relationships in Power BI

Afterward, the tables in your data model should be connected, as shown in Figure 9-20.

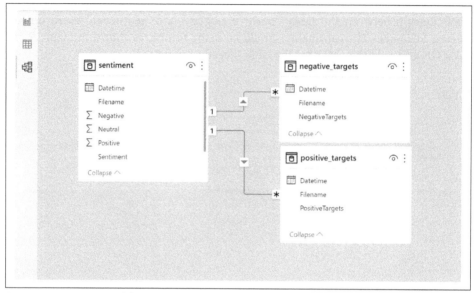

Figure 9-20. Data model in Power BI

Now that our data model is completed, it's time to move on to handling the visuals.

Building the AI-Powered Dashboard in Power BI

Let's quickly recap the situation: management wants to know if something is going on that should be on their radar. To get a high-level overview about the customer reviews, we need four elements:

- The development of customer sentiment over time to check for trends
- A list of items that customers complain about (negative targets)
- A list of items that customers like (positive targets)
- A reference back to the original data so we get more context

We could convey this information in many ways. I decided to put a report together consisting of a line chart containing the overall trend, two treemaps highlighting the positive and negative targets, and a simple table that lists all the customer feedback with plain text. You can see the final result in Figure 9-21.

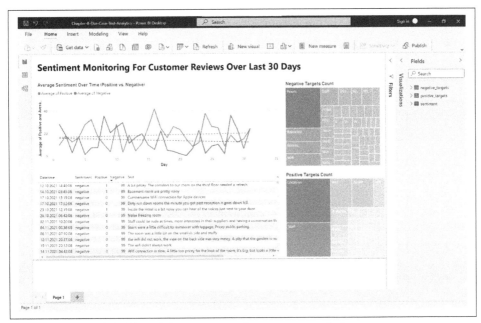

Figure 9-21. Final dashboard for AI-powered sentiment analysis

Try to re-create this dashboard by yourself in Power BI or come up with your own solution. Or, you can download the complete *User_Reviews_AI-Powered.pbix* file from the book's website (*https://oreil.ly/0uHwu*) and connect it to your own Azure Blob Storage.

So what does this dashboard tell us? For one, we can see that both the positive and negative sentiment seems to have a somewhat steady trend, with daily ups and downs. If we aggregate the visual to a monthly level, the picture becomes a bit clearer (Figure 9-22). From a monthly perspective, the negative sentiments seem to have increased a lot. If we explore the reasons, we can find out that most complaints are about the rooms, the breakfast, and the WiFi. While the rooms might be hard to fix in the short term, the breakfast and WiFi provide clear action items that can be addressed quickly by management.

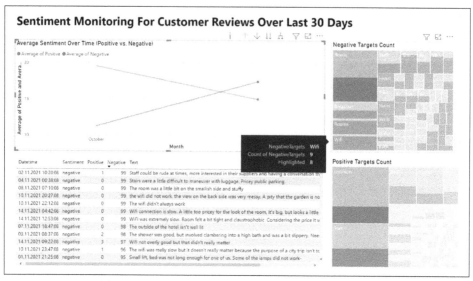

Figure 9-22. Monthly sentiment analysis

Also, since we have created the relationships among the tables, Power BI allows us to filter for certain data points. For example, if we select a date from the line chart, the rest of the dashboard will update accordingly and show only the relevant data that was collected on this day, and vice versa. What exactly is it that customers complain about with regards to the room? Just click Rooms in the Negative Targets treemap and see what customers say by exploring the original text at the bottom. This provides a great way to explore the dataset and find out more about the actual customer feedback.

While this dashboard only touches the top of the iceberg of text analytics, I hope you have seen how powerful it can be to analyze text data at scale. Thanks to AI services, this can be done with a few lines of code and integrated in any BI system.

Use Case: Parsing Documents with AI

Have you ever seen a business that does not use forms? Forms are for businesses what APIs are for programmers. Forms have a great advantage. They typically work well to exchange information between humans. Given a specific form and some descriptions, you should pretty quickly be able to figure out how to read the form or how to fill it in.

The drawback often comes when forms need to be processed by a computer. Often forms still live as paper documents or their electronic counterparts, PDFs. If you want to process them at scale, you often don't have any other choice than to look through them manually and extract data from these PDFs by hand for further analysis.

Receipts can also be considered a form; they provide a recurring data structure that is easy for humans to read, but hard for machines to interpret. In this use case, we will learn how AI will help us to read documents at scale and extract values from it to display them in a BI system.

Problem Statement

In our next scenario, imagine that we are working for a medium-sized company that provides consulting services. The business is located in Germany, where sales representatives travel frequently to potential customers to prepare or close deals. The travel is mostly done via high-speed trains that connect the big cities of Germany, called InterCity Express (ICE).

Our travel management department keeps control of the overall expenses. The process for business travel is as follows: sales reps can book their train tickets over a self-service portal from the train operator (Deutsche Bahn). These tickets are paid for with a company credit card. The travel management team oversees the credit card billing at the end of each month to get an overview of the travel expenses. However, the credit card statements do not provide any further detail except for the amount spent and the date. To optimize travel expenses and better understand which business trips are causing the most costs, the travel management team wants more insights about the trips, including a breakdown by popular travel routes (train origin and train destinations).

This information can be found in the booking receipt that the sales representatives automatically receive via email after every successful booking. Figure 9-23 shows an example of such a receipt.

In particular, the team is interested in extracting the following information from this form: booking date, trip origin, trip destination, and ticket price. The travel management team wants to find out if there is a way to extract this information automatically and ideally report it using the existing BI. They have provided us with a sample of 162 receipts from a single sales representative to work on a first prototype.

Figure 9-23. ICE train online ticket

Solution Overview

In this scenario, we're going to extract information from a document by using optical character recognition (OCR). Now, this technique isn't new and has been around for a while. However, AI will help us with at least two layers of this problem. The first layer is to improve the actual OCR—that is, recognizing single text characters and converting them into machine-readable form (plain-text string). The second part is making sense of the characters, to find out which ones belong to a word or a sentence, or even recognizing more complex structures like tables.

Take a look at Figure 9-24 to review the overall architecture of this use case.

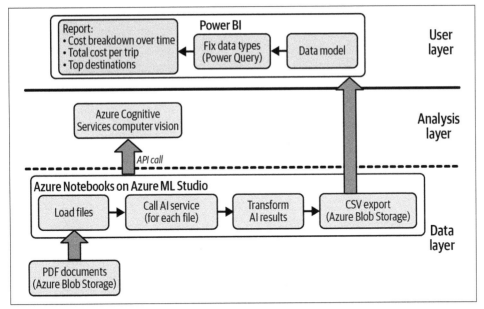

Figure 9-24. Use case architecture for parsing documents

To tackle this problem, we will follow a similar approach to that in "Use Case: Getting Insights from Text Data" on page 261:

1. Deploy an out-of-the box AI service on Microsoft Azure—in this case, Cognitive Services for Computer Vision (analysis layer).

2. Load the data into a staging area—in this case, again using Azure Blob Storage (data layer).

3. Prepare a small ETL script that loads the data from the staging area, applies the AI service, and transforms it to a flat CSV (data layer).

4. Upload the CSV file to a location from where it can be easily accessed and visualized with our BI tool (user layer).

Let's go!

Setting Up the AI Service

Go to your Azure portal (*http://portal.azure.com*) and type **cognitive services** in the search bar. Select Cognitive Services from the suggestion list and proceed to the respective resource page. Scroll down to Vision. You should see the available services shown in Figure 9-25.

Figure 9-25. Cognitive Services for Computer Vision

Select "+ Create" from the "Computer vision" box, and you should be greeted with the now well-known form to set up a computer vision resource. Again, select a resource group, give your resource a name, and select the free F0 pricing tier. Don't forget to select the checkbox at the bottom that you agree to the "Responsible AI terms" of use.

Take a minute to acknowledge these terms. They essentially mean that you don't violate personal rights by using the AI. Remember, every image or document that you send to the API will be processed by services owned and operated by Microsoft. So, especially if you deal with personal data, you have to ensure that you have the consent and permission to do this. For our use cases, we are dealing with fictional or public domain data so there is no risk involved. However, in a business setting, think twice before you start sending documents about your customers or employees to a remote AI service.

Click "Review + create" once you've completed the form, and Create after the automatic validation passes. After a few minutes, your service should be deployed, and you can access it either by clicking the notification link or by searching for your resource name through the search bar in the Azure portal. If you open the resource page, you should see a screen that looks similar to Figure 9-26.

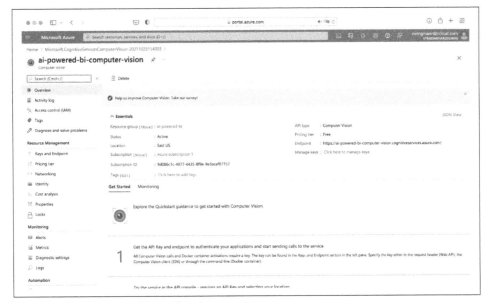

Figure 9-26. Computer Vision Service overview

The quick start looks a bit different from the previous AI service but essentially contains the same information: you will find a link to your access keys and some code examples to get started quickly. For now, you can navigate to Keys and Endpoint, where you will find the resource HTTP endpoints and secret access keys. Leave this page open, because we will need these keys in a bit.

The AI setup is complete, so let's move on to load and process the PDF files.

Wait a second, you might say. Why didn't we use the dedicated Azure service Form Recognizer for this? Form Recognizer is a specialized service that tailors computer vision to form recognition and value extraction. The service is more focused, but also needs a certain degree of custom training and setup before it works; it is no out-of-the box service. On the other hand, the computer vision API is a multipurpose service that works like Plug and Play. It is easier to implement, but you will hit limits when the task gets too specialized. It will also be useful for you in scenarios other than form extraction. My recommendation is to start with the general computer vision first and switch over to more customized or tailored services later, if needed. If you want to learn more about Form Recognizer, see "Azure Form Recognizer Documentation" (*https://oreil.ly/XfqAK*).

Setting Up the Data Pipeline

Let's first upload our PDF files to an Azure Blob Storage container so we can access them easily. Open a new Azure portal window and navigate to Azure Blob Storage by using the search bar or looking in your recent items in your dashboard. Navigate to Containers and create a new container called **pdfs**, as shown in Figure 9-27.

Figure 9-27. Creating a new storage container in Azure Blob Storage

Now, download the *pdfs.zip* file from the book's website (*https://oreil.ly/0uHwu*) and unzip it on your local computer. Download all the contents from your local *pdfs* folder to the container in Azure Blob Storage. At the end, all PDF files should be stored in the "pdfs'" container on Azure Blob Storage without any subfolder or any ZIP file, as shown in Figure 9-28.

Figure 9-28. PDF files in Azure Blob Storage

Now that the files are ready for analysis, we can move ahead to the ETL process. As in the previous example, I will walk you through the code step by step, and we will run the script in Azure Notebooks. Of course, you can also use your local IDE if you prefer.

First things first, download the *ETL_For_Document_Analysis.ipynb* file from the book's website (*https://oreil.ly/0uHwu*) to your local computer. Open Azure ML Studio (*http://ml.azure.com*), select your preferred workspace, and click "Get started." Navigate to Notebooks and choose "Upload files," as shown in Figure 9-9. Select the *ETL_For_Document_Analysis.ipynb* file and upload it to Azure Notebooks. After the upload, the notebook shows up on the right side of the screen. Don't forget to connect your notebook to a compute resource as we did in the previous use case. When everything is ready, your screen should look similar to Figure 9-29.

Figure 9-29. ETL notebook for document analysis

I will now walk you through the code and explain what is happening section by section. Please follow along by executing the code cells in the order covered here.

First, section 0, Packages and Setup, again is the place where you need to input your custom Azure connection string as well as your custom key and endpoint for your computer vision service. Do you still have the window open? Good, then you can just copy and paste both values here. In the following section, the code ensures that all required packages are imported, and we define some custom functions. I will explain these functions in more detail once we are going to use them. Now, run the first code cell by placing the cursor inside and pressing Shift+Enter.

Section 1 covers the file download from Azure Blob Storage. This one is quite straightforward and identical to what we did in the previous use case. Run this code cell as well. As a result, you should see a *pdfs* folder in the file browser. If not, click the small refresh icon in the file browser.

Section 2 is again a short one. Here, we are just calling the AI service and fetching the raw results from the analysis. We have two important things to note here.

You might notice the `time.sleep(6)` command in the code. I included this line to make sure we are not exceeding the free tier limit of 20 requests per minute. So why do we wait 6 seconds and not only 3 (3 seconds × 20 requests = 60 seconds)? This is because in the case of computer vision, we are running an *asynchronous operation*.

Remember that in the previous example for the sentiment analysis, we just sent the text to the API and immediately received the response with the AI results. In the case of computer vision, the operation is more complex and the results can take a while (like seconds). Therefore, for each document, we need to make two API calls: one POST request to send the document to the AI service, and one GET request to fetch the results. If you look carefully into the function `document_analysis` under section 0, you will notice both API calls. And, in fact, we are waiting two seconds each time before we make the GET request to increase the chances that the result is there for every call that we make.

If you move to a paid plan, you can safely delete the `time.sleep(6)` line from the loop in step 2. But I do recommend keeping a short pause between the first POST and GET request; otherwise, you will run into a lot of empty (but still billed) API calls. Considering the limitations of the free plan, the overall analysis for the 162 PDF documents should take around 30 minutes. Run the code cell. And now it's time for a coffee break before we head to the dirty work!

Calling the AI service so far has been pretty easy. Extracting the information from the response can be messy, though. To understand why, let's take a look at what the result from the AI looks like. To do this, we can't just print the result object. The result object is a nested structure that we need to unpack. Fortunately, the GitHub documentation with Python code examples (*https://oreil.ly/305e3*) shows us how to do this:

```
# Inspect the first result
read_result = results[0]
# Print the detected text, line by line
if read_result.status == OperationStatusCodes.succeeded:
    for text_result in read_result.analyze_result.read_results:
        for line in text_result.lines:
```

```
            print(line.text)
            print(line.bounding_box)
```

The preceding code will yield the following output (truncated for brevity):

```
DB
[0.6349, 0.5273, 1.0222, 0.5165, 1.0222, 0.764, 0.6349, 0.764]
Online-Ticket
[3.0799, 0.5784, 4.6416, 0.5784, 4.6416, 0.7642, 3.0799, 0.7642]
ICE Fahrkarte
[0.5206, 1.1069, 1.4109, 1.1069, 1.4109, 1.2117, 0.5206, 1.2117]
...
Betrag
[0.5614, 3.5237, 0.873, 3.5237, 0.873, 3.6278, 0.5614, 3.6278]
92,00€
[1.109, 3.5237, 1.455, 3.5237, 1.455, 3.6197, 1.109, 3.6197]
...
Datum
[0.5621, 3.6571, 0.8733, 3.6571, 0.8733, 3.7384, 0.5621, 3.7384]
02.02.2018
...
Halt
[0.5207, 4.6438, 0.7449, 4.6438, 0.7449, 4.7352, 0.5207, 4.7352]
Datum
[2.4111, 4.6438, 2.7826, 4.6438, 2.7826, 4.7352, 2.4111, 4.7352]
Zeit
[2.9165, 4.6429, 3.1326, 4.6429, 3.1326, 4.7352, 2.9165, 4.7352]
Gleis
[3.4701, 4.6429, 3.7657, 4.6429, 3.7657, 4.7358, 3.4701, 4.7358]
Produkte
[4.104, 4.6438, 4.6302, 4.6438, 4.6302, 4.7352, 4.104, 4.7352]
Reservierung
[4.852, 4.6429, 5.6354, 4.6429, 5.6354, 4.7605, 4.852, 4.7605]
Hamburg Hbf
[0.5214, 4.8136, 1.2506, 4.8136, 1.2506, 4.932, 0.5214, 4.932]
02.02.
[2.4063, 4.8167, 2.7382, 4.8167, 2.7382, 4.9068, 2.4063, 4.9068]
ab 16:36 5
[2.9179, 4.8148, 3.5288, 4.8148, 3.5288, 4.9068, 2.9179, 4.9068]
ICE 1527
[4.1059, 4.8209, 4.6115, 4.8209, 4.6115, 4.9153, 4.1059, 4.9153]
1 Sitzplatz, Wg. 38, Pl. 12, 1 Fenster,
[4.8551, 4.8209, 6.8913, 4.8209, 6.8913, 4.9404, 4.8551, 4.9404]
Leipzig Hbf
[0.5213, 4.9636, 1.1351, 4.9636, 1.1351, 5.082, 0.5213, 5.082]
...
Seite 1 / 1
[7.1081, 11.2414, 7.5931, 11.2414, 7.5931, 11.3253, 7.1081, 11.3253]
```

To make sense of this, let's compare the output to the original document, as shown in Figure 9-30.

Figure 9-30. Online train ticket (full PDF)

In both the code output and Figure 9-30, I have highlighted the elements of the document that we are interested in (Date, Price, Origin, Destination).

If we compare the AI output with the original document, we can see that the AI parsed the document line by line. It starts with "DB" and "Online-Ticket" from the top left and ends with "Seite 1/1" on the bottom right.

Each line of text is an element of the result object, and the numbers that follow are the bounding boxes for these lines, indicating where the line was positioned in the document. The six numbers correspond to the x and y coordinates, as shown in Figure 9-31, with the coordinate system starting at the top left of the document with coordinates ($x = 0$, $y = 0$). Each list of coordinates is mapped as [$x1$, $y1$, $x2$, $y2$, $x3$, $y3$, $x4$, $y4$].

Figure 9-31. Bounding boxes used by the computer vision service

To extract just the information we want from the document, we need to rely on the assumption that the document was parsed in western reading order (from left to right, top to bottom); this can be adjusted for the AI service if needed.

Let's start with the date information by running the next code cell labeled Part 1 of section 3. In this code cell, most work is done by the custom function get_text_by_keyword(result, "Datum"). The function, which was defined in section 0, takes a given keyword argument, in this case Datum (German for *Date*) and returns the item that follows just after that in the AI response. Since the AI parses the text from left to right, the result will be the actual date that we are looking for. We do some postprocessing to turn it into a more conventional date format, and that's it. Extracting a form value that has a distinct form label next to it is pretty straightforward.

Now we move on to part 2, extracting the origin and destination information. This part is a bit trickier since the information is not listed on the same line, but on different lines in the document, similar to a table structure. To make it even more complicated, this list can be even longer if connecting trains run between the origin and final destination. How do we tackle this? We will use a combined approach of a keyword search and a bounding box filter. Let's take a look before we run the cell.

First, we call the function get_text_between_keywords(result, "Halt", "Wich tige Nutzungshinweise:"), which will give us all text elements between the start and stop markers. In our case, that is the first column header of the table (`Halt`, German for *Stop*) and the first text object that follows after the table (`Wichtige Nut zungshinweise`, meaning *Terms of Use*). This function will extract all text elements in the table, as shown in Figure 9-32.

Ihre Reiseverbindung und Reservierung Hinfahrt am 02.02.2018					
Halt	Datum	Zeit	Gleis	Produkte	Reservierung
Hamburg Hbf	02.02.	ab 16:36	5	ICE 1527	1 Sitzplatz, Wg. 38, Pl. 12, 1 Fenster,
Leipzig Hbf	02.02.	an 19:42	11		Panorama / Lounge, Nichtraucher,
					Ruhebereich, Res.Nr. 8091 3012 3081 12
Wichtige Nutzungshinweise:					

Figure 9-32. Table data contained in the PDF

However, we don't want all text elements, but only the items of the first column. How do we get them? There are possibly many ways to approach this, but I found it easiest to just locate this information by using the respective bounding boxes. The idea is that, from the text fragment we have just collected, we extract only the part indicated by the dashed line in Figure 9-33.

Ihre Reiseverbindung und Reservierung Hinfahrt am 02.02.2018					
Halt	Datum	Zeit	Gleis	Produkte	Reservierung
Hamburg Hbf	02.02.	ab 16:36	5	ICE 1527	1 Sitzplatz, Wg. 38, Pl. 12, 1 Fenster,
Leipzig Hbf	02.02.	an 19:42	11		Panorama / Lounge, Nichtraucher,
					Ruhebereich, Res.Nr. 8091 3012 3081 12
Wichtige Nutzungshinweise:					

Figure 9-33. Relevant column in PDF table

So how do we get the coordinates for this dashed box? We take the lower-left corner of the first column header `Halt` and define it to be the upper-left corner of our dashed box. To get the width of the box, we take the x coordinate of the lower-left corner of the text `Datum`, because we know this will always be the second column. This will become the $x2$ value of our dashed box. And finally, to get the height of the dashed box, we search for the highest $y3$ coordinate in our extracted text area. These coordinates are all we need to draw a rectangle.

Now that we have defined our "filter" box, we can keep the text findings where the bounding box is inside the boundaries of our filters. This is what the function `get_text_by_position(result, filter_box)` is handling for us. This function will return a clean list with all the train stops. Now, we just need to take the first and the last item of this list, and voilá—we have our origin and destination values. With the conceptual understanding of what's going on here, run the code cell for part 2.

Part 3 is again a bit simpler. In this case, we are extracting the price information based on identifying the keyword `Betrag` (indicating the price) in the document, similar to the way we extracted the date. The only difference is that this time we are extracting not only the next item after the keyword, but also the next two items after the keyword, as you can see by the parameter 2 in the function `get_text_by_key` `word(result, "Betrag", 2)`. Why is that? The short answer is, it makes our script a bit more robust. We can safely identify the price information based on the € sign and we know it should come soon after the label `Betrag`, but it does not necessarily have to be the first item; it could be the second. Go ahead and run the cell.

Now only one step is left for the data transformation, and that is bringing our results together and writing the CSV table. By now, you should have four list objects—`dates`, `prices`, `origins`, and `destinations`—all having the same length. In this last step, we are binding them together to a dataframe and exporting this as a CSV file. Run this last cell and you should see the new file *public-transportation-costs.csv* in the file explorer on the left after a quick refresh. The result table is shown in Figure 9-34.

	Date	Origin	Destination	Cost	Receipt
0	2017-10-29	München Hbf	Hamburg Hbf	122.00	KKZ2A1.pdf
1	2018-06-08	Leipzig Hbf	München Hbf	101.25	8M1XML.pdf
2	2018-05-21	Leipzig Hbf	Hamburg Hbf	92.00	SYGLKK.pdf
3	2018-07-21	Bonn-Oberkassel Nord	Frankfurt(M) Flughafen Fernbf	56.10	bahn-B3QNOU.pdf
4	2018-04-06	Hamburg Hbf	Leipzig Hbf	89.50	OG4EB6.pdf
...	...	...	...	...	...
157	2020-01-11	Leipzig Hbf	Hamburg Hbf	81.90	bahn-17B6DU.pdf
158	2018-10-02	Konstanz	Bonn Hbf (tief)	109.10	bahn-UKW9RT.pdf
159	2018-11-18	Leipzig Hbf	Hamburg Hbf	89.50	bahn-G4SUFW.pdf
160	2017-10-22	Leipzig Hbf	Hamburg Hbf	87.75	GBEOH3.pdf
161	2017-11-12	Bonn Hbf	Hamburg Hbf	77.75	vhl8hb.pdf

162 rows × 5 columns

Figure 9-34. Structured output for extracted PDF data

Finally, let's upload our result to our container called "tables" on Azure Blob Storage. The last code cell in section 4 will handle this for you. Run this cell and give yourself a pat on the back; the biggest part of the work has been completed. We can now move ahead and visualize the results in our BI.

 Don't forget to stop the Azure compute resource after you finish the script to avoid any ongoing charges!

Model Inference with Power BI Walk-Through

Let's move on to the fun part. Open your favorite BI and load the CSV that we just created to get more insights. I will walk you through the process again with the example of Power BI.

In Power BI, create a new report and choose Azure Blob Storage from "Get data." Provide the name of your Azure Blob Storage account, as shown in Figure 9-35.

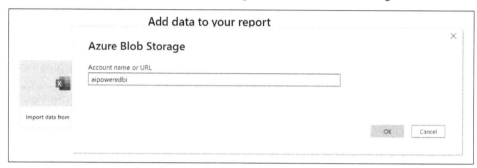

Figure 9-35. Importing data from Azure Blob Storage

You should see the file list of your blob storage. Navigate to the folder *tables* and click Refresh, as shown in Figure 9-36, if you still can't see the new file *public-transportation-costs.csv*.

Select the checkbox for the *tables* folder and click Transform Data to open Power Query. Click the Binary link next to the name of the CSV file *public-transportation-costs.csv*.

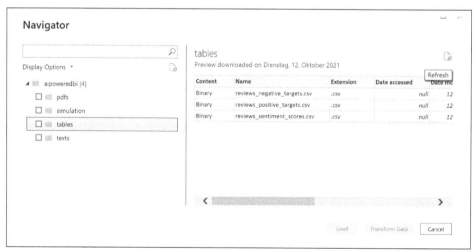

Figure 9-36. Refreshing a data preview in Power Query

You want to make sure of two things here. First, the date column should be correctly identified as a Date data type. Second, ensure that the prices are converted to a numeric value. If Power BI does not automatically recognize the correct data types, right-click the Date column and select Date, as shown in Figure 9-37.

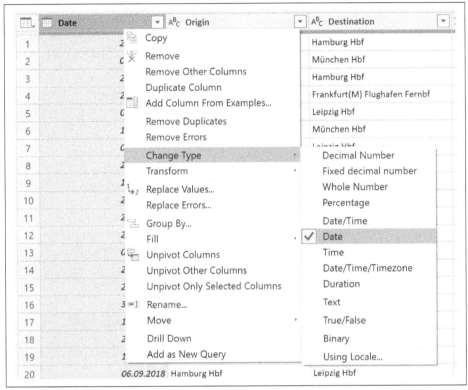

Figure 9-37. Changing the data type in Power Query

If the prices are not showing up as numeric values, right-click the column and choose Change Type → Using Locale, as shown in Figure 9-38.

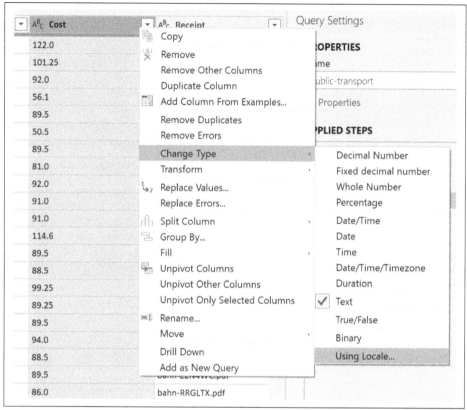

Figure 9-38. Parsing decimal numbers by using the locale in Power Query

Change the data type to Decimal Number and set the locale to English (United States), as shown in Figure 9-39.

Figure 9-39. Changing the data type with the locale in Power Query

Finally, your table should look similar to Figure 9-40. Close Power Query by clicking Close & Apply.

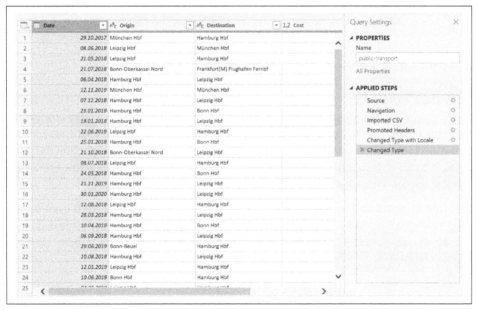

Figure 9-40. Transformed dataset in Power Query

Building the AI-Powered Dashboard in Power BI

Head over to the report and create some new visuals. I decided to show the total travel expenses per year in a line chart, the total number of business trips as a metric, the top destinations as a horizontal bar chart, and, finally, all routes (combinations of origins and destinations) as a treemap in which the size equals the money spent. Figure 9-41 shows the visuals.

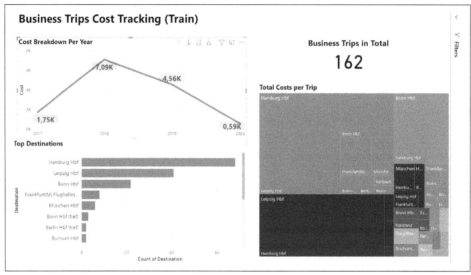

Figure 9-41. AI-powered expense-tracking dashboard

With these visuals, the travel management team can clearly see the overall cost trend and absolute trip numbers. And the team can also identify which routes contribute the most to the overall travel expenses. In this example, we can see that the connection from Hamburg to Leipzig and back accounted for the largest proportion of travel costs. We can also see that most trips started in Hamburg, with Bonn and Frankfurt being the second and third most popular destinations from this origin.

Feel free to re-create this dashboard on your own or see if you can find even better ways to display the data. If you want to see the final dashboard that I created, you can download *Document_Analysis_AI-Powered.pbix* from the book's website (*https://oreil.ly/0uHwu*).

Use Case: Counting Objects in Images

With the previous use case, we have only touched the vast capabilities of computer vision. In the following scenario, I will show you how to use the existing infrastructure even further—namely, to detect objects in images. For this, let's take a closer look at the problem at hand.

Problem Statement

We are working for a transport and road authority that tries to improve overall traffic management and traffic flow to minimize road congestion. One important factor is to control the speed limits on highways. To set speed limits, the authority needs an ideally constant measurement of the traffic flow on the roads. While new roads are equipped with respective measurement sensors and technology, old roads often have only closed-circuit television (CCTV) cameras installed that were used by traffic managers for manual traffic inspections.

The operations team approached us to check whether it is possible to count the traffic by using the existing camera infrastructure and has provided us with sample CCTV footage for testing purposes. Figure 9-42 shows an example of the CCTV footage.

Figure 9-42. CCTV camera footage. Source: Kaggle (https://oreil.ly/yHY0w)

The CCTV images for this use case were provided via a dataset on Kaggle (Highway CCTV Footage Images).

Solution Overview

To tackle the problem at hand, we are building on the existing computer vision AI service from the previous use case. Since we are using the same service, the overall use case architecture is almost identical to the previous computer vision use case, as you can see in Figure 9-43.

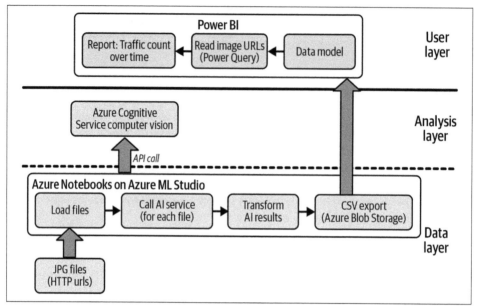

Figure 9-43. Use case architecture for counting objects in images

Instead of a Read operation, we are now calling a service called "Detect objects." In this case, we want to analyze data on the fly. So instead of loading a dataset to Azure Blob Storage, we are consuming the CCTV footage directly from a web URL and will feed this web URL into the AI service. We will still have a small ETL job in place that consumes the HTTP URLs, calls the AI service, and writes the output as a flat CSV file to Azure Blob Storage so we can consume it with our BI tool. Let's start!

Setting Up the AI Service

We are using the same AI service that we deployed previously in "Use Case: Parsing Documents with AI" on page 282. If you haven't completed it yet, go to the previous section, complete the steps listed under "Setting Up the AI Service," and come back here. If you did it already, just follow along; there's nothing more you need to do.

As it turns out, computer vision has many use cases that run under the same service. With the computer vision service that you have just deployed, you can not only extract text and detect objects, but also recognize brand names, popular landmarks, tag images, and many more. For a complete guide, check out "Computer Vision Documentation" (*https://oreil.ly/m3UD7*) for Azure Cognitive Services.

Setting Up the Data Pipeline

Download *ETL_For_Image_Analysis.ipynb* from the book's website (*https://oreil.ly/ 0uHwu*). Just as before, open the file in your local IDE or upload it to Azure Notebooks. In addition to this file, you will also need *image-urls.txt*, which needs to be located in the same directory as the notebook file.

If you open *ETL_For_Image_Analysis.ipynb*, you will see that it looks similar to the files that we used previously, as you can see in Figure 9-44. I'll quickly walk you through the main steps.

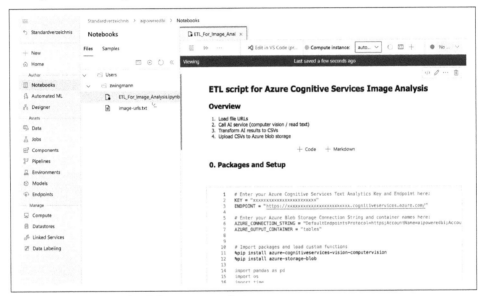

Figure 9-44. ETL notebook for image analysis

In section 0, update your Azure credentials. These are the same as those you used in the previous use case. After you enter them, run the first code cell.

In section 1, execute the code cell to import the TXT file with the image URLs. Make sure that you downloaded the file from the book's repository and placed it in the same location as the *.ipynb* file.

Section 2 calls the computer vision AI service. In contrast to the use case before, object detection is a synchronous operation, so we need only one API call per image and can reduce the wait time to three seconds after each image to stay within the 20 images per minute limit of the free tier. If you are on a paid tier, you can safely delete the line `time.sleep(3)` from the script.

Execute the code cell. While you wait for the results, this is a good time to draw your attention to some restrictions or preconditions for the object-detection AI service. These also apply, more or less, to other providers, not only Microsoft Azure. As we can read in the Azure documentation (*https://oreil.ly/dDToz*), the following limitations apply:

> It's important to note the limitations of object detection so you can avoid or mitigate the effects of false negatives (missed objects) and limited detail.

> Objects are generally not detected if they're small (less than 5% of the image).

> Objects are generally not detected if they're arranged closely together (a stack of plates, for example).

> Objects are not differentiated by brand or product names (different types of sodas on a store shelf, for example). However, you can get brand information from an image by using the Brand detection feature.

Most importantly we have to consider the first point. We basically have to make sure that the objects of interest are large enough compared to the overall picture size. If you pay close attention to the image URLs in the text file, you will note that we are not passing the raw footage to the AI service but instead cropping these images on the fly using a content delivery network (CDN). This way, we can focus on the parts of the image that actually matter to us and ensure that a potential car object covers more than 5% of the image area. So, if you see poor results with an object-detection AI service, try cropping the image or splitting it into parts.

By now, the AI service should have done its job, and you can run the following code cell to print out an example result (Figure 9-45).

```
1   # Print a sample result
2   results[0].as_dict()

✓

{'metadata': {'format': 'Jpeg', 'height': 400, 'width': 900},
 'model_version': '2021-04-01',
 'objects': [{'confidence': 0.862,
   'object_property': 'car',
   'parent': {'confidence': 0.872,
    'object_property': 'Land vehicle',
    'parent': {'confidence': 0.872, 'object_property': 'Vehicle'}},
   'rectangle': {'h': 89, 'w': 107, 'x': 521, 'y': 185}},
  {'confidence': 0.729,
   'object_property': 'car',
   'parent': {'confidence': 0.744,
    'object_property': 'Land vehicle',
    'parent': {'confidence': 0.744, 'object_property': 'Vehicle'}},
   'rectangle': {'h': 135, 'w': 122, 'x': 336, 'y': 263}}],
 'request_id': 'a0248e40-98a8-4dd0-bd4e-0d86e3f82a1e'}
```

Figure 9-45. Example output of the computer vision service for one image

As you can see, the AI service provides not only the names of the detected objects but also a little more context, such as the position of the object in the image and additional semantic information. Let's move on to section 3, data transformations, where we want to parse these results to get the count of vehicles in an image.

The approach here is rather simple. We are calling a function called count_objects(result, "Car", 0.7) that is filtering the outputs from the result according to two criteria: the object property name and the confidence score of the detection. I chose 0.7, which translates to something like "the AI service is 70% sure that the detected object is a car." Feel free to experiment with the value and find out where the sweet spot is for your use case. Run this code cell and you will see a list with the counts.

The only task left is to put this into a nice table format that also includes the original image file URL to reference back to the data source and an index that makes sorting the data easier. Execute the second code cell of section 3 and you should see output similar to Figure 9-46.

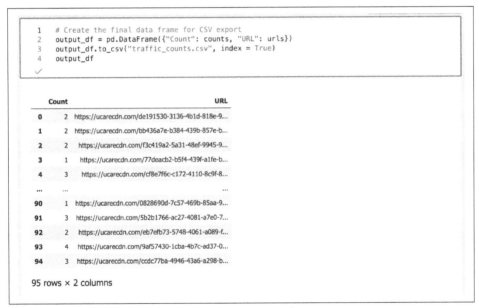

Figure 9-46. Tabular data output from the image analysis service

Finally, run the last code cell in section 4 to upload the CSV file to our Azure Blob Storage. And that's everything we had to do for our prototype ETL job. Let's move on to visualizing the results in BI!

Don't forget to stop the Azure compute resource after you finish the script to avoid any ongoing charges!

Model Inference with Power BI Walk-Through

Since we have stored the AI results in a flat CSV, any BI tool can make use of this data. I will show you again how I have done it with Power BI—and there will be a little surprise!

First, create a new Power BI file. Choose Get Data → Azure Blob Storage, provide your storage account name, and select the container called "tables." Click Transform and click the Binary link in the row where the new table name *traffic_counts.csv* is shown (see Figure 9-47). If you can't see this file, refresh the preview in Power Query.

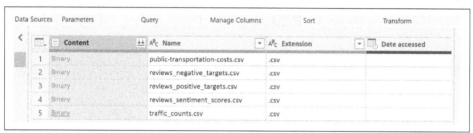

		Content		AᵇC Name	AᵇC Extension		Date accessed
1	Binary			public-transportation-costs.csv	.csv		
2	Binary			reviews_negative_targets.csv	.csv		
3	Binary			reviews_positive_targets.csv	.csv		
4	Binary			reviews_sentiment_scores.csv	.csv		
5	Binary			traffic_counts.csv	.csv		

Figure 9-47. Azure Blob Storage files listed in Power Query

In the Power Query Editor, we don't have much to do. Just give the index column a name by right-clicking the column name and choosing Rename, as shown in Figure 9-48. Rename the column to **Index**.

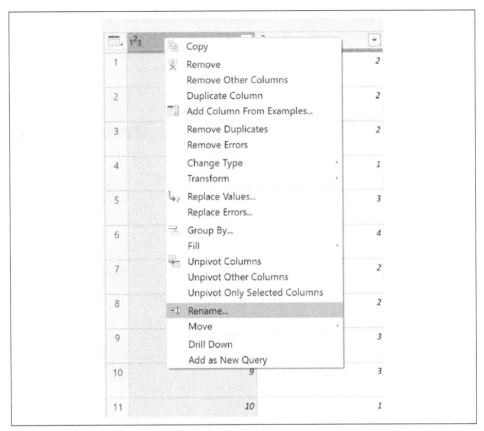

Figure 9-48. Renaming the column in Power Query

Double-check that all three columns are in the table: the index (numeric), the count (numeric), and the file URL (string). Confirm the query by clicking Close & Apply.

Before we head over to build the report, let's include one small but powerful feature that Power BI is offering for us. Click the small table icon that is located between the data model and the report icon on the left side (Figure 9-49). In this window, select the URL column and choose "Column tools" from the menu pane on the top. Find the field "Data category," which is a bit hidden in the top menu, and change the data type from text to Image URL, as shown in Figure 9-49.

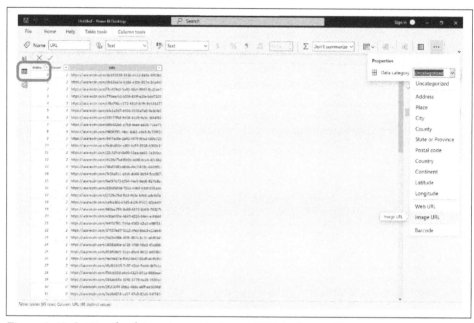

Figure 9-49. Setting the data category to Image URL in Power BI

Building the AI-Powered Dashboard in Power BI

Now, let's move on to the report page. In this example, I chose only two components: a line chart for the count over time (in our case, the index) and a table showing the count, index, and image URL. And because we have formatted the URL field as an Image URL data type, Power BI will fetch the image from this URL and show it in our dashboard. Isn't this marvelous? Take a look at Figure 9-50 to see the final dashboard in action.

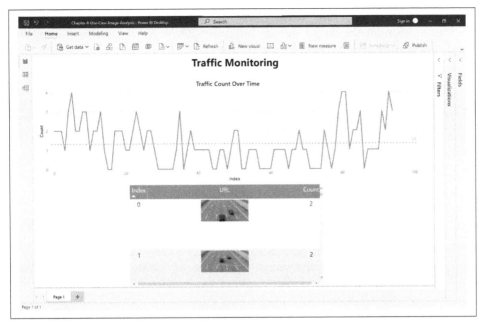

Figure 9-50. AI-powered traffic-monitoring dashboard

Of course, this table inherits the full interactivity that you expect from a Power BI visual. So when you select, for example, one point with the highest traffic count on index 80, the table will show the relevant image for this data point, as Figure 9-51 shows. This way, we can also ensure that the AI detection was correct by spotting four cars in the image.

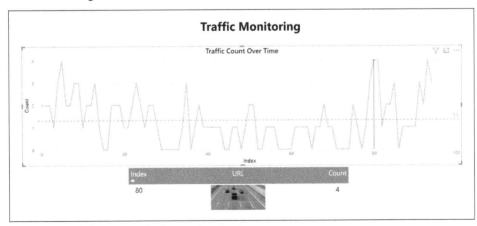

Figure 9-51. Selecting single data points in the report

Feel free to re-create this dashboard by yourself or modify it as you like. You can find the final version on the book's website (*https://oreil.ly/0uHwu*) by downloading the *Traffic-Monitoring_AI-Powered.pbix* file.

 Cleaning Up Resources

Consider stopping or deleting the following resources we have used in this chapter to avoid any ongoing charges:

- Stop the compute resource in Azure ML Studio.
- Delete the Azure Cognitive Services that you have deployed.
- Delete all files from Azure Blob Storage.

We will still need the Azure resource group for the use case in the final chapter. If you don't plan to continue, you can delete all resources at once. Select "Resource groups" in your Azure portal, select the resource group that you created, and choose "Delete resource group." Confirm the resource group name and click Delete.

Summary

This chapter has only touched the surface of what AI services can do with data sources that are not in the usual CSV or Excel format. I hope that you had fun trying out these AI services, and I wish even more that you gained more inspiration on how to use these tools for your own use cases.

This chapter concluded the building blocks of AI services that can empower your BI. In the next chapter, we will take a look at how to combine what you've learned in order to build a fully functional BI dashboard with multiple AI services at work.

## CHAPTER 10

Bringing It All Together: Building an AI-Powered Customer Analytics Dashboard

You have come a long way in this book and (hopefully!) learned a lot of new things about how AI services can be deployed at various levels of the analytics stack. In this chapter, I will show you how these layers of analytics and AI services can be combined to provide a better experience for BI users and harness the potential of AI and BI by blending the two approaches. In fact, you should see that different AI services are not an either/or decision but that they can complement each other. For example, we can turn unstructured data (raw text) into structured data (sentiment scores table) so we can use it to do supervised learning (use sentiment scores to predict customer churn).

By the end of this chapter, you will be able to mix and match multiple AI services to develop even more powerful use cases. To keep programming effort to a minimum, we will use Azure Machine Learning Designer as a no-code tool to create advanced ML workflows that allow for more customization than the AutoML service you learned about in the previous chapters.

Problem Statement

In this scenario, we are part of the data analytics team of a telecommunications provider. The head of sales and marketing of the consumer division has initiated a project to look further into the topic of customer churn. As per the business' definition, churn happens at the moment a customer cancels their contract, no matter the remaining duration of the contract (the business is offering monthly and 24-month contracts).

The business is currently facing the following challenges:

- Churn rates are measured, but marketing and sales can't yet make sense of them. The churn metrics seem to go up and down sporadically, and the staff is struggling to get any meaningful insights from these metrics.

- As an effective measure to counter churn, the business has identified counteroffers to be a viable strategy. Offers are presented to customers who are quitting their contract as a means to win them back or prevent them from quitting at all. The offers turned out to be effective, but costly. Therefore, the business wants to know which customers are most lucrative to be targeted by such counterchurn offers and would ideally like to predict churn before it happens to ensure a good fit between the offer type and the customer segments.

- The business is running regular surveys among customers that include a lot of open-text feedback. Looking at samples of the survey data, the survey team suggests that the text answers could provide important signals for churn modeling.

- The business expects a certain level of interactivity to comb through the data in order to get a feeling for what's happening with regards to customer churn in various customer segments.

The data analytics team is expected to identify viable ways to present the requested information to the business stakeholders—of course, as soon as possible and with heavy budget constraints.

Solution Overview

Take a look at the use case architecture in Figure 10-1. As you can immediately see, this will be the most complex use case we are building in this book. But don't worry, we are essentially reusing concepts and techniques that you learned in the previous chapters.

To understand what's happening in this architecture, let's start at the top with the user layer and find out what our output should actually look like. We want to have an interactive dashboard in Power BI that lets us analyze customer churn in multiple ways; we want to do the following:

- Understand where churn happened and provide a seamless experience for users to interact with historical data (descriptive analytics). We will use the Power BI Q&A visual for that purpose.

- Understand which fluctuations in recent customer churn should be flagged as "too high." We will use anomaly detection for that (diagnostic analytics).

- Predict customer churn for the future to understand what revenue is at risk in which segments (predictive analytics).

- Analyze feedback from customer reviews to inform our churn report to understand what it is that customers are complaining about (unstructured data).

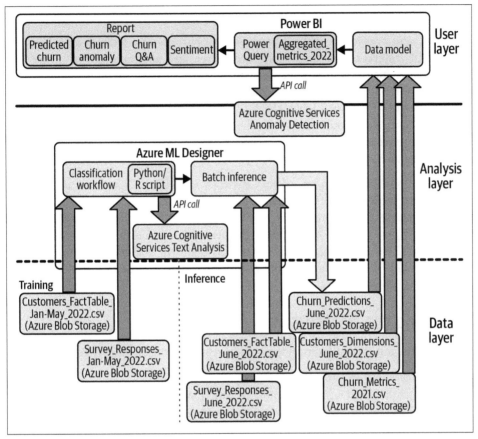

Figure 10-1. AI-powered customer analytics use case architecture

Before we look at what's happening in the analysis layer, let's jump to the bottom and examine the data layer we have for this use case. Our BI system will mainly be fed by three data sources:

- The source *Churn_Metrics_2021.csv* contains aggregated historical information about customer churn.
- The source *Churn_Predictions_June_2022.csv* contains the most recent customer data with respective churn predictions.
- The source *Customer_Dimensions_June_2022.csv* contains demographic information about our customers that we can use for further explorations or drill-downs.

This data would be typically stored in a data warehouse, but in our case we're fetching them as CSV files from Azure Blob Storage to keep things simple. While the files *Churn_Metrics_2021.csv* and *Customer_Dimensions_June_2022.csv* are given, we need to create *Churn_Predictions_June_2022.csv* by using analytics.

Now, let's head over to the analysis layer. For our purposes, we will use an ML model that will be trained on historical data (structured and unstructured) in Azure ML Designer. The historical customer fact tables we have been provided stretch over the past five months and already include a churn label calculated by our in-house analysts. Besides the churn label, the fact tables contain a flag indicating whether customers accepted a counterchurn in the past. The training data will also include sentiment information from user surveys provided as raw text in *Survey_Responses_Jan-May_2022.csv*.

To make sense of the open-ended text answers, we will run sentiment analysis on the customer feedback and see whether these sentiment labels will help us increase the performance of the predictive model. Instead of handling the workflow for this manually, we will use Azure ML Designer, which comes as part of our Azure subscription. The ML Designer is a no-code AI platform that allows us to build and deploy managed ML workflows in the Azure cloud with as little technical friction as possible.

Preparing the Datasets

Download the following files from the book's website (*https://oreil.ly/XKoQk*):

customers_factTable_Jan-May_2022.csv
Information about customer metrics and churn labels for January through May 2022

survey_responses_Jan-May_2022.csv
Customer feedback from a survey of a sample of customers conducted between January and May 2022

customers_factTable_June_2022.csv
Customer facts for the current month of June 2022

survey_responses_June_2022.csv
New survey data from June 2022

Open Microsoft Azure Machine Learning Studio (*https://ml.azure.com*), choose your preferred workspace, and you should see your dashboard (Figure 10-2).

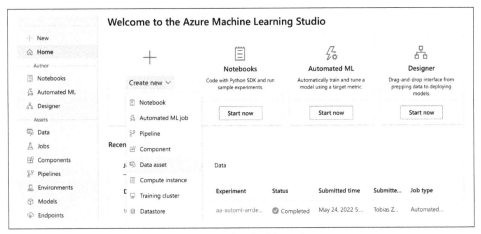

Figure 10-2. Azure Machine Learning Studio dashboard

First, we will upload all four CSV files as datasets (data assets) into Azure ML Studio, one by one, in order to be able to access them through the ML Designer later. Click the plus icon and choose "Data asset" or select "Data" from the menu on the left.

For each of the CSV files, select Create → From local files. Provide the names for the dataset as in the filename—for example, `customers_factTable_Jan-May_2022` for the file *customers_factTable_Jan-May_2022.csv*. Follow along through the form, upload the CSV files, and check the data preview if everything looks fine. The delimiter in all files should be Comma, and the encoding is UTF-8. When it comes to the schema, you have to make some adjustments.

Please make sure that the schema is as follows for the customer fact tables (Note: the columns Churn and OfferAccepted don't appear in the file from June, as this represents the most current month and the churn info isn't available yet—that's what we are going to predict in a bit.):

- customerID: String
- tenure: Integer
- Contract: String
- Monthly Charges: Decimal (dot)
- Churn: String
- Don't include: OfferAccepted
- Don't include: Month

For both survey files, make sure the columns match the following schema:

- id: String
- text: String

By the end of this, you should see the following four datasets within ML Studio:

- customers_factTable_Jan-May_2022
- survey_responses_Jan-May_2022
- customers_factTable_June_2022
- survey_responses_June_2022

Allocating a Compute Resource

Now that we have the data in place, we need to make sure that resources are available where the actual computations can happen. To add a compute resource, select Compute from the menu on the left of ML Studio, as shown in Figure 10-3.

Figure 10-3. Adding a compute resource in Azure ML Studio

Here, you should still see the compute resource that you used throughout the previous chapters. If you see the resource, but it hasn't been started yet, select the resource and click Start. If you don't have any resource yet or you deleted it previously, click New and create a new compute resource with the default settings and the cheapest machine type (STANDARD_DS1_V2) that will be sufficient for this case study. Once you have at least one compute instance up and running, you can proceed to the ML Designer.

Building the ML Workflow

Choose Designer from the menu on the left (Figure 10-4). The ML Designer will be our drag-and-drop interface to build ML pipelines. We can train our own models, but we can also do some basic data preprocessing and run custom scripts.

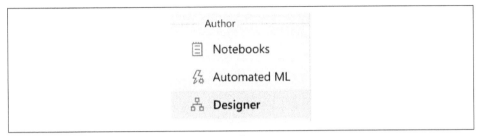

Figure 10-4. ML Designer in Azure ML Studio

Create your first pipeline by clicking "New pipeline." You should now see the empty canvas for the ML Designer (Figure 10-5). The ML Designer has three main components: the *library* on the left, where you can toggle between data assets and components; a *canvas* on the right to build your pipeline; and a *toolbar* on the top to Save, Edit, and Submit the entire pipeline.

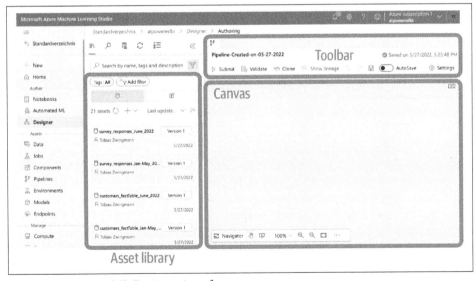

Figure 10-5. Azure ML Designer interface

Before we can start, assign the running compute instance to our session. If the settings window did not pop up automatically, you can access it by clicking the cog icon next to the pipeline name in the toolbar. Speaking of pipeline names, change the pipeline title to **Customer-Churn-Predictor** in the settings.

We can now start to populate the empty canvas. The idea is that you build a custom workflow by using the prebuilt modules on the left and combining them on the canvas. Each module can have input and output ports and provides different settings.

From the assets library select the dataset *customers_factTable_Jan-May_2022* and drag and drop it onto the canvas, as shown in Figure 10-6.

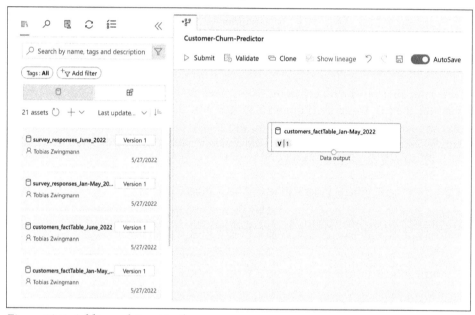

Figure 10-6. Adding a dataset to the canvas

The pipelines will be executed from top to bottom. So everything will start by loading this dataset. If you like, you can preview the data by right-clicking the module and selecting "Preview data." Previewing outputs of individual modules on the canvas is an intuitive way for debugging, especially at the beginning, when you are just familiarizing yourself with the interface.

Next, let's do something with the data. Our goal is to build a simple ML pipeline that will predict the Churn column given our input features, similar to the AutoML use case from Chapter 7.

Switch from Data assets to components in the library by clicking the respective icon. Search for **select columns in dataset**. The purpose of this module is to get rid of the columns we don't need for the predictions, such as the Customer ID. Drag the module onto the canvas below the Dataset module. Close the settings for now, if they pop up automatically. Connect the output port from the Dataset module to the Select Columns in Dataset module, as shown in Figure 10-7.

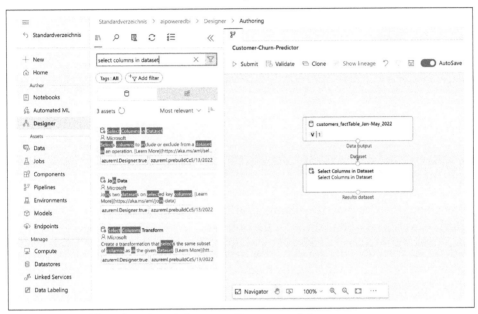

Figure 10-7. Adding the Select Columns in Dataset module

Drawing a connection between two modules allows for metadata to flow downstream in our pipeline. That means our Select Columns in Dataset module will now know the available column names. Double-click the module on the canvas to open the settings once again. Click "Edit columns" and choose to select columns "By name," as shown in Figure 10-8.

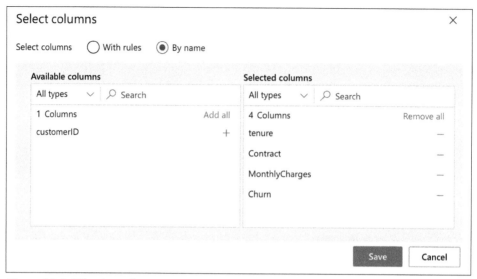

Figure 10-8. Filtering columns

Select all but the CustomerID column. Confirm by clicking Save. Close the module's settings pane to make more space for the canvas.

Next, we want to split our data into a training and a test set. Search for **Split Data** in the modules search bar and drag the module onto the canvas. In the module settings, define the following split parameters:

- Splitting mode: Split Rows
- Fractions of rows in the first output: 0.75
- Randomized split: True
- Random seed: 1234 (for reproducibility)
- Stratified split: True
- Stratification key columns: Churn

With these settings, we are doing a stratified train-test split, with 75% of the data for training and 25% for testing. *Stratified* means that the class distribution for the Churn label will be the same for both the training and test sets.

Close the settings and connect the output port of the Select Columns in Dataset module to the input port of the Split Data module. As you can see in Figure 10-9, the Split Data module has two outputs now, one for the training (left) and one for the test dataset (right).

Figure 10-9. Adding a Split Data component

We can now add the Train Model component. Search for it in the module pane and drag it onto the canvas. You will realize that this module has two inputs: the left one expects the training algorithm, and the right one expects the training dataset. Connect the left output node of the Split Data module to the right input port of the Train Model module. We still need to tell the Train Model component which column we actually want to predict. So double-click the component to open the settings and provide Churn as the Label column.

Now it's up to us to provide the actual training algorithm. In contrast to AutoML, we have to choose the training algorithm ourselves. Now, this isn't a Machine Learning Fundamentals book, but in most supervised learning scenarios, you will achieve pretty good results by choosing an ensemble method such as decision forest or boosted trees as a first baseline. These models try to combine several weak learners such as decision trees to a strong learning algorithm that tries to minimize the prediction error on your training dataset. These models work for both classification and regression problems, so they are good all-round algorithms, although they are rather complex. The good thing about the ML Designer is that you can easily try out different, even simpler algorithms such as linear or logistic regression, and see how they perform on your dataset.

For our exercise, search for **Two-Class Boosted Decision Tree** from the module pane and drag it over to the canvas. We can leave all its settings to the defaults for now. Connect the Decision Tree module to the Train Model component, and your pipeline should look like Figure 10-10.

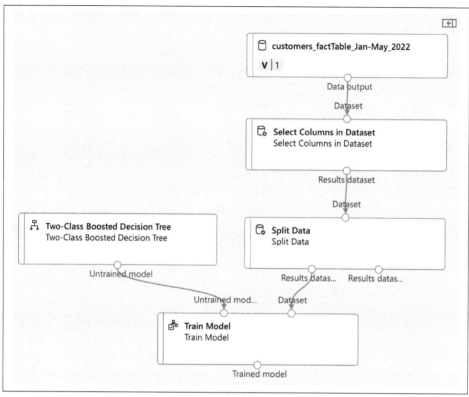

Figure 10-10. Adding the Decision Tree and Train Model components

We're almost there! Only one thing is missing, and that is adding a component that scores actual predictions based on the trained model and calculates evaluation metrics for it.

Search for the **Score Model** component and drag it over to the canvas. Connect the output port from the Train Model component to the left input port of the Score Model component.

Then connect the right output port from the Split Data component to the right input port of the Score Model component. This will allow us to calculate predictions for the test dataset by using our model trained on the training dataset. Finally, find the Evaluate Model module, pull it over to the canvas, and connect the Score Model output port to the left input port of the Evaluate Model component. Your final pipeline should now look similar to Figure 10-11.

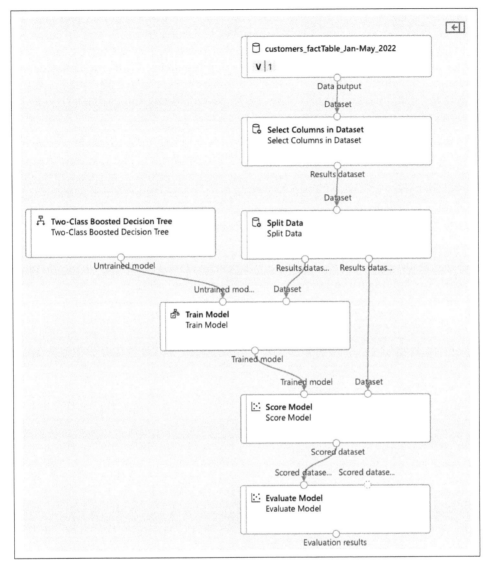

Figure 10-11. First end-to-end workflow in ML Designer

Congratulations! You have just built your first ML pipeline from scratch. Click the Submit button to run the pipeline. All runs will be gathered in *experiments*, as we are used to from the AutoML scenario. I suggest creating a new experiment for this pipeline so you keep your work organized. Create a new experiment and provide a telling name such as **customer-churn-prediction-training**. Click Submit and lean back while Azure ML Studio does its magic behind the scenes.

To follow along with the training click "Job detail" under "Submitted jobs" on the left part of the screen. Here, the ML Designer will indicate which step is currently running and which step is completed. Note that you have just left the Designer and switched to the Jobs section, as you can see from the menu. While the Designer lets you create the pipelines, Jobs will allow you to monitor the actual pipeline execution and trigger the final deployment. The whole job should take approximately 10 to 15 minutes.

The reason this is taking so long is that Azure is spinning up separate processes for each module, which creates some overhead. The advantage is that this interface will also work well for really large datasets because each module runs independently from the other. That is why running the ML Designer for some rather small datasets as in our case will actually take longer compared to running them on your local notebook. But the larger the dataset gets, the more performance advantages you will see.

When the process has finished, you should see the Completed badge on the last Evaluate Model module. In this case, double-click the module to view the Evaluation results. This should give you the outputs shown in Figure 10-12.

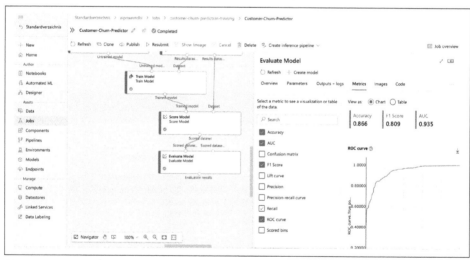

Figure 10-12. Evaluation metrics for first workflow

Click the Enlarge icon to make more space, and the whole interface should look familiar, like what you've seen in previous chapters. With our initial run, we have reached an Accuracy of 86.6% and an F1-score of 80.9%. That's not bad for a first try, but let's see if we can improve this metric even more by blending our training dataset with more data.

So far, what we have done is just another unsupervised ML workflow that we could have easily done with the AutoML service from Chapter 7. In fact, if this was it, I would recommend using the AutoML service instead of Azure ML Studio. However, we are not done yet, as we still want to insert insights from unstructured data (sentiment scores) and incorporate them into our final model. This workflow would not be possible with the AutoML service alone, so we choose ML Studio for this task.

Adding Sentiment Data to the Workflow

Close the evaluation metrics and go back to the Designer. This time, we want to add the analysis of the customer feedback and see if that helps to improve our customer churn predictions. The way we approach this is that we build a second pipeline next to the one we already have and feed the results into the right input port of the Evaluate Model module. This will give us a direct comparison of both modeling approaches.

Let's tackle this step by step. First, drag and drop the Dataset module for *customers_factTable_Jan-May_2022* from the module pane on the left to the canvas. In addition, locate the Dataset module for *survey_responses_Jan-May_2022* and drag it next to the other two Dataset modules. Your canvas should now look like Figure 10-13.

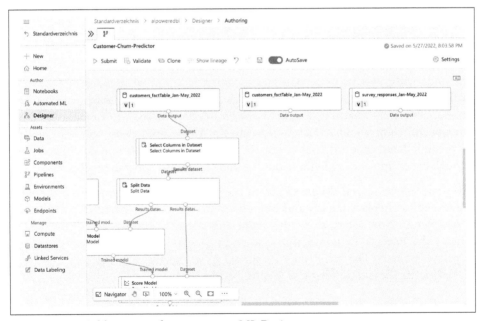

Figure 10-13. Adding more data sources to ML Designer

To get more familiar with the survey data, right-click the module and select "Preview data." The dataset contains only two columns, the customer ID and the text response, both values that came from the original customer survey results.

So far, our ML model can't handle the raw text inputs very well as predictive features. To make them more accessible, we will read the open-ended text answers from the survey dataset, send them to Azure Cognitive Services, and get the sentiment value for each text. The classification "negative" or "positive" will then become an additional feature for our classification model. For this purpose, we will use the Azure Cognitive Services for Sentiment Analysis, which we deployed in Chapter 9.

Let's bring this AI service component to the canvas! Believe it or not, Azure Cognitive Services has no prebuilt module that you can just drag onto the canvas in the ML Designer (at least not at the time of this writing). But what we can do is simply add a module that runs Python or R code for us. And that is just the approach we are going to take: we will take the responses from the survey, send them to a remote AI service API using Python or R, and feed the results back into the ML Designer pipeline.

To start, search for **Execute Python Script** or **Execute R Script**, depending on your preference. Drag it over to the canvas. Connect the output port of the *survey_responses* dataset to the first input port of the script module.

The way the script module works is that it expects up to two dataframes (tables) that can be then modified within a function called `azureml_main`. The result will again be returned as one or two dataframes.

The underlying Python or R runtimes come with a limited number of packages. To find out more about them, check the Microsoft documents "Run Python Code in Azure Machine Learning Designer" (*https://oreil.ly/ksZi8*) or "Execute R Script Component" (*https://oreil.ly/YdexI*), respectively. All we need to do now is to replace the prebuilt demo code with our custom code for the task we want to do. I'll walk you through the example using Python, but the same steps also apply to the R script.

Open *ml-designer.py* (*ml-designer.R*) from the book's website (*https://oreil.ly/XKoQk*) in a text editor. Replace the key and endpoint with your custom parameters, as shown in Chapter 9. Now select all of the script and copy it. Replace all of the sample code of the Execute Python Script module in the ML Designer with the contents of your clipboard. The script module should now contain only the code from the *ml-designer.py* file and nothing else (Figure 10-14).

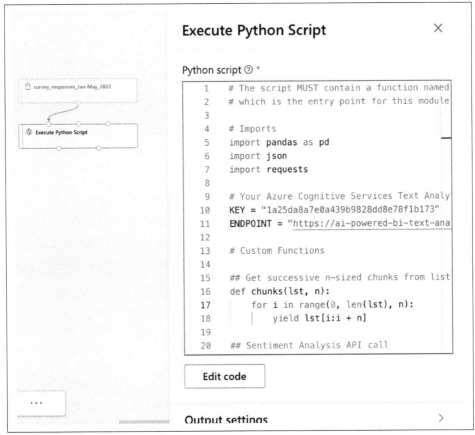

```
                    Execute Python Script                          ✕

                    Python script ⦾ *
                       1     # The script MUST contain a function named
                       2     # which is the entry point for this module
                       3
                       4     # Imports
                       5     import pandas as pd
                       6     import json
                       7     import requests
                       8
                       9     # Your Azure Cognitive Services Text Analy
                      10     KEY = "1a25da8a7e0a439b9828dd8e78f1b173"
                      11     ENDPOINT = "https://ai-powered-bi-text-ana
                      12
                      13     # Custom Functions
                      14
                      15     ## Get successive n-sized chunks from list
                      16     def chunks(lst, n):
                      17         for i in range(0, len(lst), n):
                      18             yield lst[i:i + n]
                      19
                      20     ## Sentiment Analysis API call

                      Edit code

                    Output settings                                  ❯
```

Figure 10-14. Python scripting module in Azure ML Designer

The code will basically read the dataframe as input and shape it to a format that the API service can handle. It will return the original dataframe with the sentiment predictions attached. Now, click Submit to run the new graph. Go to Jobs and verify that everything is running as expected.

Note that all steps we ran previously on the left side of the graph will not be re-executed since we didn't change anything here. Instead, this run will only read in the new dataset and feed it into the script module. After some minutes, you should see that the script was executed successfully. If an error comes up, click the script module and take a look at the log files. The error message there will help you to debug, for example, if your resource key is not valid or your free quota has been exceeded.

When the run has been completed, right-click the script module in the submitted training job and choose Preview data → Result dataset. As shown in Figure 10-15, you should see that each customer feedback entry has now gotten a sentiment label.

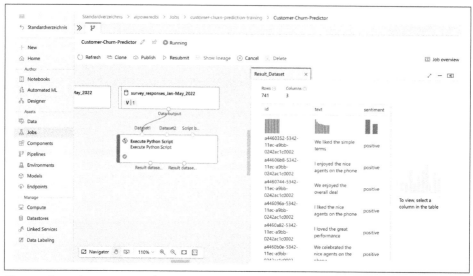

Figure 10-15. Sentiment analysis results in Azure ML Designer

Our goal is to add this information to our main dataset that is used for training the churn model. We need to join this table to the main table without losing any records in the main table; remember that this survey wasn't done for all customers, but only for a sample. This joining of data is called a *left outer join*; the left table is our main dataset, and the right table is the dataset from where we want to join additional information. Go back to the Designer and find the corresponding component by searching for `Join Data` in the asset library.

Drag the Join Data module to the canvas. Connect the first output port of the previous scripting module to the right input port of the Join Data module. Then connect the output port of *customers_factTable_Jan-May_2022* (the one we didn't use yet) to the left input port of the Join Data module. Double-click the Join Data module on the canvas to bring up its settings. We have to define the key columns on which both datasets will be merged. You can edit the key columns by clicking "Edit column" for both the left and the right dataset. For the left dataset, choose the column customerID, and for the right dataset the column "id." Set the join type to Left Outer Join and set "Keep right key columns in joined table" to False. Your settings should ultimately look like those in Figure 10-16.

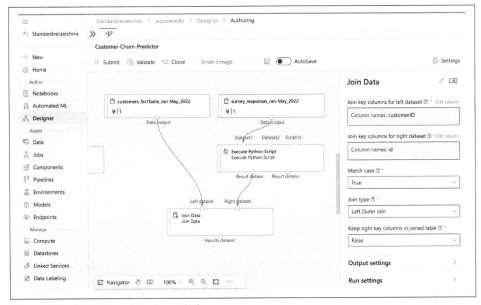

Figure 10-16. Joining data from different sources

Run the pipeline by clicking Submit to verify that the join works as expected. Your merged dataset should have seven columns and 3,814 rows, which you can verify by right-clicking the Join Data module and choosing Preview data → Results dataset after the run has been completed.

We now pretty much have to re-create the rest of the pipeline as we did previously. I won't go through these steps in detail, as these are repetitive. In brief, add the following modules and apply these settings:

Select Columns in Dataset
Select columns by rules: include all listed columns except "customerID," include column name "sentiment," and exclude column name "text."

Split Data
Same as before, 0.75 stratified sample on the column Churn.

Train Model
The Label column is Churn.

Two-Class Boosted Decision Tree
Leave the default settings.

Score Model
Connect the last output port from the Score Model component to the right input port of the Evaluate Model component we created before.

The final pipeline is shown in Figure 10-17.

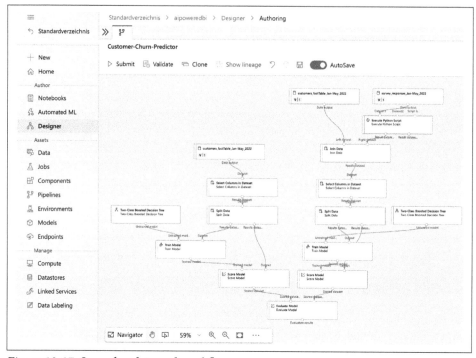

Figure 10-17. Second end-to-end workflow

Click Submit to run the whole graph. If you think that it's time for another coffee, you're right! The whole process might take a couple of minutes. Check back when the process has been completed.

When the run has completed, let's check our evaluation module to see if the model performance could be improved. Go to Jobs and select your completed training job. Right-click the Evaluate Model module and choose Preview Data → Evaluation Results. Figure 10-18 shows the output.

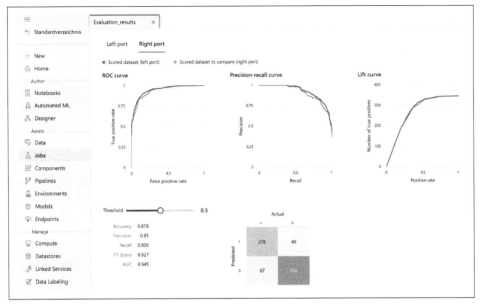

Figure 10-18. Evaluation metrics of second workflow

From the evaluation metrics, we can see that the accuracy has improved by another percentage point, to 87.7%, and the F1 score has increased to 82.6%. While not groundbreaking, this is still a solid performance improvement considering that the sentiment label was provided for only a fraction of the data. This means that the sentiment information itself has very high predictive power for our use case. So it's good to keep this information in our dataset and use it whenever possible.

If we wanted to increase the accuracy even more, we could try training on more data (rows), use a different algorithm, or try more features (columns) to get better results. There's no general rule for what accuracy value is sufficient, as it depends on your use case. But in general, having an existing baseline (as in Chapter 7) gives you a good benchmark, as your ML model should be able to significantly outperform that baseline. Otherwise, it wouldn't be worth all the extra effort.

Now, our model training is complete. Congratulations! You have just combined an out-of-the-box AI service with an advanced ML algorithm to craft a powerful custom AI model yourself! It's now time to put the model to work and make it ready for inference.

Before we proceed, let's tidy up our graph by selecting all parts on the left and deleting them. In the Designer, open your workflow and click Clone from the top menu bar to create a copy of the graph.

To select multiple modules, choose the selection tool from the toolbar and select all components on the left side of the graph, as shown in Figure 10-19. Right-click on the selection and choose Delete.

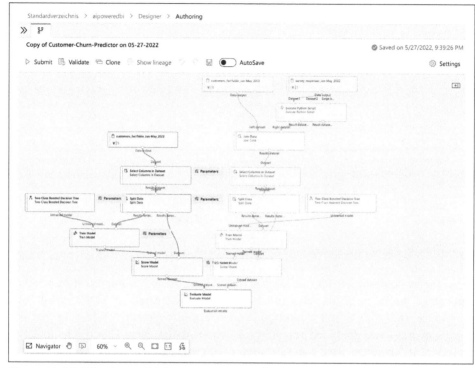

Figure 10-19. Selecting multiple components on the canvas

Finally, reconnect the Score Model module to the first input port of the Evaluate Model module by selecting the existing connection between both, deleting it, and redrawing to the first input port. Submit the training pipeline for a last time; this will be quick since it will recalculate only the results for the last module.

Deploying the Workflow for Inference

We can deploy this graph now as an inference pipeline. All we need to do is go to Jobs, open the latest experiment, and select "Create inference pipeline" from the top menu and then choose "Batch inference pipeline" (Figure 10-20).

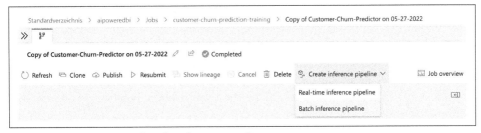

Figure 10-20. Creating a batch inference pipeline

The main difference between online and batch inference pipelines in this case is that the batch pipeline takes a blob dataset as input, whereas the online pipeline takes data submitted through an online API.

In any case, the training pipeline will be converted to an inference pipeline, which I renamed to "Customer-Churn-Predictor Batch Inference," as shown in Figure 10-21.

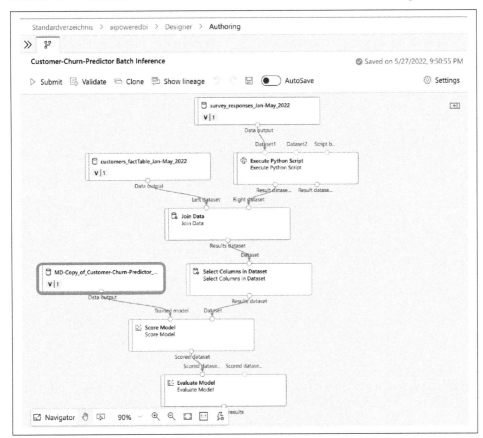

Figure 10-21. Batch inference pipeline (raw)

The main difference between the training and the inference pipeline is that the inference pipeline does not contain any training components. Note that the Boosted Decision Tree model and the Train Model modules have been replaced by a new module called MD-Customer-Churn-Predictor-Train_Model_Trained_model, as highlighted in Figure 10-21. This module will automatically reference our trained model so we can use it for inference. The rest of the data preparation pipeline, including our Python script, will remain the same.

To run inference for new data, replace the input datasets with *customers_factTable_June_2022* and *survey_responses_June_2022*, respectively. These two datasets represent new data from customers; we don't know yet if they are going to churn. To replace the datasets, simply delete the existing datasets from the canvas and pull the new datasets over from the asset library. Your canvas should look like Figure 10-22.

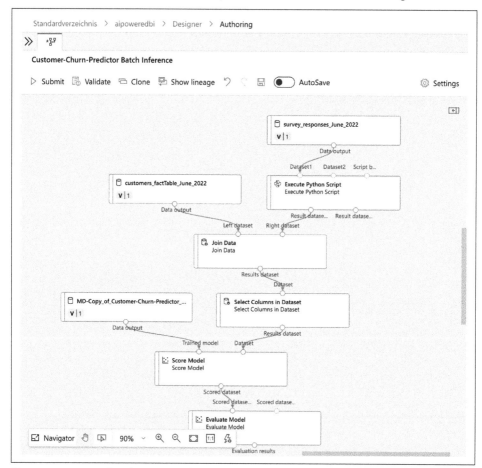

Figure 10-22. Batch inference pipeline (new data)

Before we can run the inference, we still need to make some small adjustments. Locate the module Select Columns in Dataset on the canvas. It still contains the column Churn we used for training. We don't have this column during inference (that's the one we want to predict!). So edit the settings and delete the Churn column from the module. Also, keep the column customerID, because we will need this later to match the churn predictions to the customer records. Double-check that the column sentiment is still included.

If you jump to the end of our pipeline, you will still see the Evaluate Model module as the last component here. However, we don't need this component at this stage, because we don't have any ground truth to compare to. Instead, we want to export the scored data to a location. To do this, delete the Evaluate Model component from the canvas and drag the Export Data component from the asset library to the canvas.

In the Export Data module settings, select Azure Blob Storage as the datastore type. For the Datastore, click New Datastore and give it a name such as **churn_model_scoring**. For the storage account, choose the storage account that you used in previous chapters and select "tables" under "Blob container." Your settings should look similar to Figure 10-23.

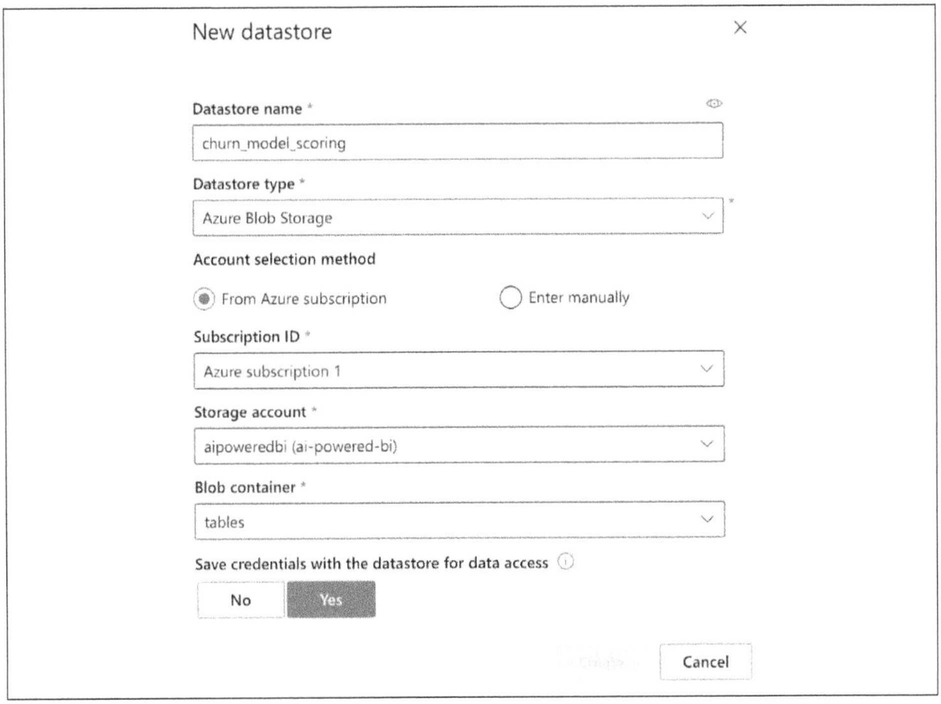

Figure 10-23. Creating a new datastore

Scroll down and paste your Account Key from the Azure Storage Account resource to the respective field in this settings window. Click Create and you should find yourself back in the Export Data settings. Double-check that your newly created datastore has been selected and assign your output file the name **churn_predic tions_June_2022.csv** in the Path field. Finally, set the file format to CSV. Figure 10-24 shows an example of the export settings.

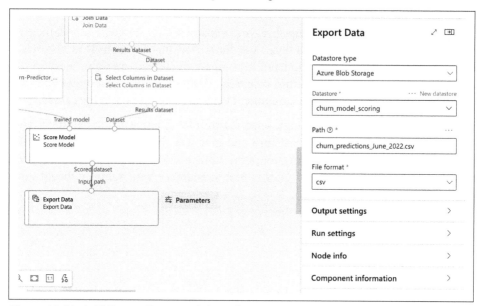

Figure 10-24. Add Export Data module and settings

Lastly, connect the Score Model module to the Export Data module. The final pipeline is shown in Figure 10-25.

Now, click Submit to run your inference pipeline. To keep things organized, create a new experiment such as **customer-churn-inference** that separates your inference runs from your training runs. The inference run will take a couple of minutes. Again, we're doing this on relatively small data samples here, but the process itself does scale pretty well to very large datasets without scaling proportionally in time.

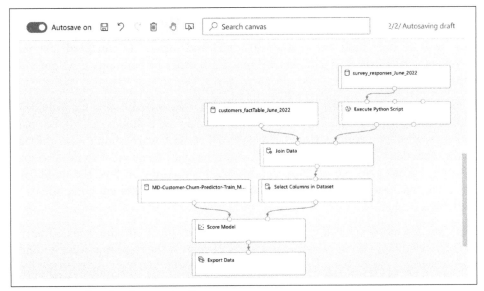

Figure 10-25. Final inference pipeline

Once the inference run has been completed, you should see the new file *churn_predictions_June_2022.csv* in your *tables* folder in your storage container (Figure 10-26).

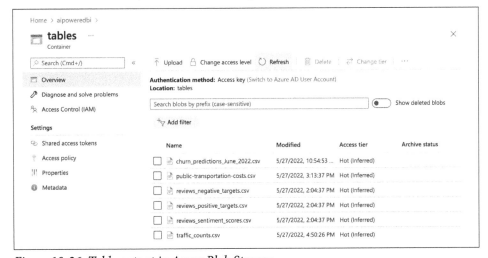

Figure 10-26. Table output in Azure Blob Storage

Time to head over to our BI!

Building the AI-Powered Dashboard in Power BI

Now that we have built our predictive model and turned unstructured text into easy-to-analyze categorical data, let's bring it all together by building an AI-powered customer dashboard.

Remember, our goal was to build a dashboard for marketing and sales that provides a high-level overview of how customer churn is developing, if things are "still normal," and how effective counteractions were taken. The dashboard should also provide further functionality to dive deeper for custom insights. In contrast to the previous chapters, I won't give you detailed step-by-step instructions on how the dashboard was built, but instead focus on the main concepts and the different components at work here.

You can download *Customer_Analytics_AI-Powered.pbix* from the book's website (*https://oreil.ly/XKoQk*) or re-create it yourself. I've used the steps that were outlined previously.

 For a step-by-step video tutorial on how to build the dashboard, visit *https://www.aipoweredbi.com/chapter-10*.

To build our customer dashboard, we will need the data model in Figure 10-27, which is based on the following four tables:

churn_predictions_June_2022
> This table includes the scored churn dataset that we got from the ML Designer.

customer_dimensions_June_2022
> This table contains further BI data for customers such as tenure, services, and demographic information. It has a one-to-one relationship to the table churn_predictions_June_2022 based on the field customer ID.

Churn_Metrics_2021
> A table that includes aggregated churn rates and offers acceptance rates per month from previous months. This data could come from a SQL data warehouse; in our case, it's provided as a CSV file on Azure Blob Storage.

Aggregated_metrics_2022

This table is generated by Power BI by taking the dataset churn_metrics_2021 and adding the predicted churn rate for June 2022. It will take this time series and send it to Azure Anomaly Detection to infer the expected lower and upper bounds for the metrics and set a flag for anomalies found.

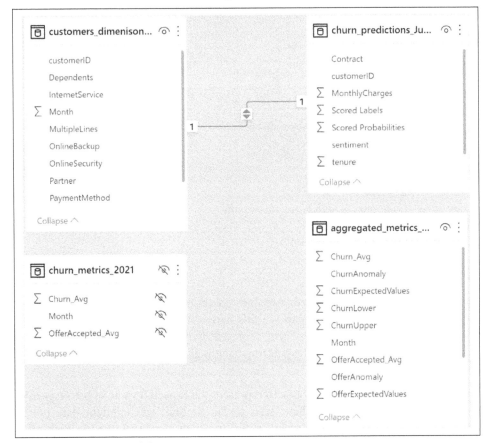

Figure 10-27. Data model in Power BI

With this data, we can generate a dashboard that looks like Figure 10-28.

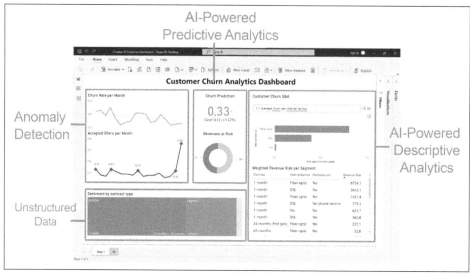

Figure 10-28. Components of the final dashboard

Let's unpack the various components.

Anomaly Detection

At the top left of the dashboard, two line charts show the churn rate and offer acceptance rate by month. You can see this part of the dashboard in Figure 10-29. While the line charts themselves "just" represent basic descriptive analytics ("What happened?"), we are enriching the chart by blending two more pieces of information here.

First, we are showing a light gray line to represent the expected value of the respective metrics based on the data we have seen so far. Second, we highlight data points that show an abnormal positive spike (either too high churn rate or too high offer acceptance rate). These anomalies are depicted by square data markers. With this additional information, we can see that the overall churn trend seems to be negative (which is good!), and at the same time we did not really observe any clear outlier, although the line seems to be rather wriggly. For the offers, we can clearly observe that the high spike in the last month was detected as an anomaly, but so were some data points before. The overall trend therefore seems to be rather steady, except for some outliers. All this information came from the anomaly detection AI service that we were calling with an R or Python script directly from Power BI.

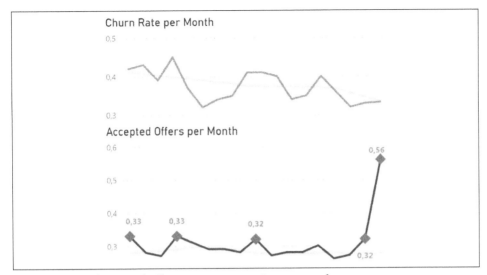

Figure 10-29. Churn and offer acceptance metrics per month

Predictive Analytics

The predictive analytics section of the dashboard combines historical information with the AI predictions. Figure 10-30 shows this visual. This includes the predicted customer churn rate for the current month, as well as a translation to what this means to revenues at risk. The predicted customer churn rate for the current month is a KPI that we are calculating as a summary metric based on the individual AI predictions we have seen from the model we used in the ML Designer. We can compare this metric to a goal, which in this case is defined as a churn rate of 0.33—a criteria that is probably met in the current month.

To make this information more accessible for business users, we are blending this metric with a donut chart called "Revenue at risk," which sums up all the revenues of the current month from customers marked with a `churn flag = 1`. Note that this metric is rather simplistic, as it does not account for customer lifetime values. We could add this information if we wanted, but for the sake of this demo, I decided to stick to the basics. The core idea here is that we can blend AI predictions with historical or transactional BI data to make the predictions more relevant for the business. We will see another, more detailed example of this in the next component.

Figure 10-30. Churn prediction KPI metric

AI-Powered Descriptive Analytics

In the AI-powered descriptive analytics part of the dashboard, the AI at work is the most seamless, yet possibly the most intuitive for users. The AI-powered descriptive part of this analysis consists of two charts, shown in Figure 10-31. The upper part is a Q&A tool, and the lower part is a table visual.

Let's explore the Q&A tool first. This tool combines churn scores with BI data to allow queries such as, "What's the average predicted churn rate in segment *xyz*?" This visual can be used to run natural language queries against our data models. Thanks to the relationship between the predicted churn outcomes and the dimensional BI data from the warehouse, the user can seamlessly blend AI-powered predictions with additional properties about the customers. As shown in the example, the user can query the "Average churn per internet service" and see that the churn rate for fiber optics is much higher than in the other internet service categories. The only settings we needed to make for this is to define synonyms in the Q&A tool so that "average churn" can be matched to the data field "scored labels," as it is called originally in the source data table.

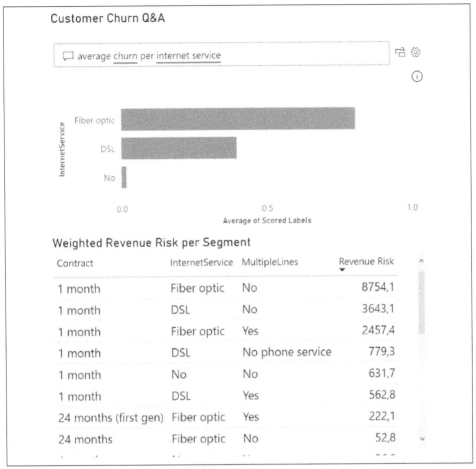

Figure 10-31. Descriptive analytics component

The lower part of the descriptive analytics component is a table that leverages a combination of historic BI data and AI predictions. The user can calculate revenue at risk by combining churn prediction with current revenues. To do this, the table uses a new field called Revenue Risk, which was generated in Power BI as a quick measure that multiplies a customer's monthly revenue with their individual churn probabilities. If we now sum that up over various customer categories, we can easily spot the customer segments where most money is going to be lost, making the aggregate churn number even more actionable for sales and marketing. If we look at Figure 10-31, we can clearly see that the segment of customers who are on a monthly contract with fiber optics internet service and without multiple lines provide the biggest leverage to defend revenue, with a revenue risk of $8,754 per month. If marketing was to think about personalized counterchurn offer incentives, this should be an interesting category to look further into.

Unstructured Data

And lastly, the unstructured data area of the dashboard provides more insights on the sentiment scores in combination with dimensional data. The sentiment analysis of the unstructured data eventually became part of our churn prediction model, but it can also stand on its own to provide further insights.

The treemap visual, shown in Figure 10-32, contrasts the sentiment labels to any customer dimension we want—in this case, the contract type. From this visual, we can see that while most customers are actually happy with regards to the sentiment of their survey comments, the majority of all customers who provided negative feedback were on a monthly plan. Considering the high churn likelihood of customers in this category, it should be the first priority to look into this category about what's fundamentally going wrong here.

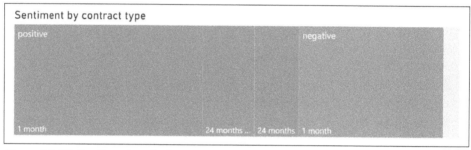

Figure 10-32. Sentiment analysis

If we pull everything together and look at the dashboard itself (Figure 10-33), we can provide the marketing and sales staff with a customer-centric dashboard that uses AI under the hood not to show off, but with one goal in mind: to make data more actionable and more meaningful to business stakeholders.

Try it out yourself, by opening the accompanying Power BI file on your computer and playing around with the components therein. Which information would you add, change, or delete altogether?

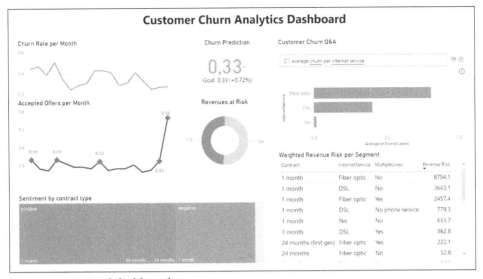

Figure 10-33. Final dashboard

Cleaning Up Resources

When you're done with the use cases in this book, I recommend deleting all resources used to avoid ongoing costs on Microsoft Azure. To delete all resources at once, visit the Azure portal (*http://portal.azure.com*) and select "Resource groups." Select the resource group that you created for this book and choose "Delete resource group." Confirm the resource group name and then click Delete.

Summary

I hope that this chapter has shown you that using AI services in your BI isn't an either/or decision. In fact, the biggest benefits come from combining multiple AI services. However, don't let the technology pull you down a rabbit hole, where the BI functionality is overloaded with AI components at work. Remember that each AI service that you add also adds another layer of technical debt: someone has to eventually take care of the models, the Q&A tools, the data integration, and so on.

Pulling various AI services together, however, is a great way of validating that the business benefits from further insights or of carving out what it is exactly that the business is looking for. With your flexible analytics stack ranging all the way from accessing unstructured data, to descriptive analytics, up to prescriptive analytics, from within the same platform, you're in a great position to find the sweet spots between adding technical complexity and delivering actual business value.

Congratulations, you've successfully built your first prototype, which contains no fewer than four AI services! But what's next? As mentioned, it is a prototype, and it still has a good way to go before we could ship this dashboard to a production environment. In the next chapter, you will learn more about what it takes to move from prototype to production and how to tackle the complexities that come with it.

## CHAPTER 11

Taking the Next Steps: From Prototype to Production

If you have made it this far and have followed along with the examples and case studies, you should have acquired a solid knowledge of the main AI/ML techniques and their application in the context of various BI scenarios. Congratulations! This is truly a great achievement and puts you in a great position to successfully launch your own AI use case.

In this chapter, we will finally discuss some of the key points of bringing a prototype solution (that's what we did so far) to production. Conversely, we'll also discuss why moving a prototype to production might not actually be a good idea. To resolve this apparent contradiction, we need to look at two concepts, originally borrowed from product management: product discovery and delivery.

By the end of this chapter, you should have an intuition about the next steps you should take if your goal is to roll out your AI-powered solution across your organization.

Discovery Versus Delivery

The practical use cases we have discussed so far have been prototypes. You've done what product managers call a *discovery process*. Discovery is about validating value, usability, feasibility, or viability of a product (or a use case).

It's worth noting that most prototypes are unlikely to survive the discovery phase. That's the nature of the game: you want to learn fast and fail fast. That's fine. By now, you shouldn't have too many resources invested and, ideally, you have other ideas in your backlog to pursue.

But what happens if your prototype survives the validation phase? What happens if it takes off?

Let's say your early BI test users love the new feature or the model predictions. Everybody gets excited about your new solution, and some people may even spread the word about it in the company. How do you scale your prototype for production?

The simple answer is: you don't scale it at all. In our prototyping example, we did everything ourselves: we created the virtual machine for computation jobs, we managed the access key for storage, and we even set the security policy for our containers. You may have guessed it: this is not what you should do in a production scenario. The Azure cloud platform (and all other platforms) may look super intuitive and easy to use after some training. But in reality, they are super complex landscapes that require expert knowledge to manage and control securely and effectively. Otherwise, you risk a data breach or a skyrocketing resource bill, or both.

If a prototype turns out to be successful and passes the tests for impact and feasibility, it's time to let go of it and move on to a different stage: delivery. In enterprise organizations, delivery is about much more than just creating a "clean" version of your code and dashboard. When you proceed to delivery, you should prioritize the following aspects:

- Scalability
- Reliability
- Performance
- Maintainability

In addition, prototypes usually have multiple security vulnerabilities because they are not properly tested at this stage of development. Therefore, you should not immediately move a prototype into production, but rethink across these dimensions. Let's unpack these concepts briefly.

Scalability refers to both the technical and nontechnical challenges of making your solution available to more users. Technically, it's about the upper bounds of how many users can access the solution simultaneously, which is limited by your infrastructure. In nontechnical terms, you want to figure out how processes can hinder the deployment of an application. For example, if you'd manually set up the dashboard for each user, the maximum size of your solution would be limited by the number of people you can assign to it. If you deploy the dashboards automatically or use a dedicated BI server, you can run your solution at a much larger scale.

Reliability simply means that your solution does what it is expected to do. When a failure occurs, can it be fixed easily and with little or no downtime? Sooner or later, you will need to respond to user inquiries and often provide online help. How quickly can these problems be fixed?

Performance refers to the speed at which your application responds to user requests. As the number of users increases, this becomes an important factor. First impressions are crucial, and slow-loading applications or sluggish interactions can hinder growth. After all, you want users to be able to complete their tasks as quickly as possible without experiencing delays.

Maintainability is about how easy it is to make changes after the solution is up and running. Can features be added or changed without requiring a programmer? Is your code properly documented so that no unexpected errors occur when a new user works on it?

Your production application should have scalability, reliability, performance, and maintainability baked in from the start. The actual priorities depend on the needs of your business. If you want to provide your solution to many users, scalability is important. On the other hand, if an enterprise application is designed for only a certain number of users, it's OK to deprioritize the scalability goal and document this constraint in your delivery project.

Either way, in most cases, your prototyping stack doesn't meet these delivery principles because you've sacrificed them for speed and developer convenience. That's why you shouldn't try to scale a prototype but should rebuild it properly, step by step.

Success Criteria for AI Product Delivery

So how do you achieve a successful transition from the discovery to the delivery phase? To develop a successful enterprise AI product in the context of BI, you need to consider five dimensions: people, processes, data, technology, and MLOps, as shown in Figure 11-1.

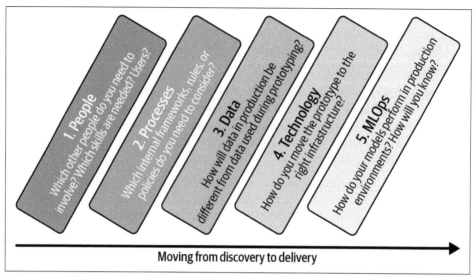

Moving from discovery to delivery

1. People
Which other people do you need to involve? Which skills are needed? Users?

2. Processes
Which internal frameworks, rules, or policies do you need to consider?

3. Data
How will data in production be different from data used during prototyping?

4. Technology
How do you move the prototype to the right infrastructure?

5. MLOps
How do your models perform in production environments? How will you know?

Figure 11-1. Success criteria for AI product delivery in the context of BI

Let's go through the five dimensions in more detail.

People

People determine the success or failure of your AI product. During the discovery phase, your team probably did not exceed the two-pizza rule, which states that all people on the project team could be satiated by two large pizzas. That's usually a maximum of 10 people.

Once you aim for delivery in enterprise scenarios, this will change. Enterprise AI projects are essentially enterprise software projects. Instead of two pizzas, you'd likely need to order a big buffet, because all sorts of people might be involved in a new software development project. These may include, to name only a few:

- IT security
- IT application management
- IT infrastructure management
- Data governance office
- Business leaders of various other departments
- Documentation person
- Works council
- Lawyers

Consult your IT department or outside experts as needed when expanding your AI efforts. You'll need a lot of support, especially in the beginning, to avoid serious mistakes. Remember that, at this stage, your prototype has proven actual results, and you should feel confident talking about it with others.

The various functions you need to include depend heavily on the way your company is organized and its size. These people often go hand in hand with the process frameworks you need to follow. While I can't give you a comprehensive list of the people you should talk to, I have generally found it useful to organize stakeholders into a matrix that maps people along two broad dimensions: power over the project and their interest in the work, as shown in Figure 11-2.

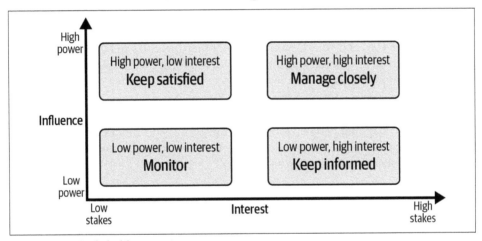

Figure 11-2. Stakeholder matrix

The goal is to identify stakeholders in each category to determine the right strategies for communicating with them. These four stakeholder categories call for four communication strategies: manage closely, keep satisfied, keep informed, and monitor:

Manage closely
    This category includes people with a lot of power and high interest in your project. These are your most important stakeholders. You need to talk to them a lot, identify concerns early, and engage to keep them on the same page and manage their expectations.

    Examples: sponsors, top management, directors, project/product managers

Keep satisfied
    These are people with a lot of power but little interest in your project. They are often under the radar, but important because they have the power to

decide whether the project should continue, depending on current outcomes or progress.

Examples: program management, financial planning

Keep informed

People with a lot of interest but little power in your project need to be kept informed on a regular basis. These are usually people who will ultimately use what is being built. Even if their formal power is small, you should communicate with them frequently. They are so involved that they are likely to influence other (more powerful) stakeholders.

Examples: end users, clients

Monitor

People with little power and interest in your project. These people may not be a priority for you, and you do not want to bother them too much. However, they still need to be monitored and informed sporadically, even if they are unlikely to cause major problems.

Examples: employees from other departments

Once you start mapping people along these categories, you should get a feeling for the complexity of your project and determine the right strategies for communicating with them as your initiative develops.

Processes

Since AI projects are essentially software projects, you need to watch out for frameworks and processes in your company that govern the development process of software artifacts. Depending on your organization, various rules may be in place, and listing all of them is beyond the scope of this book. However, if you're generally not familiar with the way software projects are handled, I'll give you some key terms to look out for to see if they might apply to your organization:

ISO/IEC (https://oreil.ly/n6L0Q)

The ISO/IEC 25000 series of standards is also known as Systems and Software Quality Requirements and Evaluation (SQuaRE). These standards aim to provide a framework for evaluating the quality of software products. If your organization uses ISO-certified standards, your project might fall under these rules and need to be set up accordingly.

Scrum (https://www.scrum.org)

Scrum is a software development framework used by companies for Agile software development. Although the goal is to enable a lightweight, iterative development process, it comes with a relatively strict overhead and fixed roles (for example, product owner and Scrum master). Check whether Scrum exists in your organization, as this will define the project structure.

Business process management (BPM)

Business process management is commonly used in large organizations to manage key business processes and their respective owners. BPM is also used in software development, and you may need to document your project accordingly.

Project management office (PMO)

A project management office is an internal department that establishes and maintains company-specific project standards. Depending on the size of your project and the way your company works, you may at least have to adhere to the PMO rules and sometimes even report to that office regularly.

Once your prototype has a chance to move to the delivery phase, I strongly recommend that you contact your IT/DevOps department (if you have not already done so during prototyping) to ensure that your project setup meets all formal requirements necessary for software development projects.

Data

By now, you should be very familiar with the data in your AI project. During prototyping, you should have been able to identify the biggest data traps, and if you made it to delivery, you somehow found a way to overcome them. The only questions that remain are as follows: Will the approaches you have taken work in production? Are they safe and reliable? Does it scale? Is there anything else you need to consider?

Coming from BI, you should have a solid knowledge of the levers you can pull in your organization to move data around as well as the requirements or constraints. These are some areas you should pay particular attention to:

Data pipelines

Remember how we manually uploaded CSV files to Azure ML Studio and stored the results in Azure Blob Storage in Chapter 7? Most likely, this approach would not work in production scenarios because too many things could break. Ideally, you pull your data from a data warehouse and store the exports according to a consistent schema in a place where your production application has direct access to it—and that can even be Azure Blob Storage.

Data cleansing and management

Once you've automated the data pipelines and created the actual ETL scripts, you need to make sure they are both maintainable and can be automated (you won't be able to do manual data cleansing). Depending on the size of the project, this data cleansing part alone can be a major hurdle for the entire initiative.

Data access

I hope the use cases in this book have shown you the importance of being able to easily access and share data throughout the various stages of the development process. If you had all the data stored in a centralized cloud data warehouse, accessing it would be "just" a matter of access rights, but not a technical hurdle. I know that many companies are still struggling to break down their data silos and improve sharing across business units. Ideally, your prototype use case has provided a clear example of the benefits of making data easily accessible and connecting your applications to those data sources with a few simple scripts. Hosting your data warehouse in the cloud can have its drawbacks, but in terms of fast and flexible development, it's definitely a big advantage.

Data protection

As you move into production and serve more users, consider whether your data is subject to other constraints compared to the data you used in prototyping. For example, in prototyping, you may have used customer data from the US and worked with it in Microsoft Azure. In production, your users might also be located in the EU, and you would need special permission to process that data if it contains personal information. Storing data outside the EU can also quickly become problematic for this user group. If you have a data governance framework in place, get your data governance team involved early enough (ideally, at the prototyping stage) to identify major obstacles early on.

Technology

In 99% of cases, the technology stack you use for prototyping will not be the technology stack you use in production. And if it is, congratulations—you have figured out what digital transformation is all about. It's far from common to use the same infrastructure for both rapid prototyping and testing new features, as well as for running production workloads at scale.

The reason is that systems for production are optimized to be scalable, reliable, maintainable, performant, and secure. As you have learned, you generally sacrifice these goals for faster and more flexible development when prototyping.

If you want to deliver a new software application or even a single feature within an existing (BI) system, you should be guided by the requirements of the testing environment. The testing stage will usually resemble your production environment and is your first milestone to deliver something that can be used for testing.

The most important questions you need to ask yourself at this point are, Which parts of my prototype do I need to re-create to deliver it to the testing environment, and which parts can I reuse?

The answer to these questions can lie between two extremes. First, you do not need to rebuild anything because the prototyping stack is the same as the testing stack. In this case, you just need to focus on actually improving things and making sure that what you built meets the production environment's criteria for scalability, reliability, maintainability, performance, and security. At the other extreme, you basically have to rebuild everything.

In most cases, you will find yourself somewhere between these two poles and will need to identify the components that you can reuse. Anything left over will need to be rebuilt and will determine the size of your development team and budget. The more complex your product becomes, the higher the cost of development and maintenance will be.

Based on the use cases we have explored in this book, here are some components we have used in prototyping that you may be able to reuse even in production:

Model endpoint APIs

> The models we have implemented using Azure ML Studio generally meet all the requirements of production workloads. Be sure to check out "MLOps" on page 356 for the criteria for ML models in production. But the infrastructure itself will be compatible.

User interface and reports

> If you are using Power BI in your existing reporting landscape, you can probably reuse the report layouts and dashboards we created in the exercises. The way you deliver them to users might be different (e.g., using Power BI Server), but the look and feel would remain the same, so you would not need to re-create these again.

Data pipelines

> We used datasets in Azure ML Studio to train our models in this book. As long as you keep the schema, you should be able to incorporate new data fairly quickly, either by importing data from a file or from other resources in Azure. As long as you manage to get your data into the datasets by using the same schema, the pipeline for data preparation within Azure ML Studio remains the same.

Documentation

> Ideally, you have used the prototyping phase to make some notes about your overall development process. This can be nontechnical documentation answering questions such as, "What problem did you solve?" or "What approaches did you take?" or "What people did you involve?" as well as more technical documentation (data schemas, API documentation, Power BI data models). You likely can reuse these components, or at least use them as a starting point for moving the prototype project into the delivery phase.

Try to reuse as much as possible and rebuild everything else properly.

MLOps

The process of managing and operating ML models in production systems is commonly referred to as *MLOps*. It is what separates companies that are serious about data science from companies that hire data scientists to "build predictive models." We've seen just how important MLOps is during the pandemic: suddenly, the data consumed by an ML model in production looked very different from the data it had seen during training. This caused many ML models across all industries to collapse or perform significantly worse than usual. Unless your company had at least a rudimentary MLOps process in place, you probably wouldn't have noticed the poor model performance until it was too late (e.g., you ran out of inventory, but your ML model still predicted that your supply chain was fine).

At a minimum, MLOps requires adequate API documentation and staff to take care of the model after it is deployed. In the best case, MLOps spans the entire life cycle of an ML solution: from data acquisition through version control, experimentation, performance monitoring, and endpoint management, to model sunset.

ML models can therefore be considered an end-to-end software project in themselves and should be managed accordingly. That's why it shouldn't surprise you that you will find some of the same concepts within MLOps that were also applied to the overall solution in which the ML model is used.

The following areas are among the most important success factors for MLOps:

People
> Truth be told, if you don't have someone to at least monitor your model from time to time and take care of its maintenance, you better not implement any ML model at all. Many things can happen after implementation. The most common phenomenon is *data drift*: the data your model sees in production becomes more and more different from the data it saw during training and makes the predictions less accurate and less reliable over time. Although tools can help automate this process, it is ultimately a human's job to decide whether a new model needs to be trained again and the data to use for that. Apart from model performance, debugging is also an important component. If the model produces errors or other problems occur, who should be responsible to fix these issues?

Automation
> One of the main goals of MLOps is to automate the process as much as possible. If you can't easily reproduce an analysis or a model training, your team won't likely be able to iterate on new models quickly enough to deliver value. For this reason, automated pipelines are considered one of the most important aspects in MLOps, especially if you run more than one or two models in production.

Reliability and reusability

If your organization is expanding the use of ML models, it's important that you establish a standard process for creating them that's reliable and whose correct operation can be easily verified each time. If you fail to do this, the cost of creating new models or making subsequent changes to existing models can exceed the value of an ML model. You also need to ensure that when a change occurs within the team, a smooth transition happens and new colleagues can take over quickly.

Security

It's important that your MLOps team understands the data it's working with and the governance rules that apply. In some cases, this data includes sensitive user information that may not leave certain geographic areas, may not be accessible to all individuals, or may have its use restricted by privacy laws. MLOps also ensures that all data and infrastructure resources are managed through appropriate identity and access management (IAM) rules and technical arrangements.

Scalability

Keeping up with an ever-growing ML resource footprint is another major concern of MLOps. One of the best ways to avoid this is by being able to scale up your infrastructure as needed, both during training and during inference. On the one hand, you want to avoid a situation where you are either limiting your ML training progress by not providing enough or not the right infrastructure. On the other hand, you don't want to reserve a large computer cluster for an ML job that is running only once every couple of months.

Dedicated ML platforms like Azure ML Studio will help you address some of the issues that MLOps deals with. But, ultimately, your organization needs a process-and-people framework to manage these aspects. Be sure to think about them before moving your own custom ML services into production. Some of these areas also apply to AI services, although in this case you usually have a vendor that will either take care of most things or support you accordingly.

Get Started by Delivering Complete Increments

I know that the success criteria for AI product delivery sounds like a lot. And I don't want to sugarcoat anything; the delivery phase is a lot! That's why you shouldn't jump from discovery to delivery (or from prototyping to production) with one big leap. Instead, take the time to make a plan to deliver in complete increments, request resources, and lay out the roadmap to delivery.

Your incremental roadmap might look like the following:

1. Gather a team and a sponsor.
2. Get stakeholders on board.
3. Get project plan approval.
4. Build the data pipeline.
5. Build the model.
6. Integrate the model.
7. Build the user reports.
8. Test everything thoroughly.
9. Deploy to production systems.
10. Iterate again over user feedback.

Be sure to complete each increment before moving on to the next. Delivering single complete increments will allow you to stay flexible, while giving you the opportunities to celebrate the small wins along the way.

Conclusion

You did it! I hope this book has given you some insight into the world of AI and how it can be used in BI. We have explored several use cases in this chapter to give you a taste of the many possibilities you can explore with ML applications. With the help of this book, you should now be well on your way to developing your own AI-powered BI applications.

So, what have you learned? Here are some concepts we covered:

- How to find use cases with business impact
- How to assess the feasibility of AI projects
- Basic things to know about ML
- How to use prototyping for product discovery and which tools to use in the context of AI prototyping
- Practical use cases of how AI can be used to improve BI results
- How to move to the next phase to take your project from prototype to production

I hope the use cases in this book have piqued your interest in how AI can improve business outcomes for BI in the areas of data collection as well as descriptive, diagnostic, predictive, or prescriptive analytics. If so, do not stop here. The next step is to build out your own BI application using AI techniques.

The world is changing at a rapid pace, but with the information in this book, you will be well equipped to navigate this field on your own. You can always contact me on LinkedIn (*https://oreil.ly/w3CEG*) or through the book's website (*https://oreil.ly/h7fE2*) if you have feedback, questions, or ideas for prototypes around AI-powered BI where you would like to succeed! I wish you all the best in your future AI journey and hope that you will launch many successful projects.

Index

M

machine learning (ML)
  accessibility of services, 3
  data requirement for ML techniques, 24
  developing an intuition for, 13-16
  fundamentals of
    common pitfalls of ML, 61-67
    deep learning, 54-55
    model evaluation, 55-61
    popular algorithms, 49-53
    supervised ML process, 45-49
  reasons for project failures, 69, 348
  workflow for customer analytics
    evaluating models, 322
    ML Designer pipelines, 317
    model training, 321, 324
    previewing data, 324
    training and test sets, 320
macro scores, 61, 161
maintainability, 349
maintenance, 48, 356
micro scores, 61, 161
Microsoft Azure Cloud Services
  alternatives to, 73
  benefits of, 73
  costs, 151
  enabling AI service on, 211-215
  evaluating model performance in Azure
    Portal, 249
  free Azure account, xiv, 74
  integrating with Power BI, 144
  working with
    Azure Blob Storage, 86-90, 254
    Azure compute resource, 83-86
    Azure Machine Learning Studio, 77-82,
      314, 357
    Azure portal dashboard, 76
    signing up, 74-75
Microsoft Azure Cognitive Services
  Anomaly Detector, 211
  Computer Vision, 285
  Sentiment Analysis, 326
  Text Analytics, 263
Microsoft Azure Form Recognizer, 287
Microsoft Azure Machine Learning Designer,
  311, 317
Microsoft Azure Notebooks
  setting up, 243-245, 269
  using, 271

Microsoft Azure Personalizer Service
  reinforcement learning with, 241-243
  setting up, 238-241
Microsoft Power BI Desktop
  alternatives to, xiv, 90
  automated insights using, 115-134
  benefits of, 73
  building AI-powered dashboards
    analyzing customer churn, 338-340
    anomaly detection, 221-233
    automating classification tasks, 177-179
    counting objects in images, 308-310
    getting insights from text data, 280-282
    improving KPI prediction, 202-207
    next best action recommendation,
      256-259
    parsing documents with AI, 300
  downloading and installing, xiv, 90
  integrating with Azure, 144
  model inference with
    anomaly detection, 218-221
    automating classification tasks, 172-176
    counting objects in images, 306
    getting insights from text data, 278-280
    next best action recommendation,
      253-255
    parsing documents with AI, 296-299
  querying data with natural language, 96-107
  summarizing data with natural language,
    109-114
  working with, 90
minimum viable product (MVP), 70
ML (see machine learning)
MLOps, 356
models
  accuracy versus labeling costs, 63
  definition of term, 47
  deploying, 48
  deploying with Azure
    automating classification tasks, 163-168
    improving KPI prediction, 194
  evaluating (see also evaluation metrics)
    basic idea behind, 56
    classification models, 57-60
    final models, 48
    multiclassification models, 61
    regression models, 56-57
  finding best using algorithms, 47
  model inference with Power BI

About the Author

Tobias Zwingmann is an experienced data scientist with a strong business background. He has more than 15 years of professional experience in a corporate setting, where he has been responsible for building out data science use cases and developing a company-wide data strategy. He is also a cofounder of the German AI startup RAPYD.AI and is on a mission to help companies adopt machine learning and artificial intelligence faster while achieving meaningful business impact.

Colophon

The animal on the cover of *AI-Powered Business Intelligence* is an African crested eagle (*Lophaetus occipitalis*), otherwise known as a long-crested eagle.

As its common name suggests, this large, dark brown eagle's most distinctive feature is perhaps the tall crest of feathers adorning its head, though it also has strikingly barred tail feathers and conspicuous white patches on the undersides of its wings—the latter of which are visible in flight.

The African crested eagle can be found across a vast expanse of sub-Saharan Africa, where it lives and hunts in woodlands and along forest edges. It is considered largely nonmigratory, with some possible exceptions in arid locations, where seasonal rainfall can vary drastically. The bird is a sit-and-wait hunter, perching near open spaces for long periods and feeding opportunistically on prey—primarily rodents—that happen to come near.

The International Union for Conservation of Nature has listed the African crested eagle as being of *least concern*, due, in part, to their extensive range and growing population. Many of the animals on O'Reilly covers are endangered; all of them are important to the world.

The cover illustration is by Karen Montgomery, based on an antique line engraving from Lydekker's *Royal Natural History*. The cover fonts are Gilroy Semibold and Guardian Sans. The text font is Adobe Minion Pro; the heading font is Adobe Myriad Condensed; and the code font is Dalton Maag's Ubuntu Mono.

Milton Keynes UK
Ingram Content Group UK Ltd.
UKHW050214080624
443739UK00003B/5